INDONESIA
in focus

Photo Editor: Peter Homan
Scientific Editor: Dr. Reimar Schefold
Journalistic Editor: Vincent Dekker
Overall final editing: Drs. Nico de Jonge

Kegan Paul International
London

ANCIENT TRADITIONS - MODERN TIMES

COLOPHON

Design: CINEMASTER,
Bergen, The Netherlands
Translated from the Dutch
by Drs. Jeff van Exel and
Drs. Tjitske Wijngaard
First published in English in
1990 by Edu'Actief
Publishing Company, the
Netherlands.
This edition published in 1991
by Kegan Paul International Ltd
PO Box 256
London WC1B 3SW, England

Distributed by
John Wiley & Sons Ltd
Southern Cross Trading
Estate
1 Oldlands Way, Bognor
Regis, West Sussex,
PO22 9SA, England
Printed in Spain
by Egedsa, Sabadell
D.L.B.: 21.874-91

ISBN 0 7103 0440 4

A catalogue record for this book is available from the British Library.

INDONESIA
in focus

CONTENTS

Introduction

Indonesia's riches

The Indonesian Coat of Arms features a motto from a fourteenth-century Hindu-Javanese text: Bhinneka Tunggal Ika, 'Unity in Diversity'. At first sight, though, Indonesia's great cultural diversity is far more striking than its unity.

Within this rich variety it may well be Bali with its temple festivals that offers the greatest number of travellers the most penetrating picture. Ever since the twenties, the grace of its inhabitants has nurtured hectic Europeans' dreams of a South Seas Paradise. Previously, it was Java with the splendour of its princely courts that greatly impressed the Dutch conquerors; the 'hidden force' of the refined etiquette that seemed to render the Javanese unassailable to any colonial interference, was a mystery to the Westerners.

All over Indonesia today's tourist will come across the Minangkabau eating-houses from West Sumatra. Throughout the archipelago, Minangkabau men are known as smart traders, while the women as guardians of the mother-right existing here, manage the beautifully decorated houses of the family groups. No travel brochure fails to mention the proud Toraja people from the Sulawesi highlands. Behind their spectacular funeral rites in which numerous buffaloes are sacrificed, lies a profound religiosity that to most tourists remains hidden. Many tours now also include a visit to the Batak in the mighty mountains around Lake Toba. Nearly all these one-time cannibals are Protestants now. But they did not give up their traditional ancestor worship. Everywhere monumental memorials silently testify to this. Some of the old ones are made of stone; the recent memorials are of painted concrete. The more recent the bigger.

Everywhere, everything seems to be different. In Jakarta we find mosques, churches, Buddhist and Hindu temples, and ancestral shrines all next to each other. The semidarkness of the tropical rain forests of Kalimantan, where the Punan, roaming hunters and gatherers, with apparent ease find an abundance of food, contrasts with the sun-drenched slopes of the fertile volcanoes with their countless terraced rice fields: green tiers that have been cultivated and irrigated for thousands of years. The colourful finery of flowers, beads and shells of tribal groups competes with the finely chiselled gold or silver ornaments in the Arab-Indian tradition of town and country. And the wealth of textiles is overwhelming: fabrics of cotton and silk, of tree-bark and plant fibres, with patterns in batik, *ikat*, *plangi* and *tritik*... There is hardly any aspect of life that from one region to another does not have a surprisingly different design. The traditional Indonesian cultures sing the praises of the richness of the human imagination.

Prehistory

This cultural wealth has historical roots. Every Indonesian ethnic group has its own past; it has adapted to local circumstances and off and on it has been in touch with neighbouring cultures. Yet some large-scale general developments in history and prehistory can be pointed out. They cannot explain the present picture, but they do offer insight into the background from which it arose.

Geographically speaking, Indonesia opens up from the South-East Asian continent. One glance at the map should make this clear. To the north we find sloping coastlines, and here the shallow China Sea looks more like an intermediate lake than an expanse of water isolating everything. In contrast, the coasts of the islands in the south-west and south drop steeply to the Indian Ocean; there are hardly any natural ports. During the glacial periods most of the China Sea ran dry, and probably Indonesia's first inhabitants crossed on foot from the Asiatic mainland. They were specimens of 'Homo Erectus', made simple blades of stone and lived in particular on what could be hunted and gathered from the sea and the jungle. The famous 'Java Man' was one of them. Discovered at the end of the last century, he was a sensation to those who were then disputing the theories of Darwin.

However, the earliest finds to which the present types of Man in Indonesia relate, date from some hundreds of thousands of years later. These finds stem from the mid-Stone Age, the Mesolithic Period, which in Indonesia started some ten thousand years ago. At the time the end of the Ice Age meltwater caused the sea-level to rise more than a hundred metres, and the bridge of land fell apart, forming the present Sunda archipelago. In Sumatra, near the coast, shell mounds several metres high have been excavated. Traces of abodes indicate that these mounds form the litter of a people who must have fed mainly on mussels and snails. On the same spot skeletons were found sharing certain characteristics with the present dark-skinned inhabitants of New Guinea, the so-called Papuas. This

◂ *Among the Minangkabau in West Sumatra the adat house accommodates several families related in the female line. In spite of 'modern times' the Minangkabau frequently restore these houses with money they earned elsewhere in Indonesia.*

▲ *How long can a proud Kubu survive in an endangered jungle?*

'Melanid' race is no longer found in western Indonesia, but there are traces in the Moluccas. In the Malay Peninsula and in the Philippines there still are groups of dark-skinned hunters and gatherers, such as the Semang and the Aeta. Like the people of the Indian Andaman Islands who resemble them, the collective term of 'Negrito' is sometimes applied to them.

Later the inhabitants of New Guinea themselves turned to agriculture, and partly even to quite intensive forms of horticulture. So far it remains unclear which external influences played a part in this transition. Many tribes in the mountainous, jungle-covered areas of New Guinea, an island second in size only to Greenland, lived in utter isolation, and nowhere else is a greater number of different languages spoken within such a limited area.

There still are other groups of hunters and gatherers in the Indonesian rain forests, but their race and language hardly differ from the surrounding tribes. Best known are the Kubu of Sumatra and the Punan of Kalimantan. Both these peoples carry on exchange trade with their neighbouring agricultural communities. It is a moot point whether they still live according to the ancient Mesolithic traditions, or retreated into the jungle at a later stage and shifted to a nomadic life style afterwards. Due to their mobility, field research among such groups is very difficult, and this mobility is increased in the event of a death in the group, by their custom of abandoning the deceased at the campsite, never to return. Their close and harmonious relationship with their natural environment, renders any further study of these hunters an interesting task, and by now an urgently needed one.

The Neolithic Period, the late Stone Age, saw the introduction in the Indonesian archipelago of shifting cultivation on swiddens. The beginnings of this cultural tradition are now assumed to date from the third millennium BC. This new development was initiated by the arrival of speakers of Austronesian languages. With the exception of some of the darker peoples in the east, nowadays nearly all the inhabitants of the archipelago speak these languages. Malay, the preceding form of modern Indonesian (Bahasa Indonesia), belongs to this language family. In their appearance these Austronesian immigrants were related to contemporary Indonesians. Their region of origin must have been somewhere in China; both the Malay Peninsula and Taiwan could have been transit areas. The new inhabitants had seaworthy boats with outriggers, as they are still found today all over South-East Asia and Oceania. They also introduced into Indonesia certain types of ceramics and a special kind of axe (the so-called quadrangular axe ground into a rectangular cross-section). It is unlikely that they also brought rice cultivation and the water buffalo, but they did bring the cultivation of tubers and bananas, as well as pig- and chicken-breeding. Modern representatives of this neolithic tradition, such as the

Mentawaians in the islands west of Sumatra, lead one to assume that these immigrants were organised in groups of a few related families, who, as a visible symbol of their community, jointly owned a large pile-dwelling in which they often also lived together. Labour specialization was unknown, and there was hardly any political integration beyond the level of the local group. Headhunting raids were undertaken against more distant groups. Alliances with neighbours were established by friendship and marriage ties. In marriage the bride-givers always enjoyed a higher status than the bride-takers, as the former provided for the continuity of the latter. In many regions this led to an asymmetrical marriage system: one group would receive brides from another, and consequently superior, group. But these in turn, would get their brides from a third group, in which relationship they would hence be subordinate. As such a relationship with a partner group could not be turned around from one day to the next, for then one would be superior and subordinate at the same time, a pattern of marriage relationships arose between all communities in a certain area, a pattern that could allay the constant threat of conflicts. Today's Indonesian tribal groups still show numerous variants of such a 'circulating connubium'.

In religious life ancestor worship played a central role. The visible world was seen as animated. To certain objects, plants in particular, religious powers were attributed, often on the basis of formal associations. This explains their use in rituals. As early as in the neolithic tradition we find the idea, so typical for Indonesia, of a dualistic cosmic order, in which opposite poles such as heaven and earth, man and woman, one's own group and the outside world, good and evil, complement each other in mutual dependence.

In most regions of Indonesia the neolithic immigrants either displaced or assimilated the earlier hunter and gatherer cultures. A somewhat comparable fate befell the newcomers themselves, when the Bronze and Iron Age penetrated Indonesia around the middle of the first millennium BC. Again the region of origin probably lay in China. For this reason perhaps, one should not speak of a new immigration wave, but rather of a lasting contact situation. In the process, the new attainments of the South-East Asian continent were gradually adopted in Indonesia. No doubt the most important of these were the knowledge of metal-working and of growing rice on irrigated fields (*sawah*). In an excavated settlement in what is now Vietnam, metal objects have been found with characteristic ornaments, especially spiral motifs, matching in detail Indonesian objects of the same period. The tradition on which the influences from that period in the archipelago are based, is named after the site of these finds: the Dongson culture.

Rice cultivation on *sawah* is only possible if several groups in an area cooperate, keeping both water balance and upkeep of the terraces well coordinated.

The 'circulating connubium' represented in a diagram:

the direction taken by the brides

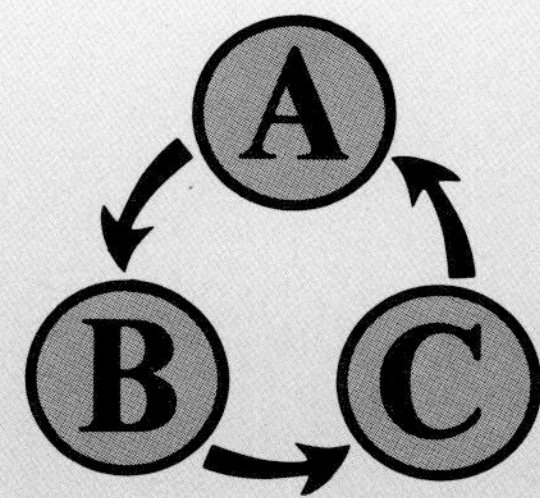

A, B and C: local groups

At least three groups are essential in this asymmetric marriage system; nearly always more groups are involved.

▼ *Sawah in Central Java.*

Only then can the soil remain in constant and intensive use, and produce surpluses. In the Dongson tradition a more complex degree of social organization was developed. A hierarchically structured community arose, with leaders, freemen and slaves. An organization still based on kinship. It was composed of groups who descended from the same mythic founder, and who jointly performed rituals. At these festivals one particular element was strongly emphasized; its seeds were already present in the neolithic cultures: the struggle for a higher status. He who distinguished himself by certain ritual acts and lavishly entertained his guests, gained prestige. Megaliths, large stones that were sometimes carved, were erected as lasting signs of this. There often was an entire hierarchy of such festivals and stone raisings, also referring to a comparable order of precedence in the hereafter. Many of the great tribal groups of Indonesia, such as those in Nias, Sumatra (Batak), Sulawesi (Toraja, Minahasa), Kalimantan (Kelabit Dayak), Sumba, and some other East-Indonesian islands, are still known for their megalithic festivities.

Historical developments

Though within these tribal groups the traditions of the Dongson culture have been well preserved, the differences in regional development are immense. There must have been similar cultures in islands like Java, Bali and Lombok. But there the old traditions are hidden under the influences of the next great culture complex to reach Indonesia: this time from India. On the basis of inscriptions, Indian influences can be demonstrated from the first centuries AD onward. This culture complex was probably introduced by way of trading contacts. Soon these contacts must have expanded enormously, due to a growing theological interest in India. Many philosophical terms of Indian origin in modern Indonesian still testify to this. The Indonesians of the Dongson period were good sailors. During that period

Memorial stone in Pagaruyung near Batusangkar in West Sumatra, with Sanskrit inscriptions from AD 1347; the text reminds the reader of the Hindu-Buddhist kingdom of Malayu. ▼

Long before the arrival of the Europeans, there was quite a lot of shipping in South-East Asian waters, as is shown in this depiction on Borobudur, the monumental sanctuary built around ▼ *AD 800.*

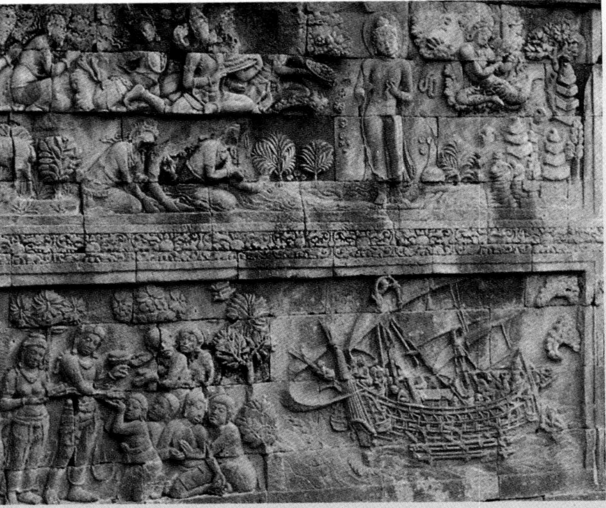

even Madagascar was populated from Indonesia. The ritual symbolism of this tradition still found in the Moluccas for instance, also expresses this quality: often villagers are represented as the crew of a boat. In this period, travellers from Java and Sumatra visited Sri Lanka and India. Sources reveal that some of them became monks there, or returned to Indonesia with Brahman priests.
In the course of the centuries many old tribal societies in Sumatra and Java, and consequently in Bali, developed into kingdoms with Hindu and Buddhist orientations. On the coast these were mainly involved in trade. In the interior realms, dominated by agriculture, a feudal system developed that forced the farmers to pay tribute to the courts. These tributaries supplied the labour for the monumental religious buildings erected in Central Java in the eighth and ninth centuries AD, such as Prambanan and Borobudur. Later the political centre shifted to East Java, where the Indian traditions became increasingly intertwined with the indigenous heritage, so that they developed in their own way. Here the ancient Javanese literature arose. The Indian epic poems of

▼ *Many reliefs on Borobudur derive from Indian folk tales.*

Ramayana and Mahabharata were modified into narratives, which to this day form the basis of *wayang* performances.
Due to the Indian influences, the ancient cosmological order of the Indonesians was expanded into a classification system that accommodated all phenomena in a firmly delineated spatial structure. Instead of kinship, it was this new system itself that legitimized the organization of society. In the same way that sacred Mount Meru rises from the centre of the divine cosmos as dwelling-place of the gods, the *kraton* – the palace from which the royal power emanates – lies in the centre of the earthly realm. Classification of all visible phenomena is based on the points of the compass; days, colours, metals, but also abstract principles are associated with them. In his daily life Man must take this arrangement into account to ensure that the divine forces will not turn against him, bringing misfortune. There is a link here with the refined etiquette Java is so famous for, and which still prescribes the proper behaviour for every class and every occasion.
In the year 1292 Marco Polo still mentions such Hindu kingdoms in North Sumatra, but he adds that there as elsewhere 'the plague of the Muslim faith' has already begun to spread. At the time Islam was disseminated in Indonesia by Arab, but in particular by Indian, traders. Especially Sufism with its strongly mystical overtones easily gained access in the Hindu regions, with the exception of Bali. In the archipelago, the populations of the areas dominated by trade, were the first to be converted. The new religion broadened the horizon and offered access to a universal community. This same period saw the first contacts with European powers, established by traders, missionaries and soldiers. The first Europeans came from Portugal; from the end of the sixteenth century the Dutch too, penetrated the archipelago. Once it had established its first bases in Java and the Moluccas, the Dutch East India Company (VOC, Vereenigde Oost-Indische Compagnie) gained power in ever increasing parts of Indonesia. From the beginning of the nineteenth century till its hard-won independence in 1949, this country was known as the Netherlands East Indies, a colony that was part of the Kingdom of the Netherlands.
The survey of the archipelago's eventful past may help to improve our understanding of the great richness of Indonesian cultures. From what history had to offer, every ethnic group has developed its own cultural forms. But a comparison of the separate traditions also reveals the common roots: the unity behind the diversity.
Java's traditional countryside shows us how, from the many successive prehistoric and historic influences and contacts, its own coherent whole developed. In society various ideological trends may be distinguished. With few exceptions, such as the Baduy in Banten, most Javanese are Muslims, but among many of them, especially the simple farmers, the ancient animistic heritage survives as a strong presence in the daily religious practice. In the literature these *wong cilik*, little folk, are sometimes referred to as *abangan*, the red group. Others, government officials in particular, base their conduct on the guidelines of the old upper class, the *priyayi*. The value they attach to discipline, ascetic meditation and strict etiquette, is closely linked to the Hindu-Javanese tradition as developed at the courts. Finally, in particular among the traders and wealthy land-owners, one finds the *santri*, who adhere more strictly than others to the Islamic laws and who consider themselves the real representatives of the only true faith.
Java's rural communities are no longer independent units, but are administered by regional centres. Yet they still have their own rituals, in which as a rule only close neighbours take part. Such ceremonies centre around the *selamatan* (from *selamat*: well-being), a shared meal occasioned by an important event in the life of an individual or of the whole group. One of these rituals is an annual common cleansing ceremony against evil influences; other reasons for a *selamatan* may be a wedding ceremony or the prayer for a safe journey. The sacrificial character of the meal is important: being offered to the supernatural powers, it has a religious meaning. In invoking these powers, Indonesia's entire past seems to play a part. Ancestors and spirits are mentioned, but also the names of gods from the Hindu pantheon. And, finally, all participants join in the formula: "There is no God but Allah and Mohammed is His prophet."
Even though all the different cultures of Indonesia have their own incommutable character, there have always been contacts between them. Throughout Indonesia, local customs hallowed by tradition are called *adat*, an originally Arabic word. The members of a community view their *adat* as a fixed point of reference that determines their daily life and in the event of problems, guides them in making the right decision. But in the course of various generations, something that at a given moment is regarded as an immutable law, proves to be subject to constant changes. Time and again the *adat* must respond to influences affecting the community from without. The result is a constant adaptation ever leading to new forms of the *adat*.
Repeatedly, the historical influences that reached Indonesia taxed the survival of the local *adat*. It may be regarded as a characteristic feature of the Indonesian cultures that they did not cut themselves off from such influences, but on the contrary opened up to them. In the process they demonstrated their resilience imperceptibly to adapt the new and to assimilate it in such a way that apparently it concerned a local and original phenomenon. This process is found in the Javanese village, and in the Moluccas too after nearly five hundred years of Christian influence.
Only in the last decades did real alternatives to this constant evolution of local traditions arise. The possibilities of a greater personal mobility and the attraction of the modern cities, may now tempt a few to extract themselves from the grip of the traditional *adat* and to build a new life elsewhere. But the most frequent motive for moving away from the old native region, is a poor economic situation. Whether the move is spontaneous or a matter of government-stimulated migration to new regions suffering less from overpopulation, 'transmigration' migrants are still eager to associate with people from their own region who preceded them.

Time bar on the basis of the Christian era

European influences
AD 1400
AD 1200 Islamization
Indian influences
AD 100
0
Dongson tradition
500 BC
Austronesian culture complex
(Neolithic Period)
3000 BC
Pre-Austronesian tradition
(Mesolithic Period)
8000 BC
('Java Man')

Content of the chapters

Several aspects that have been touched on here, will be illustrated in the present book. Examples are taken from all over the Indonesian archipelago; they are geographically arranged, from west to east.
The opening chapter begins with a 'forgotten' group of islands in the extreme west, the Mentawai Islands off the coast of Sumatra. Here we are presented with a world view in which to this day traditions dating back to the late Stone Age of Indonesia, have been preserved. This world view illustrates that a community's limited technical possibilities are no indication of a limited spiritual wealth.

We find an even older way of life among the Kubu in the Sumatra jungles. For countless generations their economy, based on hunting and gathering, has been closely interwoven with the ecology of the tropical rain forest. It is to be hoped that the modern insights and demands of nature conservation will also benefit the Kubu's chances of cultural survival.

The final section of this chapter deals with the Toba Batak in North Sumatra, and shows a different side to the present problems of a tribal group. Over the past few years many Toba Batak have moved to town, to build an independent life for themselves there. At the same time, in their home region, gigantic concrete monuments were erected to honour the mythical ancestors of the group; these may be regarded as expressions of the need to feel secure, and of the ethnic pride in one's own roots.

▲ *In addition to boar and deer, monkeys are the Kubu's most important game.*

▲ *Outer Baduy on his way home. In particular these Baduy increasingly decide to buy goods actually not allowed according to the* ***adat***.

Chapter Two starts with the Baduy in the interior of West Java. This people, living a very secluded life, shows a new facet of the ethnical ties in Indonesia. The Baduy lead rigorous lives governed by old religious rules, and are highly appreciated for their asceticism, even by their Islamic neighbours. By unique decree, the Government officially recognized their collective claim to a territory of their own.
The former dynasty of Banten in West Java maintained close relations with the Baduy. In spite of their Islamic belief, the ideology of the Central-Javanese dynasties too, is still closely linked to the old pre-Hindu and Hindu traditions. From this a religious power accrues to them, contributing to the great charisma they have among the Javanese even today.

Old religious symbolism also dominates the thought of the country people. Thus the patterns and colours in batik fabrics in North-East Java are not merely used to illustrate details of the social order; they also depict and legitimize the structure of the cosmos in a way comprehensible to all.

Despite their fixed positions within a social class, in this tradition individuals too, may gain regard. This is illustrated by the bull races in Madura, featured in the final section of this chapter. This striving for status explains why the Madurese in spite of numerous demonstrations for tourists attach real importance to these competitions merely on certain occasions. Only the officially recognized races are important; losing or winning these, determines the fame of the participants and their families.

◄ *Grave monuments on a hill in Balige near Lake Toba in North Sumatra.*

In North-East Java a woman's attire shows to which generation she belongs; it reflects whether she is a nubile daughter (top), a mother (centre),
▼ *or a grandmother (bottom).*

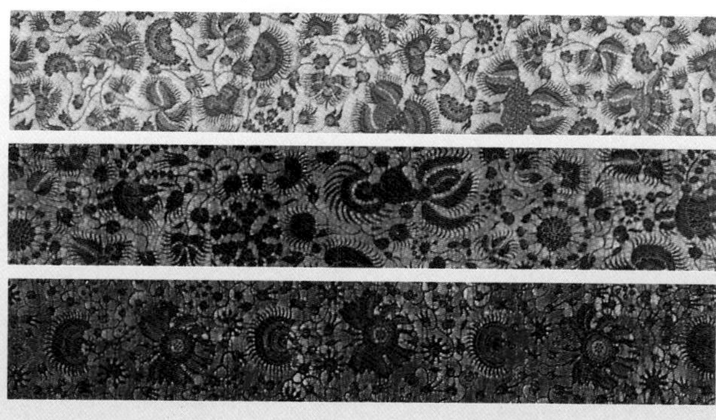

At a rapid rate, ▲ *large-scale timber-felling is destroying the life sphere of the people of Kalimantan.*

Unlike the situation in Java, in Bali Islam had no influence on the old traditions. Chapter Three shows that there a new hierarchic society resulted from the prehistoric and Indian traditions. In it, each individual has his own clearly defined place, determined by birth. Even so, in Bali too, possibilities were found to improve one's status. Due to the many rapid changes after independence, a lot of traditional claims to high positions were no longer self-evident, and at a certain moment this resulted in serious conflicts.

To the common man the daily worries are more important than such matters of status. Facing many problems considered insuperable, they invoke the help of gods and ancestors, who live in an invisible, higher world, watching over the cosmic balance. Mediumistically gifted people, usually simple women, have access to the knowledge of the wishes of these supernatural powers. In trance, these women become the mouthpieces of the divine voices, calling on people to make sacrifices or to perform other ritual acts that enable them to find a way out of their problems.

Consider on the one hand this relatively small and very densely populated island of Bali imbued throughout with a blossoming culture, and on the other, gigantic Kalimantan covered in forest, the region central to Chapter Four. Can one imagine a greater contrast? Only on the coast and along the slow-moving rivers do we find larger settlements. Yet the vast tropical rain forests are not utterly uninhabited. Here in some remote areas live the Punan, hunters and gatherers like the Kubu in Sumatra. In a way uniquely their own, the Punan have adapted to the tough life in the wilderness. Now not only their culture is at risk, but also the whole ecology of their environment due to the insatiable demand of modern industrialized countries for wood, and to the arrival of 'transmigrants' from overpopulated regions.

◄ *To the Balinese, a good relationship with the gods and ancestors is essential to a secure existence. Trance mediums,* ***balian taksu****, play an important part in this context. As a mouthpiece for the divine beings, they bring the visible and the invisible worlds into contact with each other.*

▲ *The souls of the buffaloes slaughtered during a funeral festival in Tana Toraja, accompany the soul of the deceased on his journey to the realm of the dead.*

The resilience of Indonesian cultural traditions is expressed in Chapter Five. The mountainous highland of Sulawesi is the home of the Toraja, who in many respects resemble the Batak in North Sumatra. Pride in their descent culminates in their magnificent rituals for the dead, which pave the way to the hereafter and ensure the blessing for the descendants. The splendour radiated by such a ritual, enhances the status of the host. This partly explains why family members living in the cities, keep alive the link with their native region by means of contributions. Organizing such feasts requires great financial sacrifices from everyone. And this illustrates the strength of the ties with the *adat*: individual expressions remain subordinated to tradition.

But under the influence of modern ideas alternatives have come within reach, that often lead to a reaction against the *adat*. We find a striking example among another group in Sulawesi, the Islamic Tolaki who live in the south-east of the island. To them, marriage is a crucial moment. Couples who do not want to subject themselves to the group's traditional rules, increasingly resort to a new version of the 'marriage by elopement', thus forcing the community to take their wishes into account.

The modern pursuit of personal latitude often is an extension of old forms of the struggle for power. Among the Minahasans in the north of Sulawesi, with whom this chapter concludes, that struggle was very highly developed. In contrast to many other ethnic groups, they did not consider a person's descent to be of essential importance to his status. At an early stage the Minahasa had been converted to Christianity, and they played an important role in the colonial army. Even at that time many of them acquired certain wealth; the result was a struggle for the high positions in the local community. Both the rivalry in today's politics and the tough economic competition may be viewed as a continuation of this old struggle for power.

In the Central Moluccas Christian influences date back even further. For nearly five hundred years now, the *adat* and the Church have interacted. This gave rise to a complementary relationship in which the minister and the village chief, as a symbolic married couple, divided the work to be done. Their relationship is the main theme of the first part of Chapter Six.
In the other Moluccan islands the influences of world religions are more recent. Thus the Giman in Halmahera in the North Moluccas, have only been Muslims for the past few decades. But here the old *adat* and the new rules of behaviour have already blended to such an extent that they can hardly be distinguished any longer. Due to government guidelines and improved communications, Islam as the representative of the 'world at large' is gaining ground. Yet the Babar Islands, now largely Christian, show that in the Moluccas as well, under the surface the force of the traditional ordering principles continues to make itself felt. New attainments have been embedded in society by means of old symbolic forms. For centuries the world view of these islanders was based on the model of a boat with its crew. The arrangement of new buildings and feasts show that this model still hasn't lost its strength.

The final chapter deals with Irian Jaya. This western part of New Guinea is the Indonesian region with the most contrasting scenery: here one finds both primeval jungle and perennial snow. It was only in the first half of this century, in the highlands surrounded by mountains, that the outside world got acquainted with a culture that refuted once and for all the old myth about technical backwardness of tropical peoples. There the Dani inhabit one of the world's earliest centres of intensive agriculture. Their ingenious irrigation canals must date back to some four thousand years BC. The rain forests in Irian Jaya's lowlands are far less densely populated. Here once more, we are faced with the question that recurred time and again throughout this survey of the Indonesian cultures, from west to east: how to solve the problem of the unequal distribution of people and natural resources, without irreparably damaging the regional ecological systems and local cultures?

▲ *A village in Dawera, an island in the Babar archipelago; one can't help associating this with a model settlement of a transmigration project. The houses are neatly aligned, and even their gables all point in one direction. Actually an ancient pattern underlies this arrangement, a pattern based on the proa symbolism.*

Dani in Irian Jaya like to decorate themselves, but to wear a 'necktie' of shells means more to them: it protects the throat, a vulnerable access route into the body, against disease and other evil. ▼

1 Sumatra

What used to be its tiger is now its Highway: Sumatra's appearance has changed. The remote interior has been opened up, a lot of mining is in progress. The Trans-Sumatra Highway is the artery of a new economy, and the island's development has gained momentum. Not everybody rides this current equally well. Cultural traditions disappear or are adjusted; the tiger has been put into a nature reserve.

Compared to the 'continent' of Sumatra, so far some of the islands off its west coast have been opened up to a lesser extent. In Siberut, an island in the Mentawai archipelago, there even are groups in extreme isolation. Reimar Schefold describes their world.

For the Kubu in South Sumatra, though, the old traditional way of life seems a thing of the past. Deforestation has deprived these hunters and gatherers of their habitat. Gerard Persoon compares the old situation with the new one, and sketches a perspective.

Better attuned to the modern lifestyle are the Toba Batak in North Sumatra. Various cultural expressions have been adapted and, sometimes, provided with a new content. Impressive examples are the modern accommodations for the ancestors, as presented by Lea Bolle.

Mentawai: a cosmos as network of the souls

The historical background of Indonesia's cultural diversity clarifies that the word 'unity' in its motto quoted in the Introduction, does not merely regard a modern national ideal. This motley variety conceals a common heritage, expressed in the linguistic family to which nearly all the languages of the archipelago belong: West-Austronesian. Some general characteristics have also been established in the kinship and marriage systems. In addition there are similarities in world view. Even though, particularly in this area, regional differences display an exceedingly rich imagery, time and again one encounters common notions that lend them their distinctive Indonesian flavour.

The general basic idea is that the human world is part of an all-encompassing cosmic order, and that both are subject to the same laws. This parallelism of micro- and macrocosm is linked with the idea that the whole world is 'animated', inhabited by religious forces, and held in a harmonious balance. In his behaviour Man must take this harmony into account. When he acts, he must enter into a relationship with the object of his action, avoiding everything that may upset this balance. Otherwise the forces of the cosmos will turn

◄ *In Mentawai the hunt involves pursuits that can take hours, and demands an all-out effort. Many arrows are shot before a hunter returns to the communal dwelling with his catch.*

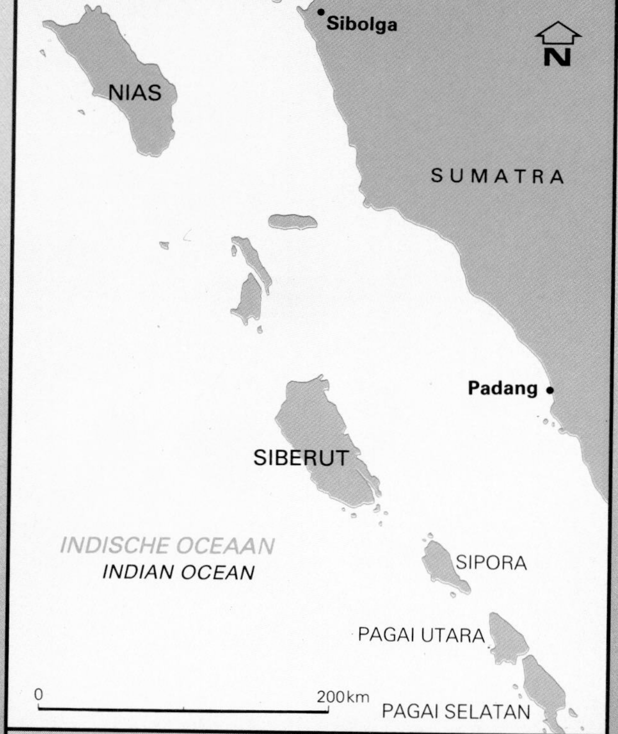

The isle of Manteu

The Mentawai archipelago lies about a hundred kilometres to the west of the Sumatran harbour of Padang in the Indian Ocean. The archipelago comprises four inhabited islands: Siberut (4480 kms^2), Sipora (845 kms^2) and North and South Pagai (1675 kms^2). All in all, there are 45,000 inhabitants. As early as 1600 Pagai was mentioned by crewmen of Dutch East India ships. North and South Pagai were named the Nassau Islands. A few years later Sipora was christened 'Goe Fortuyn' (Good Fortune), as a ship of the VOC (Dutch East India Company) had happened to encounter another East India ship in this area, adrift with one hundred and sixty victims of an epidemic aboard. The remainder of the crew, spared from the disease, had the 'good fortune' to be rescued by the VOC ship. Even then Siberut was called Mantana or Mintaon, names that like the present name of Mentawai – never used by the inhabitants themselves – can undoubtedly be traced to the word for man: ***manteu***.

▲ *In Siberut a family group of some ten nuclear families live in one communal pile-dwelling, the* **uma**.

against him and bring misfortune.
The following discussion will explain some aspects of such a world view on the basis of a society having a very direct communication with the animated cosmos. This concerns a region in Indonesia where to this day the old, prehistoric traditions have clearly been preserved: the Mentawai archipelago west of Sumatra. From a technical point of view, the traditional Mentawai way of life is simpler than that of most other sedentary ethnic groups in Indonesia. Only nomadic groups of hunters and gatherers such as the Kubu, who will be discussed later in the present chapter, lead an even more 'primitive' life. But I hope to show that this 'primitivity' has nothing to do with the spiritual value of the notions going hand in hand with such a simple way of life.

The bow and its hunter

The Mentawai Islands are covered in dense, tropical rain forest, and are sparsely populated. Traditionally, the inhabitants live off the land, cultivating sago, tubers and bananas, but they also raise chickens and pigs, and go hunting and fishing. The workload is divided among the men and the women. There is no further specialization. Neither are there any political positions; the Mentawaians have neither chiefs, nor slaves. The community is organized in clan groups of about ten nuclear families. They live in one big, common clan house, sharing the responsibility for important activities. These clan houses are built along the rivers, at irregular distances from each other. No paths have been laid out in Mentawai; the canoe is the most important means of transport, used to collect the harvest from the plantations, or to visit neighbours in the valley.

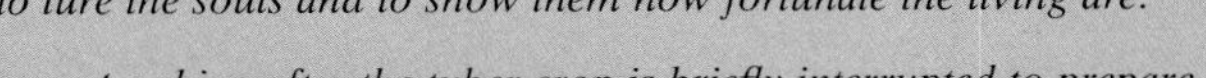

◄ *For great feasts the communal dwelling is beautifully decorated, to lure the souls and to show them how fortunate the living are.*

Cultivating the (wet) taro fields is a woman's job. ▼

Looking after the tuber crop is briefly interrupted to prepare a meal. ▼

In Mentawai, grated coconut is daily fare. ►

The Mentawaians make their few implements and utensils with a devotion far beyond any technical requirements. Special care is taken to give an object the artistic shape that traditionally belongs to it. The Mentawaians maintain that otherwise the object would not 'match its essence' (*mateu*), and such an object cannot be relied upon.

An event among the Sakuddei will clarify the meaning of the term *mateu*. This group lives in the interior of Siberut, the northernmost island of the archipelago. Once Gotta, their best hunter, taught archery. The bows are made of hard and heavy palm wood, and a lot of force is needed to bend them. The trial shots were so clumsy that the beautifully decorated top was damaged soon after they started. Gotta's face clearly showed his alarm, but all apologies were met by his reassurance that he knew it had not been done deliberately. The following days it became clear how much effort it takes to make a bow. Suitable wood had to be found, one had to shape it properly, the ends had to be carved. For hours the bow had to be honed on a grindstone, and then polished with rough leaves and finally coloured with the juice of a red fruit. Asked why he went to all this trouble, Gotta just shrugged his shoulders: otherwise, the bow would not be *mateu*, it would not 'match its essence'. At first it seemed he thus wanted to indicate that such a bow would embarrass a hunter. That was true enough, but actually he meant something else.

Gotta stated that there was little chance of even hitting a monkey with a carelessly decorated bow. This seemed to indicate that magic images were involved, and that an object gained special supernatural powers as a result of the decorations. However, this interpretation met with utter incomprehension. Only much later did I understand the real meaning of the phrase: 'the bow is not *mateu*': 'the bow does not feel matched to its essence'.

The Mentawaians see themselves surrounded, not by objects they can use, but by subjects who might allow the people to use them. For everything, man, animal and plant, but also every object, lives and has a soul. And a living being such as a bow can only be put to good use if it feels itself to be a bow, that is if its appearance expresses the bow's essence. And an integral part of this appearance are its traditional shape, and its decorations and colours, as these were handed down from the ancestors.

This way the functional and the artistic are at one. A thing grows good, because it is beautiful; not because, by means of artistic extras, it should be endowed with magic powers, but because otherwise the object would be unsound from within.

Nobody can force things, though. An object that has been shaped according to its essence, also has its own personal character. Somebody may be a good hunter and possess a formally immaculate bow, and yet frequently miss his target. If so, the bow clearly does not 'get on with' him and the hunter has no option but to give it to a friend with whom the bow might 'get on' better. The bow that got damaged during practice, did 'get on' with Gotta, and that's why he was so dismayed by the loss. The bow had had an essence matching Gotta's. Their good relationship was the condition for his success as a hunter.

◂ *In particular for festive ceremonies such as a wedding, the Mentawaians richly adorn themselves.*

◂ *Learn young, learn fair: a small boy hunting birds.*

▴ *Arrowheads for the monkey hunt are rubbed with poison; the hunter grows most of the ingredients himself.*

The less than perfect canoe

Due to the lack of any kind of labour specialization, among the Sakuddei I initially appeared in a strange light. They had kindly made me a member of their group and built a small dwelling for me, that I equipped with all my belongings, and that would turn out to be my home for the next two years. But the better they came to understand the function of all those strange things, the weirder they seemed to find me. After a while I discovered the reason: they were convinced that everything I possessed I had made myself: my watch, my camera, my tape recorder, my pens and my books full of mysterious letters. How much cleverer than they we whites must be! I tried to explain that one of us knows no more than one of them, but that everybody knows something different and that therefore ten of us know ten times more than one. Among the Sakuddei ten people know ten times the same things.

They could imagine something like this. They too, knew people who were better suited for a certain job than others, people, for instance, who were good at building exceedingly light and graceful canoes. If you yourself were not very good at it, you could go to such a person and ask him to build a canoe for you. For his trouble you would give him a pig or something similar. I asked them: "Then why doesn't one of you only build canoes? That way you would always be sure of a good canoe. And the pigs the canoe builder would get in return, he could easily trade for all his further needs." When it finally dawned on them what I meant, they started to laugh: "Gee, how boring that would be!".

◂ *With great care, the arrowheads are fashioned out of palmwood (the shaft is a reed). The shape of the arrowhead depends on the target.*

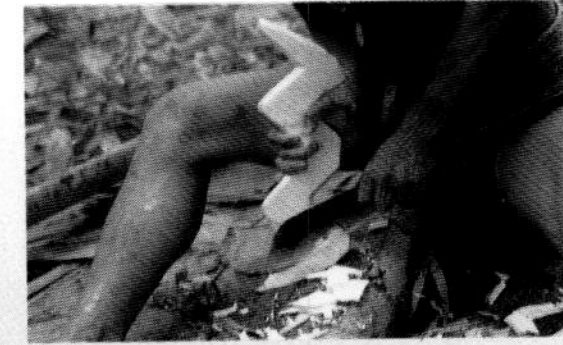

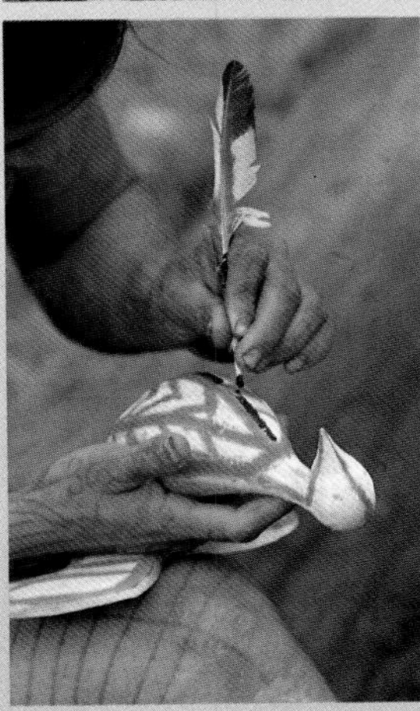

▲ *Carving and painting 'toys for the soul': a wooden bird. If during the work the woodcarver finds that the form tends toward a type different from the one he had envisaged, he will abandon his original idea, and adjust to the new development.* ▶

A toy for the soul

Hundreds of skulls attached to the cross beams of the front verandah of the communal pile-dwelling of the Sakuddei testified to Gotta's hunting successes. These were the skulls of monkeys, deer, and boar. Many of them had been inlaid with mother-of-pearl and decorated with tufts of frayed sago leaves, painted yellow. Inserted in the crown of each deer skull was a painted stick holding a small wooden bird, its wings outspread. Here too, the explanation was: 'Otherwise they would not be *mateu*'. And again, the meaning of that word lay concealed in a very special notion.

The hunted animals, too, have their own individual souls. Just like those of all other things, these souls are capable of separating themselves from their possessors. As a kind of invisible double they wander around, having their own experiences, both good and bad. But between soul and possessor a link remains, and if something happens to the soul, its possessor too, is in danger. If one morning, for no apparent reason, someone awakes in a bad mood, and all day has the feeling that everything goes wrong, the Mentawaians say that his soul has probably experienced something unpleasant.

The Mentawaians use these ideas for success in the hunt. When they come home with some game caught in the jungle, they will carefully clean the skull and hang it up in the house, hoping that the animal's soul will remain with it. Before they go out hunting again, they will make sacrifices to their trophies and beseech the souls to call their brothers and sisters, their cousins and friends to come and join them here so that they

▲ *The skulls of killed animals are beautifully decorated and hung on the front verandah of the* **uma**, *in the hope that they will lure other game from the surrounding forest.*

won't have to stay alone in the house. The souls remaining with the skulls will do as they are told, and when the Mentawaians enter the forest, they will see the game whose soul has already been lured into the house. Now this game has only one wish, subconscious as it were: to be shot.

But the spell will only work, if the souls of the captured animals do indeed stay with the skulls. That is why the Sakuddei go to so much trouble to make their stay as pleasant as possible. They offer them meat, decorate the skulls with leaves and red seeds, paint them with ingenious spirals, and inlay the eye sockets with mother-of-pearl. If the hunt has provided a deer, then as a finishing touch they will place a carved wooden bird between the antlers. This bird, too, is meant to cheer the soul; it is called *umat simagere*: a toy for the soul.

So the same basic notion applies here as in the case of implements and utensils. The beauty of the objects is a condition for their soundness, because otherwise they would be unable to function in a way that 'matches their essence'. Now for the hunt, it is the soul of the captured animal that has to be provided with a beautiful environment. Only if the soul is made happy, will it stay and summon other souls.

The decorated body

Analogous ideas apply to the people themselves. An important event in the life of the Mentawaians is the tattoo. Once body growth stops, around the sixteenth or seventeenth year, the first of a series of tattoos is applied. The completion of the decoration may take

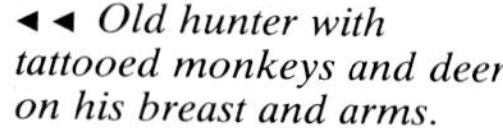

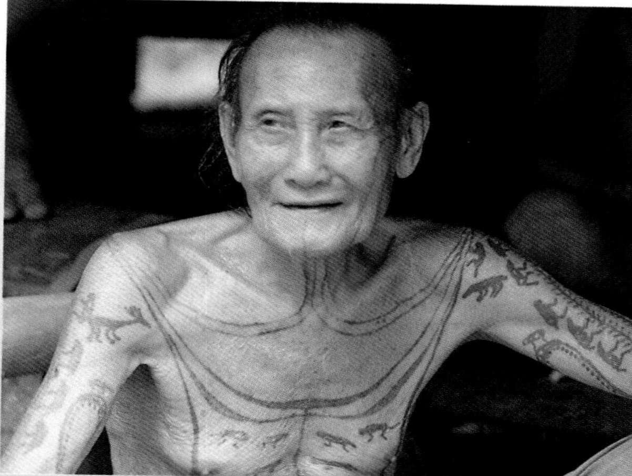

◄◄ *Old hunter with tattooed monkeys and deer on his breast and arms.*

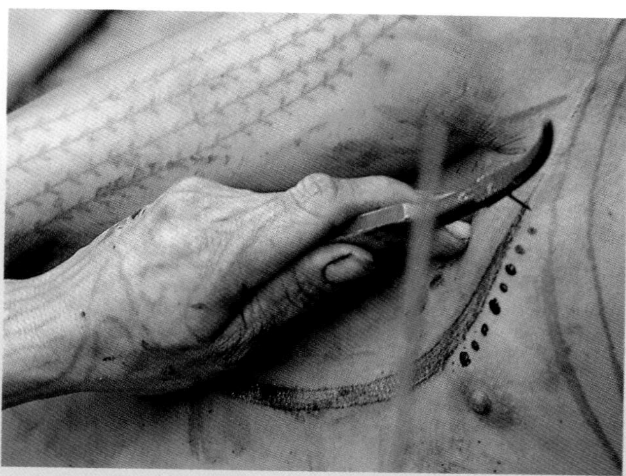

◄ *Tattooing is a painful process, but essential to a 'dignified' body. So as to render the pain bearable, a pattern is applied in several stages, in the course of a few years.*

years, as it is too painful to tattoo the whole body in one session. Many boys and girls openly admit to their fear of it. Yet none of the Sakuddei wanted to back out. The Indonesian government has banned the tattoo – like many other 'primitive' elements in the Mentawai culture. By the end of the sixties, government influence was most strongly felt in the coastal areas, and those who had themselves tattooed here, were punished by having to work without pay on policemen's plots of land for a couple of weeks. It was an easy way to find labour: many young people rather took the punishment into the bargain, than relinquish the old traditions. Here too, magic notions apparently caused this stubborn resistance. But the Mentawaians saw things differently. Only those who are tattooed, are *mateu*, and only they keep their souls sufficiently attracted to stay around, and not disappear to the ancestors. What is clearly involved here, is the idea that there is more to man than his natural growth. In the same way that education shapes the mind, thus the body too must be shaped to express the essence of an adult.

Before the actual tattooing begins, a pattern is drawn. In the case of a boy, the man doing the tattoo will take his own body as a model; in the case of a girl, a woman is asked as a model. ▼

Art for life

One day a neighbouring group invited the Sakuddei to a feast. The occasion was a sad one, so sad that it was hard to summon the festive spirit that otherwise makes all Mentawai ceremonies such happy events. And yet, it was this happiness that was the point of it all. For many weeks a man had had a tumour in his throat. He could hardly swallow, and had grown terribly thin. The medicine-men had tried everything possible. They had driven away all harmful forces, and had made sacrifices to reconcile the spirits whom the sick man might have offended by wrong behaviour or violation of taboos. But all to no avail. Apparently, his soul, for reasons known only to her, had lost her zest for life. She had become homesick for the ancestors and had gone to their villages. This meant mortal danger. For if the soul likes it at the ancestors', if she shares their meals and adorns herself together with them, the human being must die.

The medicine-men could invoke the ancestors, imploring them to set the soul free. But it was at least as important to convince the soul herself that there was something better. She had to be shown that life was beautiful and worth living. Festivities around the sick man were to give the soul the impression that being with him was so appealing that she would realize that she couldn't be better off among the ancestors. Like a bridegroom, the sick man was decorated with ornaments and garlands of flowers; hence the name of this curing ceremony: *pangurei*, 'wedding celebration'. The Sakuddei had brought chickens and pigs. From another valley too, friends had come, every one of them groaning under the weight of a live pig. For two days they had carried these animals across the mountains, lashed to their backs. In return the group of the sick man gave ceremonial presents matching the former piece by piece, as in the case of a bride-price.

Dance of the medicine men, the pre-eminent physicians ▾ of Mentawai.

During a healing ceremony, with sacred plants, medicine men cast a spell on the patient. ▴

Though here the bond to be strengthened was not the one between a groom and his bride, but the one between the sick man and his soul. All night long people danced and sang around the sick man, pantomimes were performed, life was shown at its most colourful, in all its richness. This was one great performance of artistic skills and everyone present contributed as much as possible. This time it was not an object that had to be shaped according to its own matching essence, but life itself.

The great festival

Even more important than cure is prevention. Man must take care to lead an attractive life, or else the soul will feel neglected and the human being himself will fall ill. This includes beauty of appearance, the tattoos and the pointed teeth, as well as painting one's body and adorning oneself. The beauty of the group's communal home is also part of it; the flowers planted around it, and the carved wooden figures decorating the walls. These figures too, are part of the 'essence' of a house; they are not idols, as the missionaries burning them wrongly supposed. But first and foremost, an attractive life includes many festivities, sometimes lasting several months.
During such feasts life is cleansed of harmful influences, and all benign forces are invoked. Once the feasting ground has thus been prepared, the medicine-men will sit down in front of the entrance to the house and in lengthy songs they will invoke the souls of those present. Then these are supposed to come and see how well off the living are, so that they will stay around and certainly not succumb to the temptations of the Beyond. The house is decorated, beautiful possessions are displayed, and the meat for the feast is waiting in wooden dishes. The people are wearing their finest ornaments, have put flowers in their hair, painted their faces with black dots and rubbed themselves with aromatic plants. In front of the house a large gateway has been erected with flowers and plaiting, and again the sculptured birds are hanging there to lure the souls: art for life.

Livestock of the spirits

The Mentawai look upon game as the livestock of their ancestors and the spirits. One myth is about a man who is never successful with his bow and arrow, until he finally finds himself in the regions of the spirits. Here everything is just like it is among humans, but of course more beautiful. Though compared to the human world, many things are the other way around. Here wild deer come to the spot near the house where in the world of Man the pigs are fed. The hunter is allowed to shoot one deer, and then he learns that from now on the people are to offer the left ear of all game to the spirits. To Man, left is the bad side, and an ear seems a small enough gift. Yet, both parties are content, for among the spirits everything is reversed. As a guarantee of future success in the hunt, the people are to hang the decorated skulls in their communal house.

Renewed attention for traditions

The colonial government and the Mission started their work in Mentawai only shortly after 1900. As relatively little force was exerted, the initial results were meagre. Only after Indonesian independence were modernization campaigns launched to more effect. Besides, a few years later international timber companies started the commercial exploitation of the tropical rain forest. Nowadays most Mentawaians are Christians; only a few groups in the interior still live according to the original traditions. From 1978-1981 the Dutch Ministry for Development Cooperation and The World Wildlife Fund supported a project of the Indonesian Ministry for Social Affairs, that was meant to contribute to the survival of the old ecological system. One also hoped to achieve a closer fit than in the past, between the social development and the cultural traditions of the Mentawaians.

The Kubu: survival in a protected jungle

The Trans-Sumatra Highway is an essential link in reaching Kubu country. Along this route that is both highway and village street with its chickens left to stray, its goats and playing children, here and there small groups of Kubu hang around.
Often a begging hand reaching through one's car window, is the traveller's first encounter with the Kubu. Sometimes they will suddenly show up in the middle of the road, forcing cars and buses to stop. Only after the hand has been filled, will they let people through. In those instances, the travellers' judgements vary from 'poor wretches' to 'troublesome parasites'. Whatever one may think, the sight of such a group is shocking: skinny, soiled bodies, women all of them breast-feeding a child, men wearing only grimy cotton loin-cloths, begging on the fringes of civilization.
The Kubu: Were they not the darlings of the colonial ethnographers? Weren't they the proud hunters of the Sumatra jungles? Weren't they the superior guides leading the way for gold-diggers and expeditions searching for oil? And were they not the indispensable helpers of Administration officials hunting big game? (Public officers who had their pictures taken with their catches, but without any Kubu!)
The faces of the present Kubu closely resemble those on the pictures from the beginning of the century: a chin-tuft, shocks of hair, women with a shy look in their eyes. The ever-hungry dogs are still scraping around at their masters' feet. What has induced the Kubu to stoop to begging? Aren't there any possibilities to continue their traditional way of life? How many Kubu actually still survive?
'Unspoilt children of nature' is the classical description of the Kubu in their traditional situation; a way of life that is now largely a thing of the past. Their original accommodation consisted of a simple shelter made of sticks and leaves, with a small floor just off the ground. This sufficed for several nights, and was tailored to their nomadic lifestyle. Mobility being its dominant characteristic, their existence did not call for a more permanent dwelling.
Such a hut was built within an hour. The Kubu lived in small encampments of three to eight of these huts. At night, husband, wife and small children shared one hut. From the age of eight more or less, boys slept in their own huts. But, until they had a wife of their own, they would continue to eat with the nuclear family, and give their parents anything they had caught or gathered. Widows had their own shelters too, slightly removed from the group.
The Kubu lived on nearly all the animals found in their environment: several kinds of deer, large lizards, boar, tapirs, honey bears, monkeys, birds, and in the past surely elephants as well. The one known exception was the tiger. The Kubu were supposed to have a special relationship with them.

As to the origin of the Kubu, opinions still vary widely. Some authors believe they represent old mesolithic traditions; others believe that at a later stage the Kubu retreated into the forest. ▸

▲ *At bus stations and along the road, displaced Kubu are found begging. Sometimes they offer medicinal plants and roots for sale.*

Spear

The Kubu spear, the ***kujur***, is a straight stick, about 2.5 metres long, with an iron head. In the beginning of the century the ethnographer Hagen described the ***kujur*** as a clumsy weapon, hardly manoeuverable in the dense jungle. He thought it to be a relic from ancient times, now obsolete. Apparently the Kubu disagreed, and still do. It remains their only weapon, and according to them, it is very effective. 'Throwing' the spear requires a special technique. It is thrust forward, not overarm (over the shoulder) but underarm: while one hand pushes the weapon, the other hand guides it. The game, cornered by dogs, is run through at close range. A throw from some distance would be rather useless. In the jungle trees and bushes stand in the way of a spear's trajectory. Depending on the kind of game, the Kubu use various spearheads, obtained by barter. They do not decorate their spears.

The spear was the only weapon these nomads used. Neither blow-pipe nor bow and arrow were known to them. Indispensable to any hunter was a dog to corner the game. And, of course, the dog also depended on the hunt. If nothing was caught, there would be no food for him either.

Like many other hunters and gatherers, the Kubu did not primarily live on game but on products gathered by the women. Tubers, forest fruit, leaves, freshwater mussels, snails and honey were eaten far more often, and so were fish, shrimp, tortoises and turtles. High humidity and warm weather made it virtually impossible to keep meat for any longer period. And although the Kubu were familiar with the technique of smoking meat, this didn't offer much relief either. Thus, many other groups benefited from a successful hunt thanks to an extensive network of exchange relations.

Around every hut there were some cooking-pots, a few pieces of textile, some bars of resin (for illumination at night), a small stock of tubers, a few knives and a spear. The latter two items were obtained by barter, from people in neighbouring villages. For a long time this exchange must have taken place via a system of 'silent trade'. At an agreed spot the Kubu would deposit forest products such as rattan, resin and honey and retreat into the jungle. A trader could take the goods if he left enough products in exchange: metal spearheads, knives, salt and textile. A system of signs was used to express agreement with the deal without showing oneself to the other party. At a later

A brief interval during a trip, to let fellow group members share in the success of the hunt: smoked tapir. ▸

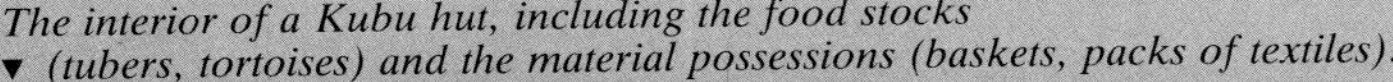

The interior of a Kubu hut, including the food stocks ▾ *(tubers, tortoises) and the material possessions (baskets, packs of textiles).*

stage intermediaries, *jenang*, got involved. A *jenang* became the link between the Kubu and the surrounding world, thus he could monopolize trade relations. As a result of their nomadic existence, the Kubu never accumulated much household gear. An itinerant existence is incompatible with great material riches. Freedom of movement would be reduced considerably, if the weight of the possessions literally exceeded the carrying capacity of the group members. All travellers who in the past, encountered small groups of Kubu in the forest – often perchance – predicted their extinction. This fate would be unavoidable as a result of either physically dying out, or assimilation into surrounding society. In the twenties, Administration official Tassilo Adam regretted that "for such a people there is no future. Soon these happy, peace-loving and benevolent inhabitants of the jungle will be 'civilized', which undoubtedly will make them less happy." A statement made at a time that one could hardly suspect which processes were to be set in motion in the region.

◄ *In brooks and rivers the women fish with various kinds of fykes made of tree bark and split rattan.*

◄ *The Kubu who by now practise agriculture, use a small axe with a helve made of light but tough wood.*

◄ *Kubu basket made of split and plaited rattan. The colour is applied with so-called 'dragon's blood', a red resin gained from the fruit of a special kind of rattan. The bands with which the basket is carried over the head and shoulders, are made of tree bark.*

◄ *Arrowheads for various kinds of game: the one at the top is meant for tortoises, the bottom one for boar and deer.*

Religion?

A cultural peculiarity that drew a lot of attention at the beginning of this century was the supposed lack of any religion among the Kubu. This was seen as pre-eminent proof that this ethnic group stood on the bottom rung of the ladder of civilization. One of the researchers: "They neither worshipped nor feared spirits or anything like that. During a heavy thunderstorm, when I observed them twice as sharply, they remained calmly seated and went on talking as if nothing were afoot. Among the Ridan Kubu I couldn't find out anything about religion, not a trace, nor did I see any object suggesting it." The heated discussion on this subject finally concentrated on the question what religion actually is. Underlying the Kubu's way of life is a specific world view. In many respects, the complex of images and notions it embraces, deviates from what is called 'religion' elsewhere. As evidence against the supposed lack of religion, one could adduce the custom of fleeing – for fear of the spirits – from a spot where one of the group members died.

Threat

Although some maps still give the impression that South Sumatra is dominated by tropical rain forest, even a superficial look around the region will show that this is no longer the case. Over the past few years, timber felling has opened up enormous stretches of primeval forest, an intervention followed by many others. Laying out coffee, rubber and palm-oil plantations has also caused the disappearance of vast forest areas. In addition, the expansion of local agriculture and reclamation for (Javanese) transmigrants took its toll. And at the moment, via the network of roads around the Trans-Sumatra Highway all kinds of newcomers are invading the area, to develop independent agricultural activities. All around one hears both these advancing farmers and the local Administration officials describe the jungle as *tanah kosong*, empty land. The fact is, the Kubu

Land titles

In Indonesia, the Basic Agrarian Law of 1960 restricts landownership per nuclear family. Land rights are linked to the cultivation method. A family practising dry rice cultivation is entitled to more land than a family engaged in wet rice cultivation. Nearly all uncultivated land, such as jungle or marshland, is owned by the state. As the Kubu neither till their land, nor use it to plant trees or raise animals, their title to the land and its products is not recognized. Nevertheless, for their survival hunters and gatherers require about 100 hectares of primeval forest per head. Since the government does not accept the traditional claims of hunters and gatherers on large stretches of jungle, in some regions farmers have started to annex the Kubu lands. In addition, timber-felling concessions have been granted, and the jungle is used for plantations or settlements. To get land claims recognized, some kind of cultivation is essential. A demand that is incompatible with Kubu culture.

▲ *Kubu boy along the Trans-Sumatra Highway near Bangko.*

are not recognised as the lawful owners of this region which until recently was unspoilt.

The loss in acreage of tropical rain forest in Sumatra means a proportionate limitation of the Kubu's environment. As pure hunters and gatherers they have been able to support themselves in this area for centuries. Their needs were limited, their means sufficient. To the outsider the jungle may be dangerous and impenetrable, to the Kubu, who have learned to interpret the signs of nature, it is their familiar environment.

The inroads made on the vegetation resulted in the extinction of a number of animal species important to the Kubu. Due to this deterioration of the animal world, the Kubu's chances of survival have further diminished, and ultimately their traditional lifestyle is at stake. In areas where deforestation was so radical that the Kubu simply had to adapt, they have in some cases embarked on small-scale agriculture, or gone to work for farmers in the vicinity.

In addition to the skulls of game, peelings and shells lying around the huts, we now find old batteries, empty tins, pieces of plastic: silent witnesses of increased contact with modern society. For their primary food supply, many Kubu now depend on the village community. Especially those who have come into contact with timber felling or the various development projects, find themselves trapped between two worlds. Ironically, these Kubu may earn their food and tobacco as night watchmen guarding the bulldozers that destroy their original habitat in the daytime. And if food cannot be earned even in this way, some Kubu ultimately take the law into their own hands. Then, aggressively, they will force the outside world, for instance along the Trans-Sumatra Highway, to dispense some food.

▲ *A small tortoise (a delicacy to the Kubu) is cleaned on a rack on which to smoke meat.*

Tobacco in any form is often the first product to link groups such as the Kubu with the outside world. A link steadily growing ▼ *stronger.*

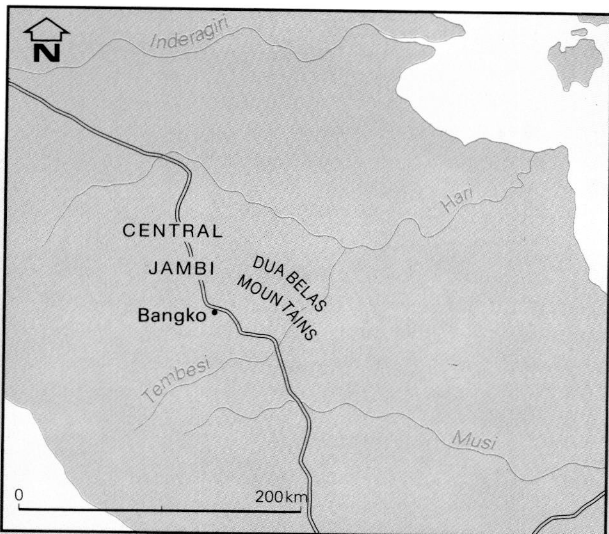

▲ *The forest is now traversed by numerous unmetalled roads along which felled timber is carried off. Over the past few years the life sphere of the Kubu has changed rapidly.*

Protection

Out of an estimated 15,000 Kubu now living in the south of Sumatra, in spite of everything a small minority persist in their traditional way of life. Though all kinds of innovations have been devised for this group as well, so far the Kubu around the Duabelas Range (Central Jambi), some 900, have resisted all 'temptations'. Over the past few years they have repeatedly rejected the opportunities to settle in villages and get used to a different, sedentary lifestyle. These Kubu did not stay passive, though. In 1984 a small delegation approached the *bupati*, the district head of Bangko. Accompanied by their *jenang*, they pleaded with this official to preserve their jungle, and asked him not to disturb their traditional way of life. The request was heard and sent on to a higher authority. For if the forest was to be saved, timber-felling concessions already granted would have to be revoked, and locations planned for transmigration would not become available.

Besides, the request ran counter to the general course set for the development of the Kubu. This people was and still is numbered among the most primitive groups in Indonesia, those most in need of development. Recognition of the land rights claimed by the Kubu for the purpose of continuing their traditional lifestyle, would be most exceptional. In Indonesia, landownership is not exclusively granted to ethnic groups. As the following chapter will show, so far there has been only one exception, for the benefit of the Baduy in West Java.

However, the bad situation of thousands of Kubu, the very limited success of many development projects and the increasing number of displaced Kubu, forced the authorities to rethink their policies. That is probably why the request was received with more sympathy than seemed likely at first. Besides, a favourable incidental circumstance was the support of the Conservation Department of the Indonesian Ministry of Forestry. The Kubu request was easily linked to the aims of this organization.

The central part of the province of Jambi is a vast stretch of marshy lowlands. As a range amidst that lowland, the Duabelas Mountains have an important function. As long as the forests on these hills remain

▲ *This man's life experience greatly differs from the prospects of the younger generation of Kubu.*

A king without a realm or subjects

The Kubu have no political organization above local level. Neither are there any Kubu to represent their people in the world outside. In part, the tragic course of Kubu history can be attributed to this. In the past no relations were developed with the region's political authorities as a channel for raising the issue of possible abuses. Lately, there has been a change. Increasingly the Kubu attempt to assert their rights. At the end of the fifties a certain Idrus bin Trees went to Jakarta, claiming to be Raja Kubu, the King of the Kubu. Particularly due to ignorance, this 'king' was received with all kinds of honours. Thus high political functionaries gave him presents, partly meant to improve relations with the Kubu. In the end his deceit was found out. Government circles grew aware of the fact that the Kubu had no king at all. Idrus bin Trees was charged with 'misrepresentation', and on 1 February, 1959, in a Jakarta court, a year's imprisonment was demanded for this self-styled king without a realm or subjects.

▲ *The Kubu distinguish at least two kinds of huts. One of these actually is only a shelter, meant for one night; under it, one sleeps on a bed of leaves on the ground. The other kind is more elaborate: it has a small floor. Such huts are found everywhere in the forest.*

intact, the water is stored for some time, and gradually released. Thus the lowland never dries out, not even if it fails to rain, while in the rainy season the water does not immediately flood the lower regions. Encroaching on the forest would greatly diminish this sponge effect and, moreover, present the danger of erosion.

In addition, saving the forest would offer the existing game the chance to survive. In other places, where the rain forest has already been turned into arable land, plantations or villages, there is no longer any niche for tigers, tapirs, honey bears and elephants, to name but a few of the larger endangered species. Hence in this district the conservationists' interests coincide with the Kubu's. If the nature reserve is to play its protective part in the future as well, then the threat of timber felling, transmigration and farmers in search of new arable land, must be averted. The outside world in particular will have to take action towards this aim. On paper the region is now a recognized reserve, but the plans mentioned above have not all been cancelled yet.

Another threat may come from the Kubu themselves: in the past it has often been suggested that hunters and gatherers consciously strive for a balance with surrounding nature. In practice, the natural resources

The Kubu oath

Many outsiders believe the Kubu will surely give up their way of life as soon as they see more of modern village life. But in practice it turns out that the Kubu deliberately reject that change. And by no means out of ignorance. They will answer any question about the future by referring to the past. Apparently their ancestors had forsworn village society, and all it entails. In a discussion with some high Indonesian officials about the desirability of a reserve, the Kubu repeated this oath:

"Just let me go,
My rice will be wild tubers;
My buffalo in the forest: the tapir and the deer;
My goat: the mouse deer and the swine;
My chicken: the pheasant and the wood grouse;
My house will be amongst the buttresses;
I shall drink water out of a wooden bowl;
(and if I fail to live up to all this)
At the top the tree will lose its crown,
At the foot it will lose its roots,
And in the middle it will be eaten away".

are chiefly maintained by a low population density, by limited technological means and by the low level of needs amongst these groups. The question is: will the Kubu be able to control the number of births, so as not to exceed the region's capacity to sustain them? In addition, they should not exploit their environment to the extent that the jungle is endangered from within. If the hunting methods change, for instance by the use of guns, the interests of the Kubu and those of the conservationists will diverge. Of course, an excessive increase in the trade in forest products such as rattan, resin and honey, will have the same result. Then the Kubu would surely lose the support of conservation circles.

By a wrong way of dealing with surrounding nature, the Kubu themselves would in the long run risk the continuation of their preferred traditional lifestyle. For its part, the outside world has assaulted Kubu territory again and again, and so far has failed to come up with any good ideas for a new (adjusted) lifestyle. It is to be hoped that a new policy will find ways to attune ecological management to the interests of the Kubu.

▲ *The flower of Zingiberaceae grows close to the ground, and provides a sweetish juice popular in particular among Kubu children. This plant is mainly found along river banks and in abandoned fields.*

In the past, Kubu women sometimes fell victim to slavery. And to this day, on the approach of strangers in the forest, they still make off. ▼

▲ *View of Lake Toba near Balige.*

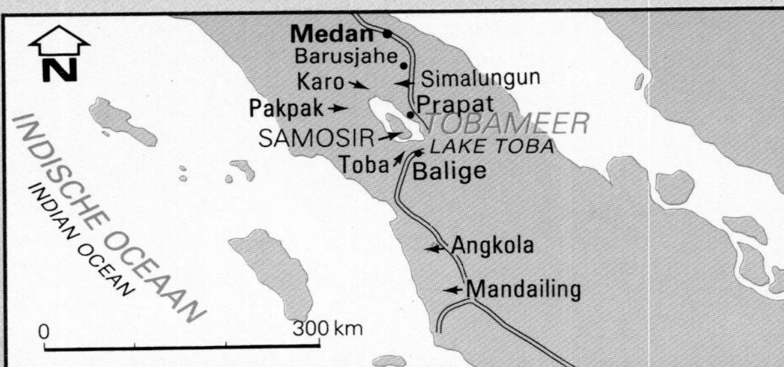

The Batak

In general the Batak are divided into groups according to their different dialects. In addition to the Toba Batak there are the Karo Batak, the Pakpak Batak, the Angkola Batak, the Mandailing Batak and the Simalungun Batak.
The two southern Batak groups, Mandailing and Angkola, are mainly Islamic, whereas the four northern groups, Toba, Pakpak, Simalungun and Karo, are Christian.
It is assumed that nowadays more Batak live beyond Batak country than within it.

Adat house of the
▼ *Karo Batak in Barusjahe.*

The tugu of the Toba Batak: a grave as a monument and a beacon

Most of the mountain country of the Batak in North Sumatra has already been cultivated. The luxuriant vegetation still offering a habitat to small groups of Kubu, disappeared here long ago.
Batak is the collective name of six ethnic groups in the region. Though they number three million, half of them belong to one group, the Toba Batak. Home to the latter is the vast mountainous area around Lake Toba, as well as the island of Samosir, in this lake.
When approaching Batak country from Medan, due to the continuously climbing road one will enjoy steadily widening vistas. The unexpected view of Lake Toba is the ultimate climax. Wherever rice fields are interrupted by clusters of trees, one finds *huta*, the villages with their characteristic Batak houses. Striking are the steeples rising above the fields.
Inevitably one's attention is also drawn by the numerous odd constructions along roads and pathways. They are decorated with all kinds of indigenous symbols, and often with the Christian cross as well. These curious concrete constructions, called *tugu* and *tambak*, are the modern dwellings of the Toba Batak's ancestors.

A landmark

The construction of these modern ancestral graves, a phenomenon chiefly encountered in the Toba area, is a consequence of recent developments in Batak culture. The initial impetus for these was given in the fifties, a period of economic revival. Many Toba Batak moved to other regions or big cities, and acquired a certain wealth. In spite of this, the bond with the family staying behind did not weaken. On the contrary, such links were, and are, increasingly emphasized. In the construction of the *tugu* and the *tambak* this is expressed in a very special way. Mainly financed by migrated Toba Batak, these monumental ancestral graves are still mushrooming.
For that matter all kin, wherever they live, have the duty to contribute to the building cost. And though the latter is by no means modest, a Toba Batak, and in particular a migrant, will not readily evade this obligation. No matter how far from home, he thus stays in touch with his original culture, and avoids feeling lost in his new environment.
As a rule a *tugu* contains the remains of one very early ancestor, whereas the *tambak*, as a family grave, houses the remains of several ancestors of more recent generations. Another difference is found in the design. According to an unwritten law, a *tambak* should not be as high as a *tugu*. Hence everywhere the latter tower over the other ancestral graves.
Though the word *tugu*, meaning (commemorative) needle, is taken from the national Indonesian language, the ideas underlying these pretentiously designed monuments are deeply rooted in Batak culture. Thus many characteristics of the *tugu* ceremony, the ritual performed at the dedication of a monument, originate

*A **tambak** in Samosir. In this island it is harder to distinguish between a **tugu** and a **tambak** than elsewhere in Toba country. This **tambak** houses the remains of several ancestors: one behind every door.* ►

7 2
1979

▲ A depiction of the **hariara** tree crowns a simple **tugu** near Laguboti (built in 1969).

in an ancient Batak tradition: the reburial of ancestors. For this reburial they used to raise a burial mound (called *tambak*, like the modern family grave). The bones of some ancestors were exhumed and transferred to such a burial mound. This was done if the progeny proved to be numerous, and preferably also rich and highly regarded. Such a reburial was accompanied by all kinds of ceremonial festivities, lasting at least seven days. Nothing was too expensive, or too much trouble. On top of the burial mound the descendants planted a *hariara* tree (a kind of Ficus), the 'tree of life' from the Toba Batak myths of origin. In these myths this tree reaches from the underworld into the upper world, symbolizing both life and the unity of the cosmos.

Around the turn of the century, when European missionaries had gained a firm foothold in Batak country, the great reburial festivals were banned or thoroughly 'adapted' to Christian norms. And the burial mounds themselves underwent a similar adaptation. Stone graves bearing a Christian cross came into fashion. They were called *semen* (from: cement, and pronounced accordingly), after the new building material. When, at a later stage, the reburial feasts were reallowed, from this low *semen* the modern *tugu* developed, that striking needle in the landscape. For that matter, reburial in a traditional burial mound is still occasionally done, but in general it is now considered less practical. The bones cannot be properly kept clean, and what is at least as important nowadays: unlike a *tugu*, a burial mound blends almost entirely into its surroundings, and is not easily recognized from afar by Toba Batak visiting their native region. But even though the traditional burial mound has a more striking shape now, the *hariara* tree depicted on some tugu unmistakably reminds the visitor of the monument's origin: what has changed is not the underlying symbolism, but its expression and hence its appearance. Apart from the traditional burial mounds, stone sarcophagi used to be made in the Toba Batak area, but their high cost severely limited their number. Only a few wealthy people could afford such an expensive grave. In addition, sarcophagi were built by communities in honour of their deserving members. A tribute now paid by building a *tugu*.

▲ House and cross: this **tambak** testifies to the merging of the **adat** and Christianity.

▼ Old sarcophagus in Tomok in Samosir.

Status and symbolism

The *tugu* is built for the founding father of a *marga*, a large patrilineal clan, a man who lived some fifteen generations ago. These forefathers, often war-lords or priests, were all held in high esteem, and became the stuff of myths. This is reflected in the symbols on the *tugu*. If these forefathers are depicted, it's always in dignified, traditional attire. Often they are holding the attributes of a great warrior, of an expert on the *pustaha* (a holy book), or of a great priest. Other symbols on the *tugu* either refer to fertility, or can be traced to the typical cultural elements of the Toba Batak (the *hariara* tree), or belong to traditional ornamentation.

In general, the size of the first *tugu*, built in the fifties, was still quite modest, two to three metres high. Thus the first monument to a founding father of a *marga* in Laguboti (erected in 1952), is hardly bigger than a modern *tambak*. Its depictions, of the attributes of a warrior, are in a sober style. The second monument erected for a *marga* founder in this area (in 1960) already is a bit bigger. On a square platform, statues of the forefather and his wife are enthroned, guarded by a stone crocodile. This forefather, a priest, could summon the crocodile to protect his region. The later monuments erected in Laguboti for founding fathers, thoroughly deserve to be called *tugu*: with their height of twelve to fifteen metres, they rise high above their surroundings.

Although the symbols on the *tugu* refer to the great life in olden times, to the power, the *adat* and the

▲ Statues of the founding father of the **marga** Sibuea and his wife, seated on a grave monument built in 1960. According to the myth, this ancestor was a great priest who could summon a crocodile to protect his territory.

A **tugu** *near Laguboti from the early seventies.* ▸
The founding father is depicted standing, and holding a staff as a mark of his rank, with his wife beside him. Such depictions of the ancestors are quite common.

In Amberita in the island of Samosir, silent witnesses in a spot
▾ *said to have been the meeting-place of powerful heads.*

religion from the era before the arrival of Christianity and the Europeans, they lack the mysticism the earlier sarcophagi radiate. Lake Toba which used to be sacred, was an important point of reference in orientating these megaliths: the 'front' of each sarcophagus had to face the lake.
On the other hand, the modern *tugu* have a less religious orientation, and face the road. The religious aspect has been relegated to the background: *tugu* now serve mainly to command respect from the passers-by, so as to lend the *marga* a higher social status. The current emphasis on the social element is also apparent in the plan to hoist a sarcophagus onto a high *tugu* in the island of Samosir. Like the traditional burial mound, the sarcophagus is now said to be too unobtrusive.

Boundary post

Apart from the loss in religious significance, and their new appreciation as status symbols, an entirely different function accrued to the *tugu*. As they are often placed at the periphery of a *marga*'s domain, they mark the borderline between the territories of the various *marga*. The monument displays the names of the forefathers, thus each passer-by will know exactly which *marga*'s territory he is entering or leaving.
People used to have an intimate bond with the land they tilled and lived on. The grand reburial ceremonies were not merely celebrations of solidarity and common descent, they also were attempts to ensure the fertility of the land, and to restore its order. Together with its people, the land formed a microcosm in itself. But new influences have radically changed the world view of many Toba Batak. No longer do they think of the territory of a *marga* as part of a greater whole. The land now stands for the roots of a *marga*, and as such it supports the latter's identity, as does the *tugu*. Both land and *tugu* have become a means of propagation, instead of an order to be carefully preserved. Now, in modern Sumatra, the Toba Batak distinguish themselves from the surrounding world by the area they live in and by their *tugu* that delimit it.

▲ *To the accompaniment of the* **gondang** *the ritual* **tortor** *is danced, and the ancestors are transferred to their new dwelling.*

Before the ancestors are reburied, a solemn ritual is performed, during which among other things, the bride-givers present **ulos**, *ritual cloths, to the bride-takers. In this case the cloths are* ▼ *buried with the ancestors, and should extend the prosperity and well-being of their descendants.*

Four days of feasting

Like the burial mound in the past, nowadays a new *tugu* is inaugurated with a great traditional reburial feast. With this ritual the members of a *marga*, the patrilineal kingroup, honour their founding fathers. The festivities now last three to four days, instead of seven as they used to. The *marga* who provides (and provided) brides for the celebrating group, occupy a very important position in these festivities. The *adat* obliges a Toba Batak man to look for a wife outside his own group, hence for its survival a *marga* always depends on other groups. All marriage bonds between two *marga* are one-sided: never may a bride be given to a group from whom a bride was once taken. This is partly why various *marga* have developed permanent bride-giver/bride-taker relationships, in which the bride-takers feel inferior to the bride-givers, called *hulahula*. That the *tugu* does not only mention the name of its own *marga*, but also the *hulahula*'s, shows how important the bride's group is.

Of all the animals killed during the ceremony, the biggest specimen will get extra attention. From this animal the so-called *jambar* are cut, the parts all having a special meaning, that are distributed among those taking part in the ritual. Thus in some contexts and regions, the bride-takers used to get the neck, as 'they carried the heaviest burden at a *tugu* ceremony'; even now the bride-takers make great financial sacrifices. At the inauguration ceremony the *jambar* must come from a buffalo, the most valuable animal to the Toba

Batak. At feasts on a smaller scale, a 'short buffalo' will often do, that is: a pig!
The reburial ceremony reaches a climax when the *marga* that provided the founding father's bride, arrives at the feasting-ground. Ritual presents are exchanged, the most important one being the ritual cloth, the *ulos*, a gift from the bride-givers to the celebrating group. The *ulos* betokens a blessing with happiness, prosperity and fertility. The ancestor in whose honour the ritual is performed, hardly enjoys greater respect than the *hulahula*. Though the *tugu* is dedicated to the forefather, respect for him is far less tangible. Apparently at the feast no direct 'contact' is sought with this or any other ancestor – none at all.
An abstinence undoubtedly due to Christian influence. Though since 1940 the Toba Batak themselves manage the Church in their regions, and its policy regarding their own culture has since been considerably eased,

Girls for sale

The group hosting the feast attaches great importance to the continuation of its relations with the **hulahula**, *the bride-givers. This is also apparent from a part of the reburial ritual that takes place on the final day, and is called 'the selling of the girls'. Girls from the* **hulahula** *and boys from the* **marga** *hosting the feast, then dance. During this dance the boy may give the girl a sprig of the* **waringin** *tree (a kind of Ficus), thus proposing to her. Marriages resulting from this part of the* **tugu** *ritual are regarded as special, very favourable unions.*

Ulos

For the traveller visiting Toba Batak country there is no better souvenir than the **ulos**, *a ritual cloth. All kinds of this hand-woven fabric are available, varying from the cloth made for tourists, to the special* **ulos** *meant to bring blessing and fertility at a* **tugu** *inauguration feast. At such a feast all participants must wear an* **ulos**, *folded over their shoulder, and the* **hulahula** *not only give the salutary cloths to the celebrating* **marga**, *but also to the ancestors whose remains have been exhumed. With the coffins, the latter* **ulos** *disappear into the new* **tugu**. *Nowadays, the cloths meant for the ancestors may also be given to their descendants.*

Gondang and Parsantian

When walking in Toba Batak country, sooner or later one will surely hear the ***gondang***, clarinet-like sounds, accompanied by the drums and gongs. No doubt a ritual is taking place somewhere in a village, often a burial or a reburial. As one approaches the festivities, the musicians can be seen on the upper verandah of a traditional pile-dwelling, seven of them if the orchestra is at full strength.
This house is a ***parsantian***, the communal sacrificial house of a branch of the ***marga***. As this house is the ancestral domain, a funeral ceremony will always take place in its vicinity. On the upper verandah, where the orchestra is now playing, the dead used to lie in state, awaiting their festive burial. According to the Toba Batak the sounds of the ***gondang*** link the living to the dead, hence no ***tugu*** feast is complete without this music.

Si Raja Batak

While honouring the ancestors is still considered important in Toba Batak society, other aspects of traditional religion have almost vanished. In 1942 the 'Si Raja Batak' sect was founded to keep the memories of the old traditions alive. The members of this sect form a small group advanced in age. Usually they perform old rituals indoors relating to rice cultivation, in which sacrifices are made to the ancestors and the gods, and for this reason they are not allowed to join the Church.

care is still taken that ancestors do not 'actively' take part in the ceremonies. Thus neither food offerings are allowed (as these might tempt the dead to 'eat'), nor trance (by means of which a deceased might enter a medium). On the other hand, the ban on the *gondang* was lifted. This traditional music is now heard again at every *tugu* ceremony. If nowadays at a reburial ceremony, the ancestors' bones cannot be reburied the same day, they will be kept in the church overnight. The church door is securely locked, and the key carefully guarded. This too, used to be different, indeed quite the opposite: the remains of the ancestors were displayed in the middle of the feasting-ground. For days they were literally the ritual centre, to be reburied only on the final day.
In spite of the bans that still exist, the Toba Batak certainly don't feel burdened by Christianity. Many even boast about being Christians, as this greatly helps to define their present identity, surrounded as they are by Sumatrans who formally adhere to Islam.

Tugu and native country

Although erecting a *tugu* demands a great deal of time and money from all members of the *marga*, nobody will try to evade a contribution. As was mentioned before, the many Toba Batak who have moved away, thus accentuate the strong ties they have with their native country. If in spite of this, someone would want to break these ties, he would risk a great deal. Thus he would have no relatives to fall back on in hard times, and he would have to do without the indispensable blessing of the bride-givers, the *hulahula*. But, worst of all, he would miss out on the *sahala*, the special spiritual power emanating from the ancestors. And if a Toba Batak were to feel too modern for these concepts, threatening social sanctions will provide for the preservation of the bond with the native country.
So, even far from North Sumatra, the Toba Batak will not forget their origins. Objections against the many requests for financial support will be easily overcome. For there will always be a place to come home to. The *tugu* will see to that.

Sahala

An important purpose of the Toba Batak feasts is to gain ***sahala***, the benevolence of the ancestors, their favours. This ***sahala*** is a special spiritual force that can be transferred and/or radiated. Although due to Christian influences the ancestors are not directly approached at a feast (for instance by offering food), they are supposed to be present. And they transfer the ***sahala*** to the participants. The amount of ***sahala*** one can receive depends on one's position in the ***marga***'s family tree. Hence a high position is desirable, and discussions about lines of descent are by no means rare (some ***marga*** have conveniently numbered the various generations starting from the founding father). In case of disagreement about the family tree, no ***tugu*** feast can possibly take place.

The much-discussed 'Highway' takes the traveller along the length of sparsely populated Sumatra (30 million people), from Aceh in the very north to Telukbetung, more than 2,500 kilometres to the south. Parallel to this route runs the Bukit Barisan, two parallel mountain ranges separated by a valley. With its many summits and volcanoes, this twin range dominates the entire island.

In this mountain country numerous rivers rise. Those descending to the west coast are unnavigable, but the rivers in East Sumatra are important as its traditional arteries, its traffic lifelines. Ocean ships sail up the Musi as far as Palembang, Sumatra's oil port 80 kilometres inland (three quarters of Indonesia's crude oil comes from Sumatra).

In the Bukit Barisan Ranges we also find the famous lakes of Ranau, Kerinci, Singkarak and Maninjau. The largest, Lake Toba, lies in the heart of Batak country. Almost fully enclosed by steep cliffs, its circumference exceeds 285 kilometres. This lake once played a part in the ancestor cult of the Toba Batak. As late as 1811 it was first officially reported, but for a long time mysterious tales had been circulating. The first white man to tell the story of his visit to the lake – in 1853 – was a Dutch scholar. For earlier attempts outsiders had invariably paid with their lives.

This secrecy seems to be a thing of the past. Lake Toba is a tourist attraction now, and lovely for bathing. Yet, the stories about ghosts who are said to reside in the unknown depths of the lake, are still very much alive. Rumour has it that in crossing to or from Samosir, the island in Lake Toba, children sometimes disappear, never leaving a trace. The lake may have lost its sanctity, its mysteries remain.

Whereas the Toba Batak were only converted to Christianity around 1900, the Minangkabau in West Sumatra have been Islamic for centuries. This people is known especially for its matrilineal organization in which the women occupy a special position. They own the land and the houses, and after marrying, a woman stays in her parental home. Her husband does likewise, leaving the responsibility for raising their children largely to his brother-in-law. Theirs is a so-called visitors' marriage. It must be added that most Minangkabau live outside West Sumatra. They are the traders of Indonesia, and their characteristic eating-houses are found throughout the archipelago.

People who do live in the Minangkabau area, albeit invisibly, are the legendary ***orang*** Bunian. Though invisible beings are known to live in nearly all regions of Sumatra, the uplands of Padang seem to be very attractive to them. ***Orang*** Bunian are like human beings, with one difference: they are visible only to those who married a Bunian girl!

From Padang and Sibolga one may reach the Mentawai archipelago and Nias, off Sumatra's west coast. Their isolated location has led to a flora and fauna different from that in Sumatra. There even are plants and animals found nowhere else.

Here, as in various regions of Sumatra, deforestation endangers the environment, and in response to this, reserves were established. In Batang Palupuh (West Sumatra), Kerinci Seblat (Central Sumatra), Berbak and Barisan Selatan (South Sumatra), flora and fauna are now protected.

Sumatra's best known national park, Gunung Leuser, lies in Aceh. Partly because of the rehabilitation centre at Bohorok for orang-utang confiscated from traders, this northern province is attracting an increasing number of tourists. Gunung Leuser is a vast area (800,000 hectares, or 3,200 square miles), covered in spectacular mountain woods and lowland rain forests. Deep in this wilderness, far from the 'Highway' rules 'he whose name is never spoken in the jungle': the Sumatran tiger.

A Sumatran tiger in Gunung Leuser. ▼

2  Java

Java. Few coasts attracted so many oppressors, were so crowded with foreigners. No island in the archipelago grew so densely populated. Bowing to all things foreign, the old never gave in to the new. Everywhere, time and again, there is the gleam of the past in Java's caleidoscopic culture.

Hidden away in the western mountains, the Baduy in particular seem to keep Java's rich history alive. Their strict, religious traditions are based on an ancient Javanese belief with Hindu-Buddhist elements. Jet Bakels sketches the special relationship the Baduy used to have with the West-Javanese princes, and explains why even today the ascetic attitude of this people is greatly admired.

In Central Java the princes actually were both king and priest. Madelon Djajadiningrat-Nieuwenhuis places their functioning in a historical perspective and concludes that, despite their diminished executive power, the princes in their role of intermediaries between god and the people still enjoy great charisma.

Like the principalities, the farming communities have undergone administrative reform. Yet, situated in regions where it seems as if time came to a standstill long ago, all aspects of life remained imbued with ancient Javanese symbolism. As Rens Heringa points out, the everyday attire in the villages on Java's north-east coast, still reflects a pre-Islamic world view.

Whereas in the dynasties of nearby Madura strong Javanese influences are apparent, many traditions in the lower social regions of the island originated from the local, social pressure to gain status. The annual bullraces, reported by Elly Touwen-Bouwsma, are among the few public occasions on which Madurese men can match themselves against each other.

The Baduy of Banten: the hidden people

Banten, the westernmost part of the province of Jawa Barat is a rather poor and forgotten region. The plains in the north are inhabited by small farming communities, and here and there a rubber or coconut estate is found. The peninsula of Ujung Kulon, Java's oldest wildlife reserve, is at the extreme south-western tip of the region. The tidal wave resulting from the eruption of nearby Krakatau in 1883, was so gigantic that the few villages on the coast of Ujung Kulon were washed away. Ever since, the rhinoceros and the panther rule in the vastnesses of this luxuriant tropical rain forest.

In the south of Banten lies the highland of Kendeng, where like a threatening crown, dark wooded peaks tower over the land. The mountain range is rugged and steep, the ravines are deep. And here, in the seclusion of the Kendeng Range in the subdistrict of Lebak, lives a remarkable and self-willed community of over five thousand people: the Baduy.

Less than one hundred and fifty kilometres from the capital of Jakarta, under the lee of history, they have managed to preserve their characteristic way of life. In voluntary isolation, almost completely concealed from the outside world, they live from one generation to the next in strict accordance with the *adat*. Thus they are links in a chain going back to times long gone elsewhere.

They distinguish themselves from the surrounding population both in religious and in social respect. Their religion is a mixture of ancient Javanese cosmology and Hindu-Buddhist influences. Ancestor worship plays an important part, and the Baduy also have a supreme god, Batara Tunggal, borrowed from the Hindu pantheon. The Baduy themselves call their religion Sunda Wiwitan, meaning something like 'originally Sundanese'. The Sundanese of West Java look upon the Baduy with a mixture of respect and fear. They can tell you tall tales about the magical powers of the Baduy. For instance, they are said to be clairvoyant and able to fly, and phantom tigers are believed to watch over their territory.

Nowadays the Baduy district, an area of about five thousand hectares (20 square miles), which the Baduy call Kanekes, is not as remote as it used to be. From Rangkas Bitung, the administrative centre of the subdistrict of Lebak, a tarmac road leading in the direction of the Kendeng Range, gets worse as it penetrates deeper into the south. After twenty-five kilometres, where hardly any tarmac is left, one reaches the village of Ciboleger. A short climb from here will take one to Kaduketug, the most northern Baduy village.

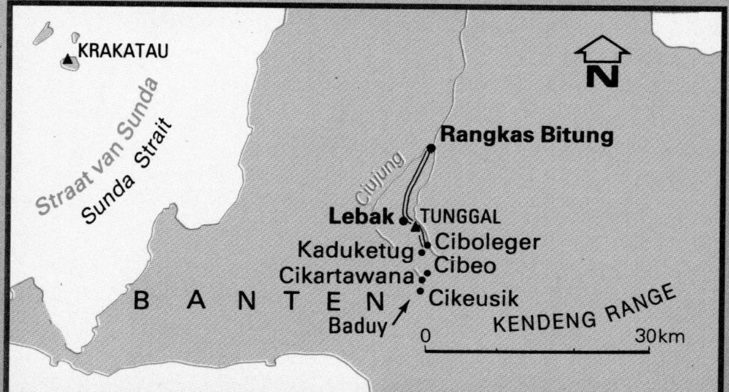

◄ *The Javanese landscape is dominated by volcanoes. Famous are Anak Krakatau, which rose from the sea off the west coast after the eruption of Krakatau in 1883, Central-Javanese Merapi, and slumbering Bromo. Here its gaping crater gives this part of East Java the appearance of a moon landscape.*

Although the trip no longer skirts the 'spooky ravines' so glowingly described by travellers from the last century on their way to the Baduy, today the appearance of a Baduy village hardly differs from that of the past. The simple houses built of plaited bamboo, have a roof of palm leaves and a front verandah.
Apart from the browns and greens of nature, only indigo blue and white catch the eye, the only colours of the traditional Baduy attire. The villages are imbued with an almost hallowed peace.
The simplicity of the Baduy's clothing is reflected in their sober households. Nowhere are there any chairs or tables, mattresses or pillows, there are no plates, no glasses, no plastic utensils... They sit on the floor, sleep on a mat, eat off palm leaves and drink out of wooden mugs or half a coconut shell.
Not that the Baduy aren't familiar with the products of modern society: in the neighbouring markets everything is for sale. But the *adat* bans the purchase of these modern articles; after all, the ancestors didn't have them either. There is a famous Baduy saying: 'What is long, may not be shortened, what is short may not be lengthened.' Thus everything stays the way it is, and always has been.
During the day the villages in Kanekes lie virtually deserted, as everyone is working in the fields. There the Baduy grow their staple food, rice, and some additional crops. They do not use irrigation systems or practise terraced cultivation. Children, too, help in the fields; there are no schools in Kanekes. 'A Baduy does not go to school, for then he would get smart and be able to cheat other people', is the Baduy's argument.
There has been a great deal of speculation about the origin of the Baduy, for here earlier researchers hoped to find the key to their way of life, so strikingly bound by tradition. Some assumed them to be the descendants of fugitives from the old Hindu-Javanese kingdom of Pajajaran that disappeared in the sixteenth century, due to the rise of Islam. The Baduy themselves have always contradicted this theory.

Mandala

The Baduy's ascetic way of life has a lot in common with that of the so-called *mandala* communities, as described in ancient Javanese texts. These were small religious groups living in isolation, and on the basis of an old Javanese faith with Hindu-Buddhist traits. Settled in a sacred spot, such as a mountain-top or the source of a river, they worshipped the gods of nature dwelling there. This worship also entailed that the natural environment of these spots was not to be disturbed.
In the Javanese world view there is a close coherence and interaction between microcosm (the ordinary, visible, daily world) and macrocosm (the all-encompassing universe with its supernatural powers). If a human makes mistakes in his daily life, he also endangers the balance in the macrocosm. It was the pre-eminent task of the *mandala* community to maintain the constantly threatened balance between micro- and macrocosm. Therefore, the members of a *mandala* community were bound to a very strict regimen, and led a very sober and ascetic life. Were they to give up their traditional way of life, the harmonizing power would be lost and the field of force disturbed. Rivers would flood, volcanoes erupt, the earth would tremble...
Mandala communities maintained close ties with the Javanese princes. After all, one of the prince's tasks was to perpetuate the harmony in his realm. Besides, to the princes in their lowlands, the elevated sources were of great strategic importance. Their waters irrigated the fields and thus enabled rich harvests of rice. The proceeds of surpluses paid for the prince's court and army.

Inner and Outer

The Baduy share many characteristics with the *mandala* community: the isolation, the ascetic way of life, being strongly bound to the *adat*, and in particular, the sense of responsibility for harmony in the realm. This realm used to consist of the West-Javanese principalities; now the Baduy feel responsible for the Republic of Indonesia. They consider it their highest duty to keep the spiritual heritage of their ancestors unsullied. The isolation this required, has even influenced the organization of their society, in that it is a dichotomy of Inner and Outer Baduy. The Inner Baduy form the religious centre of society, and inhabit its geographical heart, the core of the region. They live in the so-called inner villages: Cibeo, Cikartawana and Cikeusik. In each of these villages a *pu-un* resides, the highest authority in the Baduy hierarchy, in which religion and politics are closely interwoven.
In a semi-circle around these three inner villages lie the forty settlements of the Outer Baduy. Although they, too, are supposed to observe the *adat* rules, they have more leeway in this respect than the Inner Baduy. Thus they form a protective hedge as it were, around the inner area.
This protection also applies to the terraced sanctuary of the Baduy, Sasaka Domas, 'many stones'. This lies hidden in the 'forbidden forest', deep in the mountains near the source of the river Ciujung. Around the

▲ *A Gibbon (Hylobates moloch).*

Ujung Kulon

In 1921 Ujung Kulon was proclaimed a nature reserve. The unique and abundant flora and fauna of this peninsula required thorough protection. The marshy forests along the coast offer refuge to one of the world's rarest animal species: the Java rhinoceros. These animals are not only very rare (their present number is estimated at seventy specimens), they are also extremely shy. Biologists who recently carried out research into the behaviour of these solitary colossi, had to make do mainly with excrement, traces of feeding and footprints.
Lost without a trace is the Javanese tiger. The most recent pawprint dates from 1970. But due to the extinction of this regal raider, the panther population in Ujung Kulon increased considerably. In addition, the species sheltered in the tropical rain forest in the reserve's interior, include various monkeys, ***kancil*** *(mouse-deer),* ***banteng*** *(wild cattle), peacocks and hornbills.*

Samin, a prominent Outer Baduy. For years he was ***jaro pemerintah****, and in this capacity he represented the Baduy community in dealings with the outside world.* ▶

sanctuary, and consequently around the area of the river's source, one isn't allowed to affect anything in the forest, a ban strongly reminiscent of the *mandala* rules. Only once a year a small delegation of Baduy, led by the *pu-un*, visits the sanctuary and performs a sacred ritual there. At all other times an explicit ban on this part of Kanekes is in effect. The river Ciujung irrigates the fields of North Banten, nowadays Jakarta's rice storehouse. So, from an ecological point of view as well, it is of great importance that the sources of the river be protected.

Though the Baduy rarely show themselves, their mysterious reputation was and still is known throughout West Java. To this very day Indonesians, mostly from the big cities, visit the *pu-un* to ask their advice or (magical) assistance. But non-Indonesians are not allowed to enter the inner area at all. They have to satisfy themselves with a visit to Kaduketug, an Outer Baduy village. Even such a visit requires a permit from the Indonesian authorities.

Between the old and the new

Kaduketug is the home of the *jaro pemerintah*. This Baduy mediates between the outside world (originally the Dutch Government and later the Republic of Indonesia), and the *pu-un*. All visitors are received by the *jaro*. But it is by no means out of hospitality that this function was created. Rather, the *jaro* has to act as a buffer against increasing outside interference, and screen off the inner area as effectively as possible. The *jaro*'s house is a zone of tolerance in Baduy country. Within the Baduy community, the use of 'modern, worldly' goods such as plates, glasses and cutlery is allowed only in this house. This exception to their *adat* rules for the convenience of uninvited guests, testifies to their kindness.

Toward offenders of the *adat* within their own group, the Baduy are far less tolerant. In spite of their close ties with the *adat*, new ideas are voiced within the community too. There are members who prefer modern tableware to coconut shell and palm leaf, and would rather wear trousers than the traditional sarong. One or two now even have a radio, bought with the proceeds of commercial crops, such as cloves and coffee. This entails the violation of another *adat* rule, as the Baduy are not allowed to make a profit. Self-sufficiency that has always been the basis of their existence, allowing only for some exchange trade, still serves as their example.

Times have changed, though, and the Baduy no longer have at their disposal the vast area they once could claim. Due to population growth, both within their own group and in the surrounding villages, the acreage available for agriculture steadily diminishes. This forces more and more Baduy to find a living outside Kanekes. Some of them now work as wage-labourers for non-Baduy farmers. Others travel around neighbouring villages or set off for big cities like Jakarta and Bandung to make a living in petty trade. What they bring back with them is not only money, needed to buy rice, for instance, but also new ideas from another world. At the same time the neighbouring population is increasingly encroaching on the Baduy villages. Over the past few years the

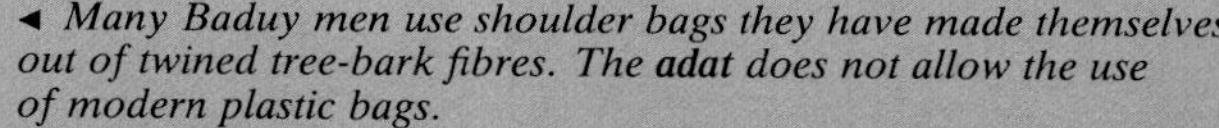

◂ *Many Baduy men use shoulder bags they have made themselves out of twined tree-bark fibres. The* **adat** *does not allow the use of modern plastic bags.*

▴ *In order to settle administrative affairs, Inner Baduy must sometimes venture beyond their territory. They may be recognized by their white headcloth, and often they also wear a white home-woven smock.*

Kanekes boundaries have even been systematically violated. Large parts of the Outer Baduy region were annexed by neighbouring farmers for their own use. For some time this slow but steady trickle of new influences seemed to be tolerated, but in 1978 the Baduy leaders had had enough. That year a kind of purification team of prominent Baduy unexpectedly made the rounds of the Outer Baduy region, purging it of all banned goods: plates, glasses, radios, clove trees, they destroyed it all.

It would hardly seem a coincidence that in the same year the Indonesian government took its first decisive steps to modernize Baduy society which it regarded as backward. For this purpose a project village was built at the foot of nearby Gunung Tunggal, some twenty kilometres north of Kanekes. Each Baduy family that settled in this project village, often forced to do so for lack of land back home, was given two hectares of land, some agricultural tools and sowing-seed. Children were to go to school, and even an Islamic prayer house had been thought of. That some forty families settled in Gunung Tunggal in 1978, was a thorn in the flesh of the Baduy leaders. They feared a dilution of the *adat* and felt threatened in their traditional existence. Purges alone would not suffice to stem this tide. Outside help was required.

What is long may not be shortened

Had not the Baduy, as an old *mandala* community, watched over the harmony in the former West-Javanese principalities? Had not they protected the sources of the river, which were still the mainspring of prosperity for West Java? And had not the prince, in exchange, always respected and protected the rights of the Baduy to a territory and a lifestyle of their own? That history had reforged the principalities of olden times into the Republic of Indonesia, didn't alter this fact. In 1985 the Baduy requested an audience with the reigning 'prince', President Suharto. They wanted to file complaints against the land robbery and other violations of their autonomous position. For this purpose the *jaro pemerintah*, Nakiwin, went to Jakarta.

The result of his meeting with president Suharto was the official recognition of the Baduy's rights to their own lifestyle and territory. They were even promised some protection. Over five hundred concrete posts now mark the Kanekes borders. It is significant that 'the father of development', as the President likes to be called, respects the Baduy's way of life and their thought, for these are both conservative. Other traditional communities, such as that of the Kubu in Sumatra, are approached with far less respect.

The cause of this 'special treatment' lies in the Baduy's unique position as a *mandala* community. The relationship between prince and *mandala* that existed in Java from ancient times, is still honoured in this day and age. The protection of the river source is safe in the hands of those who respect the water spirits. Even now the government rather derives a sense of security from the support that the Baduy's special powers have to offer, than put to the test the sorely needed harmony in the archipelago.

Recently the boundaries of Baduy country have been marked with concrete posts. The Indonesian authorities took this measure to protect that territory against the encroaching ▾ outside world.

To prepare a field for use, the Baduy fell and cut away the ▼ forest vegetation, and burn the undergrowth.

So as to combat erosion, the tree-stumps are left ▼ standing on the burnt slopes.

*Procession with an **angklung**. The Baduy play this typically West-Javanese instrument only during certain ceremonies, ▼ including the sowing ritual.*

*Before the sowing actually begins, a specialist, the **dukun**, performs the required ritual. This is meant to propitiate the rice goddess Dewi Sri, and effect a rich harvest. In the basket, the **dukun** keeps offerings for Dewi Sri. ▼*

Rice cultivation

The Baduy practise dry rice cultivation, or ***ladang*** cultivation; the ***adat*** forbids them to lay out ***sawah***. The rice fields, situated on the slopes of the Kendeng Range, which occasionally are quite steep, are used according to the method of shifting cultivation. Characteristic for this type of agriculture is an extensive use of the soil: after a field has been used for some time, it is left to lie fallow for a rest period of several years. The ***adat*** prescribes at least seven, but due to a lack of land this has been reduced to three years. In this rest period the soil can regain its fertility.

One family clears about one hectare of woodland (2.5 acres). Here they can grow enough rice to last them a year. In addition to rice, 'second-harvest crops' are planted, such as corn, cassava and pulses.

Before a field can be used, the forest vegetation has to be cut away or felled (the trunks are left standing to combat erosion), and the undergrowth burned. In October, when the first rains come, it is time to sow the rice. This is accompanied by an extensive ritual, called ***ngaseuk***, a term derived from ***aseuk***, meaning dibble. After four months the rice can be harvested. The ***adat*** forbids the Baduy to sell the rice, as this would offend the rice goddess, Dewi Sri.

▲ Soon after the first rains, like a snake the sowing procession winds its way across the field. The men are in the lead, making holes in the ground with their dibbles. The women follow, throwing a few grains of rice in every hole. ▼

The principalities

Mangkunegoro VIII, one of the Central-Javanese princes, died in 1987. Accompanied by close relatives, his body was flown to Surakarta where it was laid to rest in the family tomb. The two planes required were paid for by President Suharto.
This was not so strange as it may seem. Mrs. Suharto is a descendant of Mankunegoro III, and is related to the deceased in the fifth line. She belongs to the *trah* Mangkunegaran, a family group based on kinship on both father's and mother's side. Etymologically, *trah* seems to be derived from *truh*, meaning rain. Like the rain falling from the heavens on high to the earth down below, the blood flows from the common ancestors to their descendants. In modern Indonesia the *trah* is one of many links between past and present.
The family tomb mentioned above lies at the summit of Giri Layu, a mountain in the former Mangkunegara realm. In addition to this cemetery, the *trah* Mangkunegaran has another (natural) burial hill, Mengadeg, containing the remains of the first three princes of the *trah*. Near these hills lies Giri Bangun, a tomb recently built especially for the Suharto family. The name Giri Bangun is a contraction of the names Giri Layu and Mengadeg, both meaning: to erect.
So as to emphasize their role of mediators between gods and humans, from times immemorial the rulers of the three other former principalities have also been buried high on a hilltop. Like Mangkunegoro VIII on the Giri Layu, all former princes of Surakarta, Jogyakarta and small Paku Alaman, the three other old realms of Central Java, rest nearby on the summit of Mount Imogiri.
Even in modern Indonesia, graves, and not merely those of princes, attract many visitors; there the Javanese hope to find spiritual strength, to support them in life. But so far it was the prerogative of the princes and their kin to refer to this mediating role during their lifetimes. Death merely perpetuated their position between gods and humans; the monuments tangibly symbolize this. However, Giri Bangun, the family tomb recently built, symbolizes that modern power too, as personified by the President, claims a sacral meaning.
The death of Mangkunegoro VIII occasioned lengthy discussions in the Indonesian press. Questions arose about the charisma on which the Central-Javanese princes could still pride themselves, and people wondered whether a modern country really needs something like that. It may be assumed that Indonesia is confronted here with a very essential expression of its culture, one that is deeply rooted in the country's own history. As the following discussion will show, the charisma radiated by the princes arose and was developed during a process that took thousands of years, and into which a great variety of influences found their way: not just indigenous ones, but also from Buddhism, Hinduism, Islam and the West.

◄ *A typically urban scene: mobile cooks preparing savoury snacks from the Javanese cuisine.*

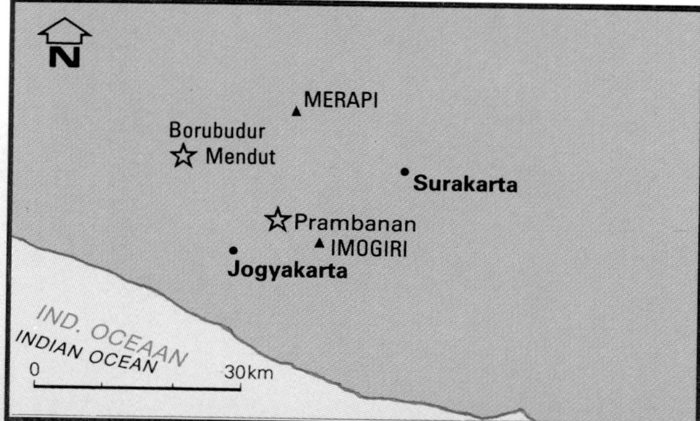

Four dynasties

Agung the Great is regarded as the founding father of the Central-Javanese dynasties. Under this powerful ruler who died in 1645, the four principalities still formed one great realm. His remains lie on the highest summit of Mount Imogiri. Beneath this spot his successors rest in two cemeteries, analogous to the division, more than a century after Agung's death, of the realm of Mataram into the two principalities of Surakarta and Jogyakarta. Further down the mountain lie the princes of Paku Alaman, a relatively small region that in the early 19th century was still part of Jogyakarta. Finally, the princes of the House of Mangkunegaran that split off from Surakarta earlier, do not lie buried on Imogiri, but rest on burial hills in the former Mangkunegaran territory.
The prince played a central role, expressed not merely in the spatial organization of his realm (a system of concentric rings around the prince, with his ***kraton*** as the nucleus of the cosmos), but also in the princes' names. Thus Pakubuwono, the traditional name of the princes of Surakarta, means 'Nail of the Universe', and Hamengkubuwono, the name of the successive princes of Jogyakarta, means 'Bearer of the Universe'. The rulers of the other two principalities adorned themselves with similar names.

Memorial on the burial hill Mengadeg, erected after the restoration by the ***trah*** *Mangkunegaran, on the initiative of* ▼ *Mrs. Suharto.*

Ancient Mataram

Hinduism in Java dates from the beginning of the Christian era. Its introduction is represented in a myth about a stranger, Aji Saka from Campa, what is now Vietnam. He put an end to the barbaric reign of a cannibal king, and brought to the Javanese knowledge and culture. He is said to have first set foot on Javanese soil in AD 78, and the Javanese regard this moment as the starting-point of their era.
The existence of a Hindu-Javanese society is first reported in Chinese sources dating from the end of the fourth century. On their trading voyages to China, navigators from India discovered the riches of Java, and settled on the western part of the island. After some time they went on to Central Java, and established the realm of Mataram.
The oldest stone inscription in Java, from 732, tells about a king called Sannaha, and his son Sanjaja. The text shows that the memories of India, their country of cultural origin, were still vivid. Probably the temples of the Dieng Plateau date from this period. In addition to this dynasty, the Chinese sources mention various other princes, including the House of the Sailendras. This dynasty which reigned Java since 778, played an important part in spreading Buddhism, and initiated the construction of famous temples, such as Candi Mendut and Borobudur.
It is almost certain that in Java, Buddhism was the religion of the princes and their inner circles only. The common people largely continued their adherence to Shivaism, worshipping the Hindu god Shiva. Whereas in India Hinduism and Buddhism fiercely opposed each other, in Java they grew closer together. Thus the Prambanan complex, built in the beginning of the tenth century on the plain of the same name between Surakarta and Jogyakarta, could become an impressive centre of Shivaism, while at the same time in nearby temples Buddhist services were held.
Not long after the construction of the Prambanan complex, Mataram must have lost much of its power. After 928, in Central Java nothing more was heard of Mataram for six centuries. Till around the year 1200 Central Java faded entirely into the background, and East Java took over its prominent role.

Majapahit

Actually, Javanese recorded history starts in the thirteenth century. Soon after, in 1350, Hayam Wuruk took over from his mother, and brought the realm of Majapahit to great prosperity. The realm embraced Central and East Java, Madura, the islands east of Java, Sulawesi and surrounding islands, as well as Malacca and Sumatra. A network of kin and priests enabled Hayam Wuruk to collect taxes on a regular basis, even from the farthest corners of his realm. Thus he could afford an enormous household. He had temples and palaces built, had a great army, and employed many officials. The centre of his realm, situated on the Brantas river south-west of what is now Surabaya, was densely populated. A poem of 1365 described this evocatively: "In its entire expanse it seems one sole city; the population of thousands and

Borobudur

Taking its inspiration from ancient Indian traditions, Borobudur forms an important peak in Java's artistic development. The fame of this monumental Buddhist creation stems from the brilliant synthesis of sculpture and architecture. The sanctuary expresses a message that in our twentieth century is just as clear as it was in the ninth, at the time of construction.
Not long after its completion, Borobudur passed into oblivion, only to be rediscovered in 1814. From 1907 to 1911 the Dutchman Van Erp carried out the first great restoration. Sixty years later, earthquakes and rainwater had again seriously affected the soft stone. In addition, the whole building threatened to subside to such an extent that once again a large-scale salvage operation seemed necessary. With the support of UNESCO, the cultural organization of the United Nations, an intensive 15-year restoration programme was carried out and concluded in 1983.
Above the base whose four sides are 123 metres each, there are four galleries which in ascending order are set farther back from the edge. The sides, with a total length of more than five kilometres, are enriched with 1460 figurative panels and 1232 decorative reliefs. In between there are more than 500 niches containing small statues of seated Buddhas. In addition, above the galleries lie three terraces with circular platforms for 72 bell-shaped *stupa*. These too are each provided with a seated Buddha. An enormous central *stupa* crowns Borobudur; here probably the builders had meant to enshrine the never finished statue of the perfect Buddha, who after a long quest for 'the Truth' finally sees 'the Light'.
According to the original Buddhist rules, one must proceed along the galleries keeping the sides to one's right. Then, as an endless strip of images and bas-reliefs, the life of Buddha passes before the beholder, and the strictly hierarchic order of the iconographic programme becomes apparent. In addition, three spiritual levels symbolize the phases into which Buddhism divides human existence.
The lowest level, Kamadhatu, the phase of 'Desires', is rendered on the base of Borobudur. The bas-reliefs here, representing profane life with depictions of love and hate, happiness and punishment, hope and hell, were discovered in 1891. A high supporting wall screens from the believer's view most of these 'hidden' reliefs and hence the worldly 'temptations'.
A number of stairs lead up to the four galleries jointly depicting the second level, Rupadhatu, the phase of 'Form'. Here all worldly temptations have been renounced, and 'Redemption' is near.
Finally, as one climbs to the three circular terraces at the highest level, en route one encounters a plateau of a peculiar design. Like the lower terraces it is square on the outside, but on the inside it is bounded by a bare wall that is practically circular. This contrast symbolizes the transition from the phase of 'Form' to that of 'Shapelessness', Arupadhatu. Here the highest level, the abstract world of the 'Unimaginable' is presented: 'Eternal Redemption', Nirwana has been attained.

LAY-OUT BOROBUDUR

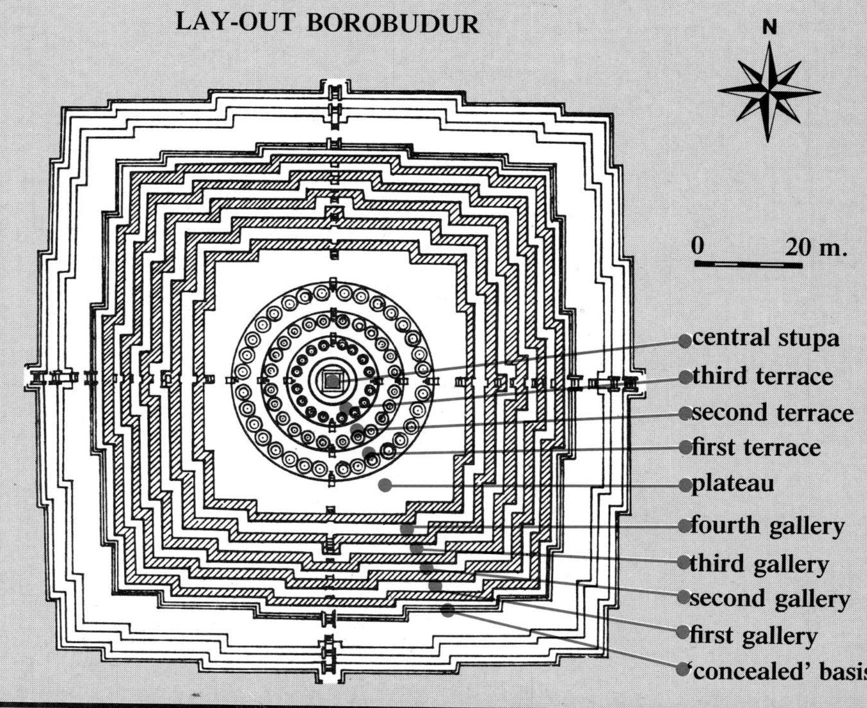

◄ *A semi-open* **stupa** *on the second terrace of Borobudur. The hand position of the Buddha statue suggests the rotation of the Dharma wheel, the wheel of life.*

thousands resembles an enormous army moving around the capital". It is as if one is shown a picture of today's Java.
A description included in the same poem, of Hayam Wuruk's quarters, reminds one of the palaces, the *kraton* as we now know them in Jogyakarta and Surakarta. Possibly in his day the *kraton* already formed the inmost circle of a realm composed of a series of concentric rings, and perhaps the prince functioned within as the sacral centre of the cosmos, a Hindu-Javanese view revived three centuries later under Amangkurat.
Hayam Wuruk's life's work did not last very long. After his death Majapahit was divided, and soon this led to the decline of the once so powerful realm.

Prambanan

The Hindu-Javanese temples of the famed Larajonggrang complex, usually named Prambanan after the village nearby, were built at the beginning of the tenth century. Here as in Borobudur, the Javanese architects display their rich knowlege of Indian styles; in Prambanan these have been combined with the Javanese traditions in a highly original way.
Due to the waning power of the princes of Central Java and the central role that East Java acquired, the interest in the temple complex at Prambanan faded soon after its completion. After many centuries of neglect, earthquakes and eruptions of the Merapi volcano finally caused the complete collapse of the temples. But from 1937 intensive restoration work has been going on, and since then various important sanctuaries have regained their old lustre.
The Larajonggrang complex embraces three great temples. The largest; 47 metres high, is dedicated to Shiva. On its south side this impressive creation is flanked by the temple of Brahma, on its north side by that of Vishnu. Opposite these three sanctuaries lie three smaller ones, of which the middle temple is dedicated to Nandi, Shiva's bull. Together with two smaller temples on either side of these six larger ones, all those buildings are situated on a central, square inner court with sides 110 metres long.
In a surrounding temple court somewhat lower down and more than twice as large, lie the ruins of 224 sanctuaries, each of which must have been 14 metres high; meanwhile some of these have been restored. In turn they are surrounded by a third temple court, a square with sides of 390 metres, again a bit lower down. Due to these slightly different levels the Prambanan complex, like Borobudur, forms a kind of 'stepped pyramid'.
The 'crown' of the 'pyramid', the Shiva temple, is enclosed by a railing with four access gates. The outside of the railing's base bears the famed 'Prambanan motif': rabbits, rams, deer, peacocks, monkeys and geese, in each case clustered on either side of the tree of life. The inside of the railing shows scenes from the Ramayana Epic. Here we find depicted how Sita, Rama's beloved wife, is kidnapped, and how Hanuman the ape manages to set her free with the aid of his army. The reliefs begin on the Shiva temple, and continue on the Brahma temple at the point where the army of apes builds a bridge to the island of Langka. The Vishnu temple shows scenes involving Krishna, the hero of the Mahabharata, another great Hindu epic. Back at the Shiva temple, via galleries and stairs, the visitor reaches the central area of the sanctuary, containing the statue of the four-armed Shiva. In three separate rooms we find the statues of Ganesa, Agastya and Durga. Ganesa is Shiva's son, with the head of an elephant as the symbol of wisdom. Agastya symbolizes Shiva as a teacher. The statue of Durga, killer of the demonic bull, and Shiva's mainstay, occupies a prominent position in Hindu-Javanese sculpture. In addition the entire complex derives its name from him: in the vernacular, Durga is sometimes called Larajonggrang, 'slim virgin'.

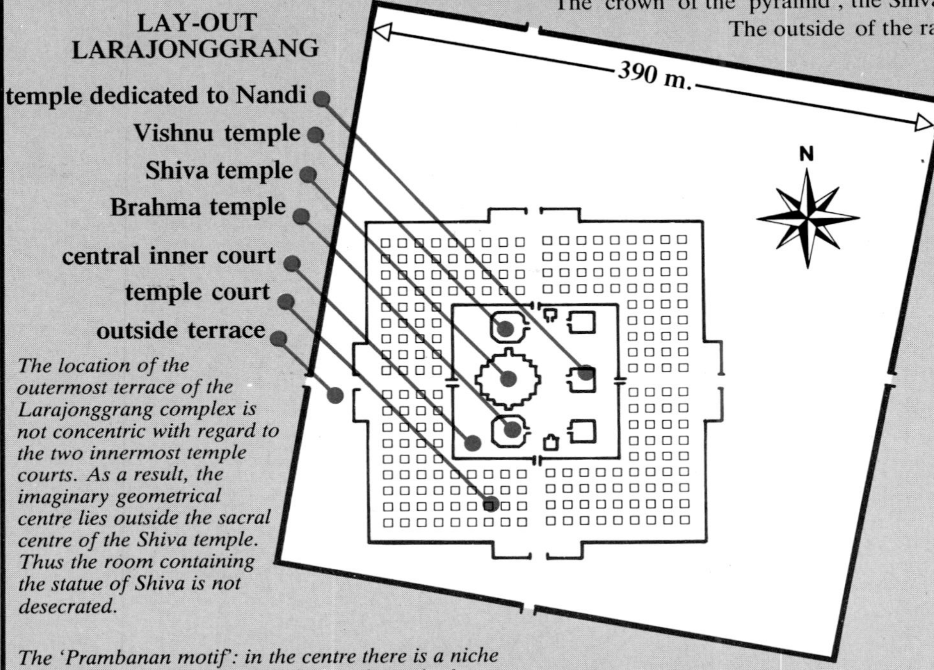

The location of the outermost terrace of the Larajonggrang complex is not concentric with regard to the two innermost temple courts. As a result, the imaginary geometrical centre lies outside the sacral centre of the Shiva temple. Thus the room containing the statue of Shiva is not desecrated.

The 'Prambanan motif': in the centre there is a niche with a mythical lion. Bas-reliefs on either side show ▼ *rams guarding the tree of life, decorated with jewels.*

An episode from the Ramayana Epic: the army of monkeys is gathering stones to build a causeway or land bridge to ▼ *Langka (what is now Sri Lanka).*

The impressive Shiva temple dominates the Larajonggrang complex on the Prambanan Plain between Jogyakarta and Surakarta. ▶

Demak

The end of Majapahit, around 1500, also spelt the end of the supremacy of Hindu princes. Islam became important. As early as 1292, Marco Polo wrote about Sumatra: "This monarchy is so often visited by Islamic merchants, that they have converted the natives to the laws of Mohammed". It can be derived from a Chinese source that in 1416 Islam had also penetrated Java. Almost a century later, in 1514, the Portuguese Governor of Malacca wrote to his king: "In Java there still are two kafir (heathen) princes, namely of Pajajaran and of Majapahit. The beaches belong to the Moors, and are managed by Governors". Not long after, the power over Majapahit came into the hands of these Moorish 'governors', giving rise to the realm of Demak; Majapahit ceased to exist. Yet in Central Java much of the Hindu culture was to survive. The realm of Demak soon came to an end, in 1546. Hence in the memory of the Javanese, Demak's hey-day is less important than Majapahit's.

New Mataram

In the second half of the sixteenth century, more than six hundred years after the fall of ancient Hindu-Javanese Mataram, Panembahan Senapati founded a new realm in Central Java bearing this name. His grandson Agung the Great, who used the Islamic title of Sultan, was the first of a dynasty that was to rule over nearly all of Java. Envoys of the Dutch East-India Company (VOC) who in the early seventeenth century stayed at the Agung's court, described the prince as an intelligent and inquisitive man. At first, in his efforts to conquer all Java, Agung was eager to co-operate with the Dutch. But when they seized Jacatra (the later Jakarta), a city Agung himself had in mind, the prince informed the VOC that it must either accept his supreme authority, or leave Java. The Dutch were not impressed, and in 1628 the VOC officer Jan Pieterszoon Coen thwarted Agung's attempts to capture Jacatra. It was clear that the Dutch had settled in Java for a long time to come. Though this defeat had reduced his prestige, Sultan Agung did manage to impose his authority on other parts of Java. In other fields as well, his influence still turned out to be quite considerable. Thus Agung provided the monarchy with a clear structure, built a magnificent palace, the Karta, near today's Surakarta, and introduced the mixed Arab-Javanese era. As his last resting-place the Sultan chose the summit of Mount Imogiri, where to the present day his successors are also buried.

In contrast to Agung, his direct successor Amangkurat I (1645-1677) did not use the title of Sultan, but the Hindu-Javanese title of Susuhunan (often abbreviated as Sunan). This was one way of opposing Islam, which he felt to be a threat to his sacral power. He reduced the influence of the Muslim leaders, and ensured that henceforth he would be the only medium between god and the people: the prince was the centre of the cosmic order. In shaping his realm into a system of concentric rings, he emphasized this central position. The Sunan's palace, the *kraton*, belonged to the inmost circle. Around it, in the next circle, lived the nobles and officials in the capital. The third circle embraced the central region of the realm, the *negoro-agung*. Finally, the outer circle was formed by the *monconegoro*, the frontier regions, with the *pasisir*, the coastal regions beyond.

The VOC praised Agung the Great

*"Agung had a fine build and a round face that usually showed the same expression. With his big wide eyes he looked about him 'like a lion'; his nose was small and straight, his mouth with which he spoke slowly, was broad and flat. He made the impression of having a good mind, and showed an interest in matters that did not directly concern himself and his realm. His clothes hardly differed from those of the other Javanese: he wore a white and blue batik sarong, held together by a belt with a gold ornament holding a kris. On his fingers he had many rings with sparkling diamonds, and a small white linen cap covered his head. Thirty or forty women sat around waiting on him with **sirih** (Piper betle), tobacco and the like in gold dishes and cups, and with a water-**gendi** (an earthenware pitcher)."*

▲ *The **alun-alun** of the **kraton** of Jogyakarta in 1910.*

Kraton

*Generally a **kraton** has an easily recognizable lay-out that has to do with the four points of the compass: east, west, north and south. The lay-out is based on the cosmological classification system used in the principalities; in this the north is associated with death, the south with life; the east refers to the male element, and the west to the female element. Thus in principle the prince's quarters are located in the eastern part of the **kraton**, and those of his wife and her servants in the western part. The **alun-alun**, a large forecourt that may serve as feasting ground, lies to the north or to the south; for the 'front' of a **kraton** may be orientated either to the south or the north, depending on the proximity of an important mountain or the sea.*

▼ *Refined court dance in the **kraton** of Jogyakarta (1983).*

Three principalities

At the end of the reign of Amangkurat I, the new Mataram threatened to fall apart, and the VOC seized its opportunity. A process of Dutch intervention started that was to last throughout the colonial period. There were abundant reasons for the VOC's interference. As a result of wars and other causes nearly every Sunan started out with such great debts that he had to ask the VOC for a loan to avoid bankruptcy. Next, instalments and forced yields bound the various princes to the VOC. In addition, every Sunan had numerous court intrigues to cope with, matters in which the VOC's help was also appreciated. In 1743 the VOC believed to have enough power to place the *pasisir*, Mataram's coastal regions, under its authority. A few princes at the court of the reigning Sunan Pakubuwono II firmly opposed this take-over. But this did not deter the VOC. In anger, Prince Mangkubumi, a brother of the Sunan, joined forces with his cousin Mas Said, a prince who had taken up arms against the Company before. A long guerrilla war ensued.
When the Sunan on his deathbed turned over all of Mataram to the VOC and asked the Company to appoint his successor, the end of the struggle seemed to be in sight. As a result, by contract the realm officially lost its independence in 1749. But in reality the agreement turned out to be a worthless scrap of paper: the VOC did have power over the prince, not over his subjects.
Meanwhile the two resistance fighters, the princes Mangkubumi and Mas Said, had fallen out with each other; to the VOC this was a signal to start a divide-and-rule policy. The Dutch made peace with Mangkubumi and induced him, in exchange for 'power' over half of Mataram ceded by the Sunan, to assist the Company in their struggle against his former partner Mas Said. Thus in 1755 Mangkubumi was proclaimed Sultan of Jogyakarta.
Not long after, in 1757, Mas Said gave up his resistance. In recognition, he too was given authority over part of Mataram, and he received the title of Mangkunegoro. The Sunan in Surakarta, appointed by the VOC and once so powerful, was left with only a small part of his original realm: Mataram had been divided into three principalities.

The erosion of power

In Europe, the following turn of the century was the age of the French revolution and Napoleon's advance. This strategist's powerful arm reached as far as Java. In 1799 the VOC was turned over to the State of the Netherlands, which at the time was a French protectorate. As a General of Napoleon, Daendels was sent to Java and he deprived the Central-Javanese princes of the last semblance of authority. Henceforth, legitimate authority was to reside only in Batavia (the former Jacatra), and after Napoleon's fall the British interim administration continued this policy. The Sultan of Jogyakarta resisted the waning of his influence, and when in 1812 a plot of his got out, he was punished by further reducing his territory: a fourth small principality, the Paku Alaman, was split off from it.

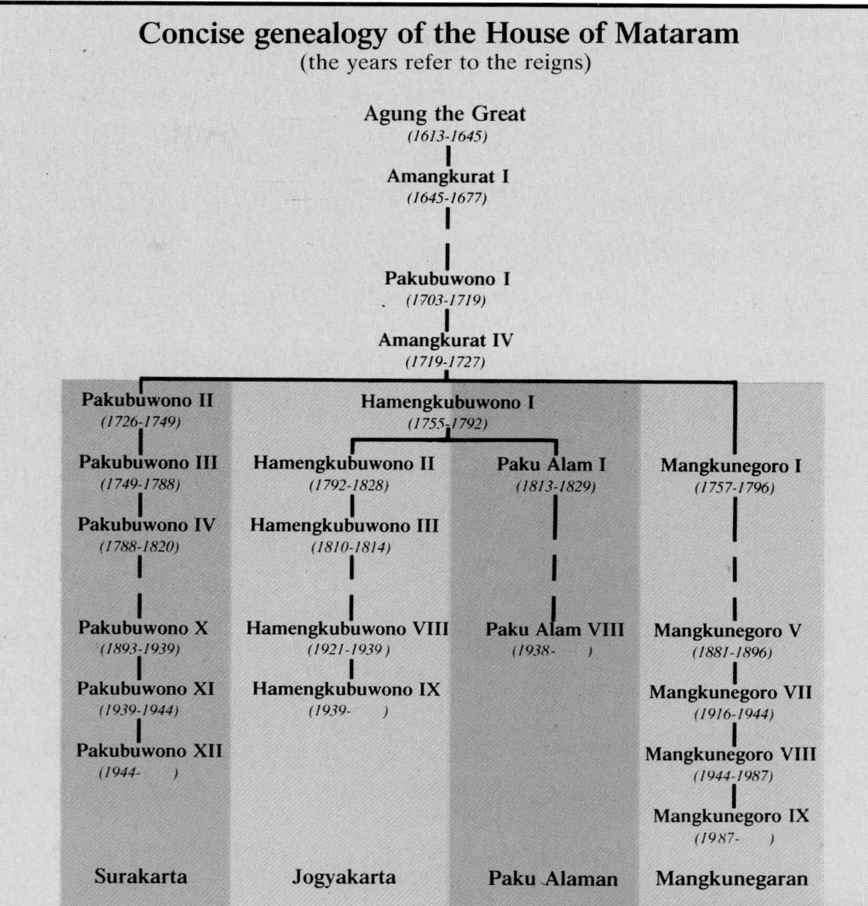

Mangkunegoro VII ►

Mangkunegoro VII and his predecessors, with one exception: Mangkunegoro I, Mas Said. Tradition has it that he always ▼ refused to be portrayed.

dressed as Central-Javanese bridegroom, and in the uniform of Colonel-Adjutant to the late Dutch ▼ Queen Wilhelmina.

Time bar based on the Christian calendar

1949 27 December: The Netherlands recognizes the Republic of Indonesia

1945 17 August: Republic of Indonesia proclaimed. Hamengkubuwono IX, Sultan of Jogyakarta, sides with the revolution

1900 Revival of Javanese nationalism

1813 Sultan Hamengkubuwono III has to cede part of Jogyakarta to Paku Alam I

1757 Sunan Pakubuwono III has to cede part of Surakarta to Mangkunegoro I

1755 Mataram divided: Surakarta under Sunan Pakubuwono III, and Jogyakarta under Hamengkubuwono I

1645 Susuhunan Amangkurat I: the pivot of the cosmic order

1613 Agung the Great becomes Sultan of New Mataram

1400 Islam reaches Java

1350 Hayam Wuruk brings Majapahit to prosperity

1292 Marco Polo reports on Islam in Sumatra

928 Last account of ancient Mataram in Central Java, Mataram moves to East Java

900 Prambanan complex is built

778 Sailendra dynasty comes to power Spread of Buddhism Candi Mendut and Borobudur are built

732 Temples built on the Dieng Plateau

400 For the first time, Chinese sources report the existence of a Hindu-Javanese society

78 Aji Saka reaches Java: introduction of Hinduism

Now the threat of war was in the air, and in 1825, due to a conflict between a Dutch 'Resident' and Diponegoro, the uncle and guardian of the new Sultan of Jogyakarta, this war actually broke out. In this so-called Java War the aristocrats, impoverished as they were by the colonial arrangement for leasing land, joined forces with Diponegoro. Among the people, he had great charisma. He was believed to be the Ratu Adil, the just prince who had been prophesied, the liberator of the oppressed. True, the princes could be deprived of their political power, but not of the sacral authority they enjoyed among the people.
Diponegoro himself had every reason to revolt. He blamed both the court in Jogyakarta and the Dutch Administration for the fact that he had not become the new Sultan. His guerrilla warfare was hard to beat. But gradually his energies were exhausted, and in 1830, after five years of struggle, he was taken prisoner. The Sultanate of Jogyakarta was held responsible for the war, and punished by further territorial reductions. For the sake of balance, the Sunan's territory around Surakarta suffered the same fate; for the Sunan, who had fought on the Government's side, this was a most unjust decision.

The cultural renaissance

Though in name the princes governed their own territories, in the course of the nineteenth and twentieth centuries they were increasingly checked by the Dutch officials in Jogyakarta and Surakarta. The princely élite compensated for this lack of political leeway by focussing ever more on cultural matters. The dance and music of Central Java grew more and more refined. In *babad* (chronicles), court writers, *pujangga*, immortalized the history and fame of the ancient realms of Majapahit and Mataram. The European court too, was used as a source of inspiration. Lighting fixtures, furniture and china were ordered in Paris. The splendour and glitter seemed more radiant than ever, but the ostentation had no political substance whatsoever.
The cultural renaissance of a glorious past, which at the beginning of the twentieth century was to become the source of inspiration for Javanese nationalism, culminated in the founding of Budi Utomo in 1908, in which Mangkunegoro VII and Paku Alam VII played an important part. The name of this movement meant both 'the beautiful endeavour' and 'a higher civilization'. Budi Utomo strove to achieve a synthesis of Western science and Eastern wisdom. This had to lead to a realm superior to the West in every respect. Both princes hoped that the movement would stimulate the formation of autonomous administrative territories, but efforts to translate this nationalism into political power failed.
Mangkunegoro VII did score success in founding the Java Institute, a cultural and scientific institution with an image obviously less ominous than that of his political reforms. In 1918 the first conference of this institute was held in Surakarta. Hundreds of delegates took part, both Javanese and European. It was decided that the institute would dedicate itself in particular to the cultural development of Java, Bali and Madura.
Hence, in matters in which the colonial authorities and the princes shared the same aims, it turned out that co-operation was not impossible. In other fields silent opposition remained an effective protest. Sunan Pakubuwono X (1893-1938) in particular, was a master of this art. On his travels, surrounded by much pomp and circumstance, he knew he could count on his great charisma. Many saw in him the real king of Java. To the Dutch government each and every one of his many successes was a warning that there were limits to patronizing.

The republic

In 1939 both the Sunan and the Sultan died. In their territories the administration had always remained very feudal. The necessary administrative reforms had not been carried out, and the population was poor. In contrast, Mangkunegoro VII had democratized and modernized his realm. It was fair to expect that from this region an impulse for renewal would emanate to all Java. But in 1944 he too, died. After the Japanese occupation his realm did not respond to the budding revolution and the cry for an Indonesian republic.
What nobody could have expected in 1939, happened in 1945. After many years the scene for political action moved once again from Surakarta to Jogyakarta: the Sultan opened his doors to the revolution. In recognition, his territory was later to get a special status, and the chance to gain limited autonomy. He reformed his administration in such a way that it came to serve as an example for the republican government in Jakarta. In the early years of the republic he played an important part as a link between the army, the cabinet and the socialist intellectuals, and even under President Suharto's administration his influence continued for quite some time. After a long colonial period of forced concentration on symbolic leadership of a religious hue, the prince's political role had regained some of its substance.

Symbol and charisma

In the course of the history of the political field of force, the position of the Central-Javanese princes had shifted from the centre to the periphery. Due to structural weakness and the Dutch supremacy, the actual exercise of their power had become more and more marginal. But at the time, despite that erosion of political influence, to the people of Central Java the princes – as the religious pivots of a glorious past – remained the only true representatives of power. Owing to the forced political inactivity of the princes, this sacral Hindu-Javanese conception could gain a clearer prominence. In addition it turned out that in this notion the princes could be quite a nuisance to the colonial oppressor. This largely explains the charisma they radiate even today. That one prince's political role regained some substance once the Dutch had left, is not surprising: his authority gave him an almost natural right to that role.
The princes' graves are symbols of the legitimacy of their former power. Meanwhile, their descendants have become ordinary citizens of the republic, but as links with the past their graves continue to play a part. The Giri Bangun, the new burial hill, connects this old charisma with the present.

▲ *On the beach, the outrigger proas lie waiting for the fishermen to put to sea before sunrise.*

▲ *Rice for a ritual meal is being pounded in a wooden rice-block. Both women are dressed in home attire: the young woman is wearing a bought batik hip cloth in Central-Javanese style and a white bodice; the older woman has wrapped a home-woven* ***sarung*** *under her armpits, combined with a dark-blue men's head cloth used as breast cloth.*

Textiles and world view in Tuban

A narrow strip of land along Java's north-east coast, Pesisir Wetan, stretches from the Java Sea to Pegunungan Kapur, the northern limestone mountains. In the centre of this region lies the district of Tuban. The level coastal area borders on a white sandy beach whose gradual slope continues far beyond the waterline. Thus the shallows extend quite a long way. The coast is lined with small fishing villages strung together. Before dawn the men put to sea in their characteristic outrigger proas, to return home around four in the afternoon. On arrival, the catch is immediately sold where it is landed: on the beach, and taken to the inland village markets.

There in the interior, the people grow rice, corn and tubers for their personal use, as well as cash crops of tobacco and peanuts. Due to low rainfall and the easily eroded limy soil, the fields yield only poor harvests. Both men and women work on the land. In addition, the men raise cattle, while the women have their households and children to look after. Moreover, the women make patterned weaves and batik cloths for themselves and their families.

On the southern mountain slopes the cultivated land gradually gives way to dense forests that have been planted here since the nineteenth century, to replace the primary forest felled in the preceding century. From times immemorial, lumberjack families have worked in these forests. Among other things they supply the timber for new fishing-boats. Thus for centuries now, the existence of the fishermen on the coast has been linked with that of the farmers in the hinterland, and with the lives of the lumberjacks in the mountains.

Until recently, many of the inland villages could only be reached on foot. Not until the mid-seventies was the Pesisir Wetan included in the development planning of the Indonesian government. In the eyes of 'cultured' urban dwellers, the people in this remote district lead a wretched and primitive life, and must surely welcome the implementation of development programmes. Even in the Dutch colonial era, the 'primordial' situation here was mentioned and plans for improvement were developed. But to a large extent, the population apparently prefers the old way of life, an attitude not always appreciated by authorities past and present. Over the years the population has earned an almost proverbial reputation for being self-willed and stubborn.

Nevertheless, over the past decade various aspects of the infrastructure have been modernized. Along the road that replaced the sand tracks, minibuses maintain the link with the district capital, Tuban. Each village is now in proud possession of one tap, for which the water comes from an artesian well, dozens of metres deep. And a new primary school stands in the field where the cattle used to graze. Thus the villagers have come into contact with things that even a few years ago were utterly unknown to most of them.

In their turn the government officials visiting the area in connection with the development programmes, discovered ancient traditions long extinct elsewhere. Textile manufacture in particular drew their attention.

In some inland villages pattern weaves and batik cloths are still made largely as prescribed by tradition, mainly in the three months following the harvest.

Textiles and mancapat

In style and lay-out, the Tuban cloths show obvious traces of Chinese and Indian influences. No doubt these characteristic features go back to a period of intensive trade contacts with these countries, between the eleventh and seventeenth centuries. However, the village women themselves, who spend countless hours on the process of spinning and weaving, and waxing the batik designs, regard the textiles as inextricably linked to their own Javanese identity. There is an abundance of cloth types, and each appears to serve a specific local purpose. Some types form part of either daily or ceremonial attire, while others play a part in certain rituals. Moreover, all social groups within the community and the positions they occupy in relation to each other, can be distinguished by their textiles.
The relationships between neighbouring villages in the area are characterized by a typically Javanese, hierarchical structure. A group of villages forms a co-operative unit, called *mancapat*. This consists of a centrally located village surrounded by four to eight peripheral villages. The aspect of hierarchy is ostensively expressed in various ways. For instance, in dealing with the outside world, the village head of the central village is the mouth-piece for the surrounding villages. In the textile process too, the centre of a *mancapat* features prominently.
The *mancapat* cluster of traditional textile-producing villages in Tuban has come to deviate slightly from the original model. At the end of the last century, for administrative purposes, the colonial authorities added a second 'central' village to the original *mancapat*. And even now, this is where the *camat* is found, the head of the subdistrict and also the local representative of the central government. Possibly this reorganization was introduced in order to get a better grip on an area that was perceived as troublesome. The central function of this additional village in the *mancapat* has since been further reinforced by the

Batik in Tuban

The main textile technique used in Java is batik: both sides of a cloth are decorated with patterns drawn in hot liquid wax with a copper drawing-pen, or *canting*. The wax acts as a resist, to prevent the dyes from penetrating the covered areas of the cloth. After the cloth has been repeatedly immersed in a cold dye-bath, and the wax has been removed by boiling, the parts that had been waxed will come out off-white, the natural colour of the cotton.
In decorating the daily hip and shoulder cloths in Tuban, the background rather than the motifs are covered in wax. This makes the patterns come out in colour on a white base, once the immersion in the dye and the boiling have been completed. Ceremonial textiles such as shrouds show the reverse: now the motifs are waxed to stay white and the unwaxed background receives the colour.
Specific for Tuban is the ***batik-lurik*** technique: batik is applied on a black-and-white chequered weave called ***lurik***. The white checks serve as a grid for small motifs composed of dots instead of lines. After the cloth has been immersed in the dye, and the wax has been boiled off, the black checks shimmer through the background that is now red, while the motifs stay white.

The regional market in the new administrative centre. Most traders ▾ are women, selling their field produce and homespun cotton yarn.

institution of a bustling local market, held here twice a week. And the terminal for the minibuses to and from Tuban, the district capital, was also established here. To the women who co-operate in the manufacture of textiles, the old central village in the area's geographical heart, remains the real centre of the *mancapat*. This is also obvious from the dichotomy maintained in this village; a division directly linked to the textile production. A road along the north-south axis divides the village into two halves. In the eastern part lies the house of the village head, its front facing the mountains in the south. Its western counterpart is the house of the *modin*, the Islamic religious official; the front of his house faces the sea in the north. Thus the political and the religious authorities in the village each have their own territory. For the textile production, the western domain is highly important. The house in which the *modin* lives, in the 'religious' half of the village, actually belongs to his wife. She functions as the guardian of the old indigo vat, in which all the batik cloths made in the villages of the *mancapat* should receive their blue colour. The *modin*'s wife is the only woman in the *mancapat* who is allowed to dip the waxed textiles into blue or red dye. The secrets of this sacral craft are handed down from mother to daughter.

Traditionally, the eastern half of the central village is seen as the 'male' territory, where the politics of the *mancapat* are shaped, whereas the western half is the 'female' domain, where ritual matters are dealt with, such as dyeing the textiles. The external element added at a later stage, Islam, has been fitted in smoothly: of course it is no coincidence that the religious official lives in the western half.

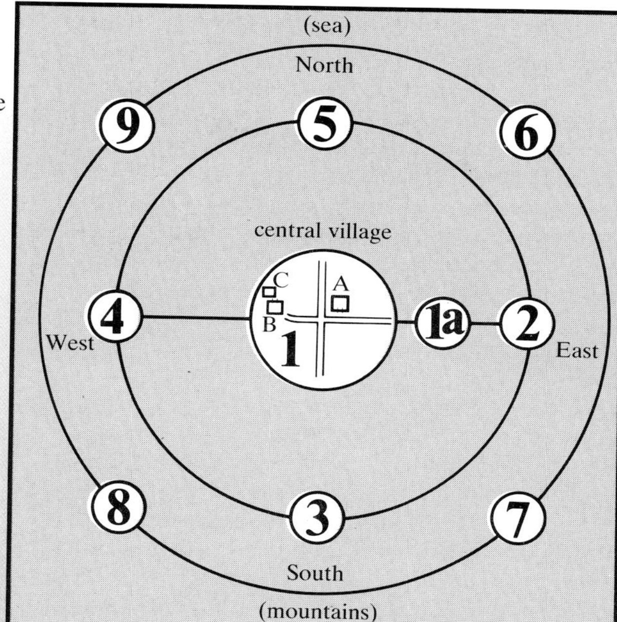

Mancapat

A diagram of the ***mancapat*** unit of textile villages in Tuban:

1: the old central village in the geographical heart
- A = house of village head
- B = dyer's house
- C = ***modin***'s prayer-house

1a: the administrative centre, a later addition
2-5: the ***mancapat*** villages situated around the central village in the four points of the compass
6-9: the ***mancapat*** villages that form a second circle around the central village

*The **modin**'s wife leaves a newly-dyed cloth to drip over the indigo ▼ vat that has a place of its own in the kitchen at the back of her house.*

The tips of the indigo shrub are left to soak for a day and a night in large earthen pots of water, to extract the pigment from the leaves. A year's supply of indigo paste is kept in the smaller pots ▼ with the narrow necks.

The shoulder cloths

In the same way that in the central village a symbolic distinction is made between the male and the female halves, within the community women as a social group are clearly distinguished from the man, by their attire. In the old days each person's attire made his or her position in the community immediately clear. At present only women adorn themselves with traditional hip and shoulder cloths. The men generally prefer western-style clothing. But on ceremonial occasions they too, wear the traditional combination of head and hip cloths, although these now often have to be borrowed or rented from a fellow villager. The main distinction between the men's and women's cloths lies in their size.

Both the male and the female group are subdivided into three generation groups. Among the women, these are the nubile daughters, the mothers and the grandmothers. At home all women merely wear a hip cloth, either a rectangular *jarik*, or a *sarung* sewn into a tubular skirt. The cloth is often simply wrapped under the armpits and folded over in front. This leaves the wearer cool and offers her much freedom of movement. When leaving her house, a woman will wrap this cloth around her hips, add a *kebaya* (a long-sleeved blouse) and knot a second cloth, long and narrow, across her body over one shoulder, like a sash. In this *slendang* or *sayut* she will carry her market merchandise, or her child. Above all the colour of this batik cloth denotes the woman's age group.

All cloths are dyed in various shades and combinations of indigo-blue or red and the natural colour of cotton. Where blue and red have fused, the cloth is black. In preparing the dyes, the *modin*'s wife and daughter will use mainly natural dye materials like their ancestors did before them. With one exception, nowadays: bright red is the only dye prepared from synthetic powder dye bought in the shop.

The colours all have a profound symbolic meaning stemming from the Javanese system of colour classification. In this system a relation is established between the points of the compass and the various periods of night and day, which are also linked to the different stages in life. White is the (non-)colour of the east, where the sun rises, and all life begins. Slowly the sun turns south, symbolized by the colour red, and reaches its zenith, as adolescence blossoms into womanhood. Yellow belongs to the third stage, maturity, located in the west. The day ends in the north, its colour is blueish black: Man's death is lik the close of day. Next, the distance from north to east symbolizes the period between death and rebirth. With the beginning of a new life, the process has come

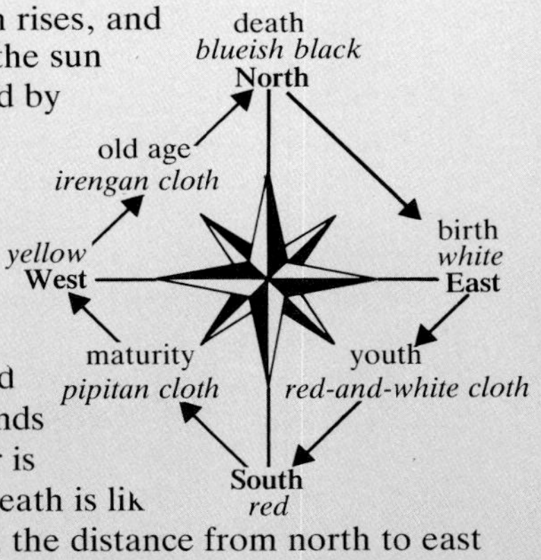

death
blueish black
North
old age
irengan cloth
birth
white
East
yellow
West
maturity
pipitan cloth
youth
red-and-white cloth
South
red

Early morning at the regional market. Formal dress for a woman beyond the immediate surroundings of her home: a hip cloth combined with a **kebaya** *(a long-sleeved blouse), and a* **slendang** *in which she carries her market merchandise on her left* ▼ *hip.*

full circle, a circle found time and again in the cosmology of other traditional Indonesian societies. This cycle is reflected in the colours and names of the types of shoulder cloths assigned to the three generations. Diagonally across her left shoulder a nubile daughter will wear a *slendang* with bright red floral and bird motifs on a natural cotton-coloured background, dotted all over with red. The bright red is the unmistakable sign that the wearer is in the bloom of her life.

Over her right shoulder a mother will knot a cloth in which bright red mingles with indigo-blue. The dots on the natural background will be blue as well. This type of colour combination is called *pipitan*, 'close together', an appropriate description of a stage in life when two social groups (man and woman) and two generations (mother and child) are closely linked. *Pipitan* also means: 'yellowish', derived from the Old-Javanese term *pita*, and apparently refers to the colour of maturity.

Finally, a grandmother will wear more subdued colours; for her, blue has been dyed over with reddish brown, so she ends up with a blueish-black shoulder cloth. Again, the name of the textile, *irengan*, has a double meaning: both 'blackish' and 'lying fallow', a dual reminder of the end of life, and of fertility.

Red are the motifs on the white background of a nubile daughter's ▼ shoulder cloth.

*This **slendang**'s combination of red, blue and black with white ▼ indicates that the wearer belongs to the group of the mothers.*

The blue-black cloth for grandmothers is the darkest of the three ▼ generation cloths.

Ikat in Tuban

In many parts of Indonesia fabrics are decorated before weaving, with a tie-dye technique: with bits of string, bundles of warp or weft yarns are tied off in places and then dyed. This resist technique is called ***ikat***, from the verb *mengikat*, to 'tie' or 'bind'. In ***ikat*** cloths woven from cotton yarn, only the warp is generally tied and dyed, while the plain weft remains invisible in the warpfaced weave.

In many islands of the archipelago a so-called ***ikat*** frame is used; its size is usually related to the weaving-loom's. A bundle of warp yarns is stretched on the frame and tied to produce the desired motifs. Then, the bundle is taken off the frame and dipped into the first dye bath. The bindings act as a resist, the dye cannot penetrate there, and the motifs retain their original colour. By repeatedly applying this process to the same bundle of yarn, complex patterns can be achieved.

In their simplicity, the equipment and method used in Tuban to tie off the yarn, differ from anything found elsewhere in Indonesia. An ***ikat*** frame as such is not known here. Two lengths of bamboo are used to separate the bundle of home-spun yarn that is kept stretched by the weaver's weight. First the pieces of bamboo are slipped through the skein of yarn and one of them is attached under the overhang of the verandah roof. Then the woman sits down on a low wooden stool, slings her legs over the second piece of bamboo, one knee on each side of the yarn bundle, and keeps it tightly stretched. Little by little she ties off small bits of the bundle, tightly binding them with strips of the outer leaf of a corn-cob. All across the skein, rows of large diamond-shaped patterns appear. After having been dyed a bright indigo-blue, the ***ikat*** thread is woven into both warp and weft of the ***kain kentol***. The carefully tied diamond shapes can no longer be recognized as such in the finished cloth; now, only white spots spread irregularly, indicate the position of the former bindings.

The hip cloths

Not only the colouring carries a message, but also the technique used in making certain hip cloths. The combination of these techniques with particular colours and motifs clearly indicates to which village in the *mancapat* and to which social class the wearer belongs.

Each village has its hierarchy of social classes to which only the married villagers belong – men as well as women. Those who do not own land or a house, i.e. the lowest group, or *mondok*, usually work the fields for those higher up, receiving part of the harvest in return. The owners of arable land, the *gogol*, form the middle group. Finally, the *wong kentol*, the descendants of the first settlers of the village territory, and naturally all of them landowners, form the village 'aristocracy'. The village head is generally chosen from their ranks.

In relation to this hierarchy, three types of hip cloths can be distinguished, each decorated in a different technique. Apart from the batik cloths there are *kain kentol*, chequered and striped weaves, with the additional feature of natural-coloured spots formed by tying them off, the *ikat* technique. The third type of cloth combines two different techniques: the white checks of a black-and-white weave called *lurik* serve as a grid for fine geometrical batik motifs composed of dots. Hence this cloth type is called *batik-lurik*.

Two of these cloth types are prerogatives of the élite. Thus the *wong kentol* in the central village of the *mancapat* wear batik hip cloths, while their counterparts in the western village dress in *kain kentol*, the chequered cloth with the *ikat* spots. A *batik-lurik* cloth is the attire of the lower strata in the hierarchy.

The hip cloth denotes the wearer's group within the hierarchy. The batik cloth of the mother carrying her child shows that she and her husband belong to the élite of the central village. The ***batik-lurik*** *cloth of the woman on the left indicates that the couple are common people.* ▸

Different depths of colour and a varying range of motifs relate the *batik-lurik* cloths to specific villages. The red background of the *batik-lurik* cloths worn in the villages in the eastern part of the *mancapat* is much more vivid than that of the villages to the south. The women in the south with their deep-red cloths tend to frown on the flashy dress of their neighbours to the east. The greater the distance between the villages and the *mancapat* centre, the further apart and the smaller their *batik-lurik* motifs tend to be.

▲ *A* ***batik-lurik*** *worn in a village further removed from the* ***mancapat*** *centre. A* ***batik-lurik*** *worn in a village closer to the* ***mancapat*** *centre.* ▼

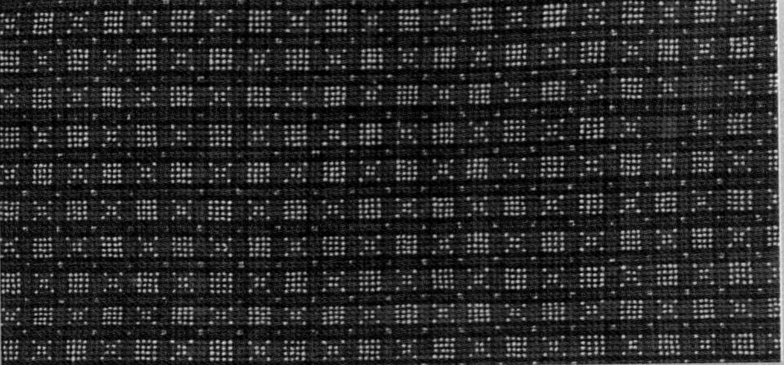

Ceremonial cloths

In contrast to the batik cloths for daily use, with coloured motifs on a relatively light background, the batik textiles for ceremonial use are characterized by light motifs on a dark background. And instead of the colour of the motifs, it is the background colour that lends its name to these ceremonial cloths.

Besides, the two types differ considerably in the style of the motifs. On the ritual cloths, instead of the freeflowing motifs of daily attire, fine geometrical patterns are used. The latter form a kind of blueprint of the *mancapat*. The heart of a stylized flower is always surrounded by four or eight petals, for instance. This highly abstract type of motif has also been compared to a centrally situated mountain with surrounding lower peaks. The patterns can be seen as

▲ *Dark blue-black shroud, with fine, patiently waxed white motifs. This pattern is called* ***kelapa sekantet****, 'coconuts from a single bunch'. This name reflects the concept of unity also expressed in the* ***mancapat****.*

a series of metaphors for the hierarchy of the villages, for the relationship with the ancestors who came from the mountains, and for respect for the gods – who, incidentally, are worshipped in a mountain cave.
The colour of the background of a ceremonial cloth is an indication of the ritual concerned. Here again, black is the colour of death and thus of the background of the cloth draped over a bier. There are only a few old women left who still remember how to draw the details of the intricate pattern type. Again, red is the colour of life and fertility, as demonstrated by the red background of the wedding cloths, preferably decorated with multi-coloured patterns.
A special category is formed by the *putihan*, the 'white' or 'purifying' batik cloths that protect one from illness and ward off evil influences. These textiles are white with bright blue or greyish motifs, while the white may also occasionally be offset by black. The motifs may be either of the floral or of the geometrical type. A young woman will receive a *putihan* shoulder cloth from her mother to carry her newborn baby safely wherever she goes. Later the cloth will often serve to cover the child in times of illness, or to transport valuable goods to the market.
The use of the *putihan* may be seen as a counter-force to break the life cycle mentioned above, that inevitably leads from the east, the place of birth, via south and west, to death in the north. A counter-force, because these cloths are associated with a reverse movement from the east to the north, in the indeterminate area between life and death. If disaster strikes the community, two halves of a *putihan* hip cloth are tied as banners to two long bamboo poles and carried in procession around the village in the same reverse direction, to safeguard the entire community. No other ritual in Tuban so convincingly shows how textiles and world view are inextricably intertwined.

▲ *A* ***putihan*** *with floral motifs.*

A ***putihan*** *with geometric patterns.* ▼

Ancestors and gods

The village community has fitted its adopted religion, Islam, into a strong framework of pre-Islamic traditions. The way in which the central village is divided into two symbolic halves, is a case in point. Other examples may be found in the worship of the ancestors.
The villagers see the ancestors and the gods, together with the living, as an essential part of the community. In every village grows a holy tree with a ***punden*** *in its shade. This is the grave of the (mythical) founder of the village, who reputedly was the first to descend from the mountains and reclaim the village territory. In case of illness or uncertainty, the villagers will bring small offerings of food and flowers to the* ***punden*** *and ask for advice and support. Once a year, after the harvest, a thanksgiving meal is offered on the graves of the ancestors. On this occasion the villagers bring food both for their ancestors and for the villagers they are related to. In this same period, groups of villagers go into the mountains to join in a ritual performed in the Gua Terus stalactite cave. An enormous rocky mass hanging down in the middle of an impressive space is rubbed like a bride with fragrant, yellow* ***boreh*** *paste. Quite possibly the rock is seen as a personification of Dewi Sri, the goddess of rice, of cotton and fertility. A second mass of stone forms the altar for the goddess. The intricate patterns on the walls, formed by the dripping water, are called* ***pari****, rice stalks – which they are seen to resemble. The real rice for the sacrificial meal is to be pounded in a special rice-block used only on this annual occasion; the rest of the year it is kept high up in a niche in the wall.*
In spite of performing ancient Javanese rituals such as these, the villagers regard themselves as Muslims.

A ***kain kentol*** *on the traditional backstrap loom. The weaver sits wedged in between the cloth beam and the wooden loin beam, enabling her to regulate the tension of the warp with her lower body.* ►

The first encounter with foreign tourists.

Madurese

The Madurese are one of the larger ethnic groups in Indonesia. Not only the inhabitants of the island itself belong to this group, but also the people living in the islands around Madura, in the Kangean and Sapudi archipelagos. In addition, a large number of Madurese has left the island to settle as farmers in East Java, and many live in cities such as Surabaya, Malang and even Jakarta. In 1985 there were about three million people in the island itself, whereas by now the number of Madurese beyond Madura has probably risen to some six million. Madura is part of the province of Jawa Timur. The island itself is divided into four districts, Bangkalan, Sampang, Pamekasan and Sumenep. Their capitals bear these same names, and are the only towns in Madura. The great majority of the population, over eighty percent, lives in villages in the interior and along the coast. Agriculture, trade, cargo sailing, fishing and the salt industry are important livelihoods. Tobacco and fruit are the only commercial crops.

Older women who no longer have young children to look after, often open a small shop where they sell ***krupuk*** *(deep-fried prawn crisps), spices and herbs, lemonade and sweets.*

The bull-races of Madura

The island of Madura, north-east of Java, is easily reached from the port of Surabaya. Three ferries maintain a twenty-four hour service between the island and Java; the crossing hardly takes fifteen minutes. Considering this proximity, it is hardly surprising that from times immemorial, the history of Madura has always been closely linked to that of the Javanese princes. The Madurese dynasties were related to those in Java, and in language and lifestyle the Madurese nobility had a thoroughly Javanese orientation. The political and economic development of Java at the time of the Dutch East India Company and under the government of the Netherlands East Indies, involved Madura as well, to such an extent that in many books and articles both islands are bracketed together. Conveniently these publications assume that in analogy to the similarity at the top, the lifestyle of the ordinary Madurese closely resembles that of his Javanese counterpart. But nothing is further from the truth. To name one important difference: so as to prevent conflict, the Madurese code of social conduct is far more strict. In contrast to the subdued Javanese, the Madurese act far more openly in matters in which their family honour is at stake. An insult or a loss of face quickly degenerates into violent clashes.

Tourist attraction or struggle for status

For a Madurese the best way to keep up his reputation is to win a bull-race. In these competitions, teams of two bulls must pull a sledge and jockey as fast as possible across a track of over a hundred metres. The Madurese bull-races are unique in the world, and due to the folklore attached they have been a tourist attraction for a long time now. The races in a town such as Bangkalan have become a household word to visitors from all continents. During this exciting sports spectacle the foreign spectators are let in on the 'secrets' of the Madurese and their island. The bull-races are the Madurese popular festival par excellence. In addition, they are told that the Madurese man is a great lover of these animals and takes good care of them.
Such statements are true enough, but don't reflect more than a fraction of the real passion with which the Madurese cherishes his bulls. To possess a brace of racing bulls is the ideal of every Madurese man. However, what is important to him, are not the competitions organized for tourists throughout the year, but the annual traditional races. These claim all his attention. With a team of racing bulls a Madurese can enter these races and become 'champion of Madura', the highest honour to be gained in the island. The traditional races are held only during the dry season, in September and October. Then, rival Madurese families engage in cut-throat competition, with one aim only: to win, win, win.
As the authentic bull-races are among the few occasions on which Madurese men can match themselves against one another, they are exceedingly

important. The honour at stake here, justifies all imaginable means to eliminate competitors, including the use of spies and black magic. In these races the suspense is tangible, for if a group of Madurese are scornfully humiliated by rivals, this might easily trigger an eruption of violence. Hence these races require permission from the local authorities, and the police is emphatically present.

Honour and prestige

In Madura there are strict rules of social conduct, to prevent conflicts as far as possible. The life spheres of men and women are so separate that one could speak of a dichotomy, and young people have to show a lot of respect to their elders. But strictest of all are the rules governing the interaction between men, the way

The head of a family in ceremonial Madurese dress. The spear is a heirloom, ***pusaka****, passed down from father to son.* ▼

Islam

The religious life of the Madurese nobility centres around the mosque. Thus the members of every self-respecting noble family want to be buried in one of the special cemeteries for the nobility which, as in Sumenep, are situated around a mosque.
Far more important to the way in which the commoners experience their faith, are saints and religious leaders, called ***kiyai***. The latter teach religion, direct religious ceremonies, give advice in case of illness, and are seen as 'intermediaries' between Allah and the believers. Often supernatural powers to promote prosperity and well-being are ascribed to them. After death, some ***kiyai*** are regarded as saints who can still effect ***selamat***, well-being and blessing. Hence pupils and followers of a religious leader often pray at his grave.

they associate and deal with each other. This is a direct result of the social pressure on a man to keep up his prestige. If he is insulted, he will defend his honour at all costs. Often he has only one answer, *carok*: given a chance, he will make a violent attempt to get rid of his opponent.

The strict rules apply to all kinds of situations. For example, a self-respecting man cannot go to a party uninvited; he would disgrace himself and his family. Doing his daily work in the fields, a man will not easily ask other farmers for help; he will prefer to turn to his sons or his wife. If circumstances force him to co-operate with other men, the division of labour and the compensation for the work to be done must first be clearly agreed upon.

In buying and selling cattle or land, men will never enter into direct negotiations, but will use a go-between. Once these intermediaries have reached an agreement on the price and any other conditions there might be, the principals will close the deal. Even then, buyer and seller cannot do without help: the intermediaries have to witness the payment.

Taking part in a bull-race means far more to a Madurese man than just an amusing pastime. Thus he shows he does not avoid a challenge, and that he is prepared to do battle with other men.

Selamatan

The Madurese are good Muslims. They pray five times a day, pay their religious taxes, and fast during Ramadan. And every Madurese hopes to go on a pilgrimage to Mecca at least once in his lifetime. In spite of this orthodox attitude to life, the religious ideas of the Madurese, like those of the Javanese in Tuban, are mixed with all kinds of non-Islamic elements. Every transition in the life of a Madurese (birth, circumcision, marriage and death), must be accompanied by a salutary meal, a ***selamatan****, for only this will ensure the good fortune of the person involved, and his family's.*

For that matter, these meals are organized on all sorts of occasions, to ward off evil influences. Whether somebody is leaving on a business trip or is about to enter his bulls in a race, a common meal is always arranged first. The prayers at such a ***selamatan*** *are addressed not only to Allah, but also to the ancestors.*

▲ *In earthen pots the rice is steamed over a wood fire.*

No salutary meal is complete without rice cones. ▼

▲ *Preparing a salutary meal.*

The meal served in the prayer house is for men only. ▼

After the meal every participant is given a small basket with some food and biscuits for his family at home. ▼

Bulls and status

Not every Madurese farmer can afford to keep a team of racing bulls. One needs more than just the money to buy the animals; masseurs and other specialists must also be paid to look after them. Only rich farmers, traders and members of rural village councils have enough capital for such investments.

One of the best known cattle markets for racing bulls is held in the village of Poteran in the district of Sumenep. Racing bulls are hardly ever bred by their owners. The animals only come up for sale when they are about three years old and reasonably well-trained. Before the future owner decides on a team, he will be shown in detail how well-disciplined the bulls are, and how fast they can run. With a brace of racing bulls that are well taken care of, an owner will be able to compete some ten to twelve times at the annual traditional races.

The bulls are preferably stabled at the owner's, and looked after by specialists from the neighbourhood. They massage the animals frequently, and keep them under close surveillance to see whether extra nutrition is needed. In contrast to the draught cattle, the racing bulls are grazed every day by attendants specially hired for this purpose. They must see to it that the animals never lack fresh fodder, grass and leaves.

It is extremely important for an owner to find a good jockey, the man straddling the skids and driving the team. A jockey must be a lightweight, no more than fifty kilos, and a real dare-devil. Experienced jockeys, who also train the bulls, like to be well paid. So every bull-owner runs a constant risk of losing his jockey to a rival willing to pay more.

In addition to care and training, the traditional equipment of the bulls is quite an investment. The wooden yoke and the sledge attached are carved and painted in bright colours, usually red and golden yellow. It is customary for the yoke to have three holes drilled in it; depending on the wealth of the owner, flags, sun-shades or sticks with beautifully carved birds are stuck into these holes. For the bulls' heads, necks and backs, special decorations are made that are attached to the animals before they leave for the race-course. However, the bulls run without this finery; before the race, each competitor shows off his team 'dressed' to the nines.

In some families the equipment for the racing bulls are heirlooms passed from father to son. It is the tradition

▲ *The cattle market, a man's world.*

▲ *Inspection by the experts.*

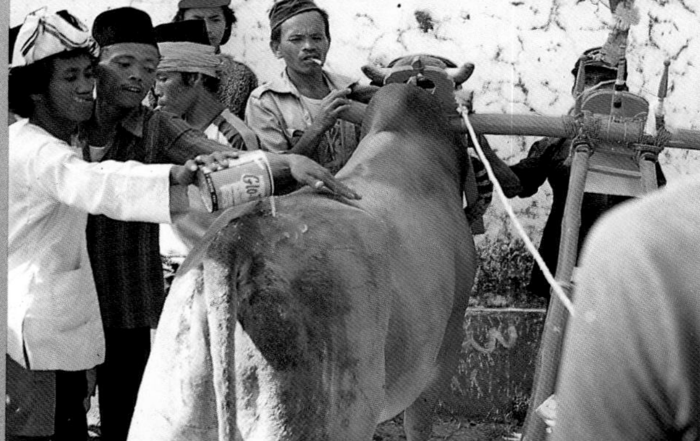

▲ *The last preparations in the stadium.*

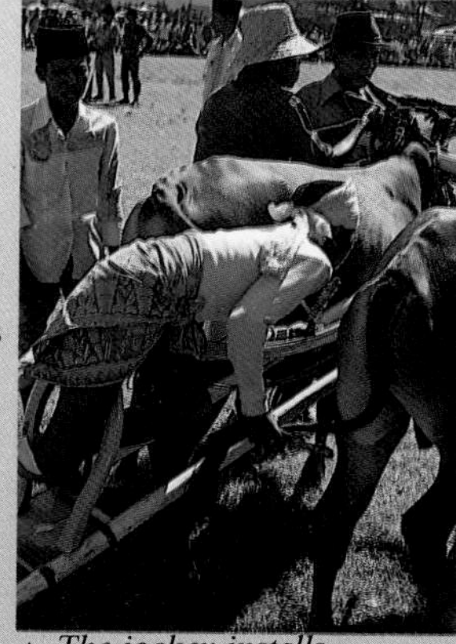

▲ *The jockey installs himself.*

Prior to the races, the bulls and their escorts make a festive ceremonial round of ▼ *the stadium.*

▲ *The sledge, to be pulled by two bulls.*

of such families that at least one man in each generation buys racing bulls and takes part in the races. Nobody with sufficient means, can evade this unwritten law. With every new generation the status of the family has to be confirmed. Besides, keeping a team of bulls is a clear and unmistakeable sign to the economic and social competitors: they will have to take the power and influence of the family thoroughly into account.

Fear of magic

During the months preceding the traditional races the bulls are taken better care of than ever. The owners, whose name and prestige are at stake, spare no trouble or expense to get the animals in top condition. In this critical period the bulls are often stabled with specialists who have the knowledge to get them into optimal shape for the competition. They massage the animals every day, and feed them not only grass –also eggs, coffee and herbal potions. Day and night the animals are guarded, to prevent them from being poisoned or harmed in any other way. To reduce the risk of injuries as much as possible, the jockey trains his bulls on a carefully levelled stretch of land.
Yet all these preparations combined, do not guarantee success at the races. Through spies, the owner gathers information about the strength of competitors' bulls, and about the care they receive. The rivalry between the owners may even go as far as frequent attempts to eliminate the other team by means of black magic. Generally feared are the spells that cause the bulls to refuse to run, or to turn around halfway. So every owner takes his own precautions and consults specialists who can break possible spells and avert evil influences. That such services are expensive, goes without saying.
Not only the bulls, but also the jockeys risk being struck by such spells. Therefore, prior to a race, a jockey will go to a *dukun*, a specialist in sorcery, and ask him to break any spells that may have been cast on him. In addition, during the race many a jockey will wear powerful amulets as a protection against evil forces.
A few days before the race, the bulls are taken back to the owner's stables. All attendants and confidants the owner has gathered around him, will now install themselves here and make the final preparations. Then it is only a matter of waiting for the *gamelan* orchestra and the *dukun*'s final instructions. He will determine the spot where the bulls will spend the last night before the race, as well as the hour of departure and the direction in which the animals are to leave the yard.
The night before the competition everybody is wide

Standing in their owner's yard, the bulls spend ▼ *the night before the races out in the open.*

awake. The *gamelan* plays, and the hours pass slowly. The bulls are in the yard, securely tied between three bamboo stakes. They are moved regularly; time and again they are turned in a direction prescribed by the *dukun*, to ward off all evil forces. A salutary common meal, a *selamatan*, concludes the nocturnal session after which the bulls are prepared for the trip to the track. Next to the animals incense is burnt with sugar, and one of the attendants sprinkles the animals with a kind of perfume in which special flowers and herbs have been soaked.
At the predetermined time and in the prescribed direction, the bulls leave the yard, to the accompaniment of the *gamelan*, and escorted by the attendants, the owner and his confidants. In a cattle-truck the team on which so much depends, leaves for the stadium...

▲ *The fodder for the racing bulls is carefully put together and measured.*

The champion

The climax of the traditional bull-races in Madura is the great race in the capital, Pamekasan. At these races the stadium is always sold out. The stand is filled to capacity and people are swarming everywhere, either involved in the organization of the races, or with a brace of bulls. Wherever possible, food and drink stalls have been set up, and a *gamelan* plays all the time.

Well in advance most teams and their escorts arrive at the stadium. Again it is the *dukun* who determines the spot where a group will stand. Here the bulls are prepared for the start. All their muscles are given a final massage and the animals get a potent pep drink: a mixture of beer, geneva, sodawater and beaten eggs. Their skin is rubbed with a bitter liniment, and *sambal* (red-pepper paste, a popular ingredient of the Indonesian cuisine) is applied to their mouth, nose and genitals. Safety pins are stuck into their tails.

Before the actual race, the bulls and their escorts make a final ceremonial round past the crowd. For this purpose the flags and sun-shades are inserted in the yokes, and the bulls are exuberantly decorated. A *gamelan* orchestra leads the procession in which the bulls are followed by the owners and their supporters. As soon as the *gamelan* starts to play, the procession is set in motion. Thus, team after team passes the jury who occupy a high platform at the finish.

◂ *An attendant sticks a safety-pin into a racing bull's tail.*

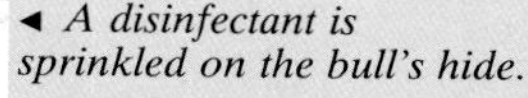

◂ *A disinfectant is sprinkled on the bull's hide.*

▾ *Madurese racing bulls dressed to the nines.*

▲ *Ready, set...*

...GO!

...the spectators watch breathlessly...

...the last round...

...the winning team passes the finish. ▼

Then a trumpet sounds: the races are about to start. The referees take up their positions, one at the start and one at the finish. The first two teams are called forward; the men have trouble keeping the excited bulls under control. The tension in the stadium mounts. The teams are lined up at the starting-line and the jockeys straddle the skids, holding a bamboo slat through which nails have been hammered. During the race he will rub the bulls' shoulders with it, literally stinging them to greater efforts.
The referee standing in front of the teams, now raises a red flag and off they go! The winning team is the first to get their front legs across the finish, and is indicated by a coloured flag.
After the race the bulls are taken care of and led back to the spot where they are looked after. Immediately their wounds are treated, and disinfected. Again the animals are given an alcoholic mixture. If the team has won, they await the call for the second round. The final race is between three teams running for the supreme honour, the championship of Madura. The names of the winning bulls, but their owner's in particular, are established for a whole year.

The great race

In Pamekasan the bulls race along a track about 120 metres long, staked out on a stretch of grass. After a preselection, twenty-four teams are admitted to the great race. Each consists of two bulls pulling a simple wooden sledge. During the races the jockey will lean on a bent support attached to this sledge.
Usually the teams compete two at a time. Only in the final round are there three braces. Before the start, the animals are held tight by a group of burly fellows. As soon as the starting signal is given, they send the bulls on their way with a few firm smacks on their backs and shoulders.
The speed of the bulls on the track is quite high, on average 36 kilometres an hour (22.5 mph). The names of the animals express their speed. To name a few marvellous ones: Si Tolop (blow-pipe), Si Koceng (cat), Si Bharat (howling wind) and Si Pana (arrow). After the race, the winning jockey performs an elegant Madurese dance on the backs of his bulls.

Java, rich in history and culture, rich in people and fertile soil, but above all rich in contrasts. In few islands of the archipelago is the tourist so inevitably confronted with Man's limitations and the uncontrollable forces of Nature: despite the skyscrapers he built, time and again an awe-inspiring chain of active volcanoes brings home to the Javanese how insignificant Man is. A trip from West Java to the east coast of the island, will take the traveller through charming villages, temples and palaces with refined court cultures, but also along gaping craters, gorges and fathomless abysses.

In West Java in the lowland in the north the Sundanese cultivates his ***sawah***, while in the southern highland the volcanoes rumble and smoke.

The high mountain country of Central Java is situated more towards the middle of the island. South of the crater summits that are under observation day and night, the traveller encounters cities where noisy traffic streams are led past serene bastions of tradition: the ***kraton*** of the Central-Javanese rulers. When in the last century the Netherlands-Indies government deprived them of their political power, the old rulers of Central Java increasingly concentrated on cultural matters, and to this day the results of that development are visible all over Surakarta and Jogyakarta. Graceful palace dances, a highly developed batik industry, the exceptional artistry of silversmiths, no one can fail to notice the excellence of these cultural expressions. Impressive examples of sculpture and architecture are found nearby: despite a series of destructive eruptions of Mount Merapi, in their restored beauty the temple complexes of Borobudur and Prambanan reflect Java's ancient religious past.

Two impressive mountains loom menacingly over the eastern highland: Bromo, a perennial trail of smoke around its summit, and Semeru, with its 3,600 metres Java's highest. Lower down, Man resumes control of the landscape; just as in the west, only reserves still show something of the original flora and fauna. On the coast the traveller runs aground in the much-praised port of modern Surabaya. ***Pasar*** full of atmosphere contrast shrilly with drab department stores, and just as in the other Javanese cities numbering over a million inhabitants, the colourful tricycle taxis are increasingly swept aside by the relentless rush of motorized traffic. It is here that the tourist experiences, almost physically, Java's greatest problem. The island seems to be buried in people, the population's density is incredible, its increase almost beyond control. Hence, in spite of all risk of erosion, the farmer lays out new ***sawah*** at ever higher altitudes. In the elevated fields of the dreamscape, the first bare rocks already glisten; for the first time the mighty mountains seem to bow: the fertility of the Javanese turns out to exceed that of his land.

A silversmith at work in Kota Gede, on the periphery of Jogyakarta. ▼

3 Bali

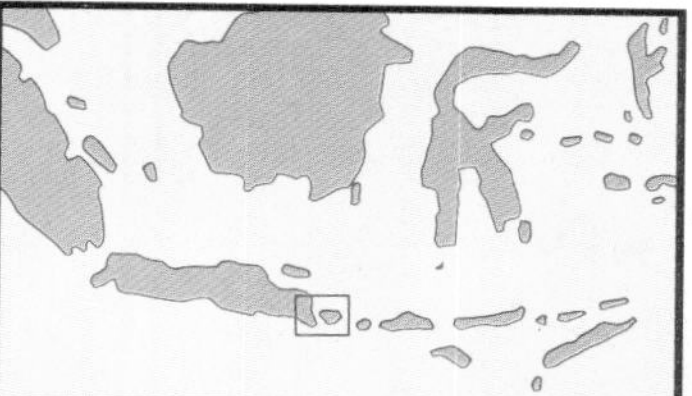

All over the world Bali is known as 'the island of the gods'; the paradise on Earth that supposedly inspired its inhabitants in their strikingly refined cultural achievements. How surprising reality is: the Balinese too, has his worries. His daily life is full of pitfalls; paradise is a long way off. And it turns out that in Bali the key to a better existence lies not in this, but in some other, invisible world.

Ancestors, residing in this invisible world, play a major role in the island. Henk Schulte Nordholt shows how important their presence is in the pursuit of power and status. Especially in the higher strata ancestor worship proves to be a formidable political weapon.
In addition to this, a good relationship with one's ancestors is seen as a condition for a safe course through life. Fear and insecurity are removed by communication with this invisible world. To many the trance medium, the *balian taksu*, is indispensable. Annemarie Verkruisen describes a consultation.

Status and ancestors

Balinese society has a very hierarchical structure. Few Balinese think they are on a level with others. Instead, they actually emphasize their mutual differences, pointing out that one person ranks higher than the other. These differences in status are reflected in their language, among other things. It befits a higher person to be addressed in polite (high) terms, and a lower person to be spoken to in neutral (low) terms. That social order is also revealed in a gathering of people of different rank. Those of higher status sit in a more elevated position than those of lower class. Higher and lower seats are embedded as it were, in the surrounding landscape. In Bali, a higher position is referred to by the term *kaja*, meaning 'to the mountains', whereas the term *kelod* (to the sea) refers to a lower position. Thus the Balinese landscape reflects the hierarchical relations.
Highest are the mountains cutting straight across the island: the dwelling-places of the gods. The wooded mountain slopes gradually blend into a gently sloping, fertile plain running down to the sea. The sea is where the demons dwell; they can cause disease and other calamities to descend on the land. Between the mountains and the sea, between gods and demons, between 'high' and 'low', live the people.

◄ ***A balian taksu** beseeches the gods to help her, while in her yard a few visitors are already waiting for a consultation. Soon, in a state of trance, she will reveal to her clients the wishes and advice of the gods and ancestors.*

Gods, ancestors and demons

Balinese religion, ***Agama Hindu Bali***, is a mixture of pre-Hindu, Buddhist and Hindu elements. This religion, professed by over ninety percent of the Balinese population, is based on the worship of a vast number of gods, deified ancestors and demons.
The gods can be distinguished into two categories. The first comprises gods from the Hindu pantheon who were given a niche in Bali's original religion. For instance Vishnu, the deity who sustains the universe. In the second category we find gods and goddesses who are linked to nature.
The Balinese worships not only the gods, but also his deified ancestors. Their souls need never return to the world of the mortals, they have forever been admitted to the realm of the gods.
The demons finally, are the opposites of the gods and ancestors in every respect: their appearance is frightening and their intentions are purely evil.

The life cycle

Analogous with the water cycle, human life in Bali proceeds in a constant cycle between the mountains and the sea. From the mountains, the water cascades down through deeply eroded gorges. There it flows out into countless little streams spreading across the rice fields and ending up in the sea. Water evaporating from the sea rises to the mountains to descend again, fertilizing the land.
The human soul follows the same cyclical course. After death the body is burned to free the soul from all earthly bonds. Next of kin ritually take the soul out to sea, from where it ascends to the mountains to join its ancestors. Like the water, the soul in turn descends from the mountains: again a human life commences on Earth. This cycle of birth and death must be repeated several times before the soul can join its deified ancestors forever. In an attempt to maintain the hierarchical order and to avert any dangerous disturbances, temple rituals accompany this uninterrupted cycle.

Living in the right direction

*The Balinese orientates himself in a way that differs from the Westerner's. He doesn't speak of north, south, east and west, but of the direction of the mountains (**kaja**), the direction of the sea (**kelod**), the direction of sunrise (**kangin**), and the direction of sunset (**kauh**). **Kaja** and **kangin** are considered auspicious directions; **kelod** and **kauh** are associated with disaster. We also find this idea in the spatial ordering of the house yard or premises:*

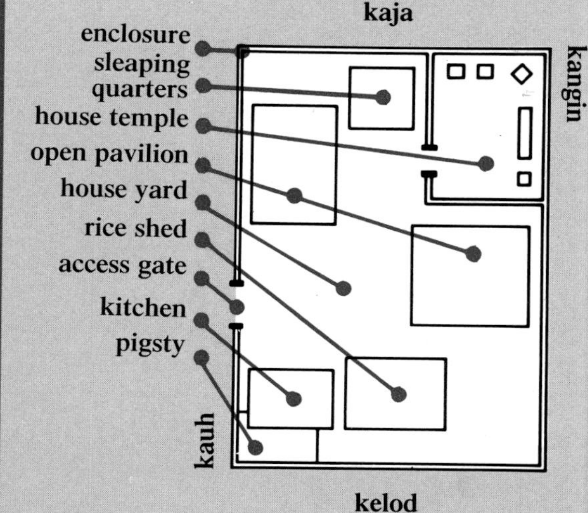

*In the yard, the house temple must always occupy a **kaja-kangin** position: as close as possible to the mountains and the rising sun. In contrast, the pigsty is invariably orientated **kelod-kauh**.*

Shrine for the gods in a Balinese temple. ▲

What am I

If a Balinese is asked *who* he is, he usually won't immediately give his name, but respond by telling *what* he is. In other words: he will first indicate his position in relation to his fellow Balinese. Only then will he give his name. The position he has in society becomes clear by referring to the family context he belongs to. The status of this family group determines the position of its members in the social hierarchy.
Family contexts are most clearly expressed in a network of small temples. Every yard has its own house temple, situated in a 'high' spot: 'towards the mountains'. All house temples of a family group are linked to the temple in the 'mother yard', from where in due course various sons departed to found yards of their own. Regularly, a family gathers around the ancestral shrine in the 'mother yard' to express their mutual bond in a fixed ritual.
Usually, a family also has a central ancestral shrine which it shares with many other families. This is the *kawitan* (literally: stock, origin), where the common forefather is worshipped. This *kawitan* is the summit of the hierarchy of family temples, and from this the Balinese derives his identity. Joining in the ritual around the *kawitan* shows that one belongs to a specific group.

Therefore, to indicate what he is, a Balinese will often refer to his *kawitan*. The *kawitan* acts as an important point of reference in life. In this spot, where the progeny meet their ancestors, one's position in society is, as it were, deeply embedded in the past. In addition, one's position in the social hierarchy is derived from the founding father's status. The *kawitan*'s status legitimizes the status that the larger family group wishes to enjoy.
If a Balinese does not know where his *kawitan* is, he does not know who his forefather was, and hence neither who or what he himself is. His position in the hierarchy is completely obscure. He does not know how he is supposed to deal with others, how to address

Social classes or 'castes'

As a result of Hindu influences, Bali has a 'caste' division, but this concerns only a minority of the Balinese. Highest are the Brahmans, followed by the Satria, and last of all come the Wesya. Brahmans, Satria and Wesya jointly form the so-called ***triwangsa***, the top layer of noble birth comprising a mere ten percent of the population. The large majority of the Balinese have a lower status. Their position with regard to the nobility is indicated by the term ***jaba***, 'outsider'. But the ***jaba*** do not form one undifferentiated mass of 'caste-less' people. For there is a great variety of lineage groups, each claiming a separate status.

*The **puri** Mayun in Blahkiuh, an **merajan gede** or house temple of a noble family.* ▼

◄ *Many shoulders support a cremation tower, a **bade**, in conveying it to the spot where the cremation is to take place. The **bade** contains the remains of a Brahman priest. The tower has the shape of a **padmasana**, the stone lotus throne of the god Shiva found in many Balinese temples.*

them, and where to sit. As his position is not embedded in the past, he feels utterly disorientated, adrift, hardly able to function properly.
Many large family groups have a written chronicle in which their origin and status are explained. First it offers a detailed account of the forefather's many heroic deeds and then, in an extensive genealogy, demonstrates his link with the present progeny.

The kawitan forgotten

An example will clarify the dynamics that this system of ancestor worship conceals. The chronicle of one of Bali's princely dynasties starts with the story of the first great ruler who, after many wars, had gained power over half the island. He lived around 1730, and was a successful warrior, feared everywhere. And yet, he struggled with a problem: he did not know who his ancestors were, so he did not really know who he himself was. Therefore he summoned his court priest and ordered him to write a chronicle. It was only then that the prince discovered that he had an exalted forefather, from whom his family could derive a lofty status. Thus the prince justified his acquired power by embedding it firmly in the past.
More than 250 years later: over these past centuries the dynasty has gone through turbulent times. After a tempestuous rise, periods of prosperity and crisis alternated at a rapid pace until, at the end of the nineteenth century, a fatal concurrence of circumstances spelt the fall of the principality. The dynasty was broken up and lost much of its former power.
Then modern times were ushered in: in the first half of the twentieth century Bali was under Dutch colonial Administration, and from 1945 the island has been part of the Republic of Indonesia. In particular the years between 1945 and 1965 were characterised by rapid changes involving great tensions. In this period the old dynasty lost its last remnants of coherence.
An unchallenged member of the family then decided it was time for action. Under his guidance the family embarked on a quest for their *kawitan*, which had been neglected since the end of the nineteenth century. "We could have known", he told his relatives, "he who does not honour his *kawitan* and forgets his ancestors, will be pursued by disaster." Finally, in April, 1983, the dynasty was reunited in the old temple in which the *kawitan* was found. This not only restored the bond with the ancestors, but also the family's feeling of solidarity. True, the dynasty had lost its former power, but in the end it had managed to preserve its identity.

Temple systems

Balinese life is, as it were, embedded in temple systems. On many levels, temples act as social points of reference and are often interlinked. Every yard has its small house temple (***sanggah*** or, among the nobility, ***merajan***), which is related to the temple in the 'mother yard' (***sanggah gede*** or ***merajan gede***). In turn, several of these temples in mother yards are linked to a larger ancestral temple, (the ***pura dadia*** or ***pura batur***), housing the ***kawitan***. In addition to these, in principle every village (***desa***) has three temples: the 'navel' temple (***pura puseh***), the village temple (***pura desa***), and the temple of the dead (***pura dalem***). In the system, the village temples rank below the regional temples, which often date from the old reign of the princes, and cover much larger areas. Higher still are the temples covering all of Bali, such as the temple complex of Besakih. A separate system is formed by the irrigation temples; these have a network of their own.
In addition we find countless other temples. Every Balinese family has connections with some five to ten temples, where they regularly make sacrifices to ensure a safe course through life.

Balinese shrine for the gods, built of traditional materials. Whereas the base used to consist of red brick or of stone, now – to save money – concrete is increasingly used. So is corrugated zinc, and for the same reason. Traditional materials, such as ***duk****, the black palm fibre, and* ***alang-alang*** *grass, do last longer (some 25 years), but are* ▼ *more expensive.*

After its arrival at the place of cremation, the body of the deceased is taken from the ***bade****, and laid in a sarcophagus to be burnt. The latter often has the shape of a bull or a cow, but may also be a simple coffin. A body is not always immediately cremated. Sometimes the next of kin have to save for years before they can afford the burning ritual.* ►

▲ *For a cremation ritual that meets all requirements, a great variety of offerings is needed. The tall cylindrical offerings are called* ***pisang jati****. A main ingredient of these is a young shoot of a banana tree, symbol of a new life. A small piece of sandalwood with a stylized depiction of the deceased is also incorporated in it. The* ***pisang jati*** *too, is sent up in flames, and is to promote a good rebirth of the deceased.*

The interchangeable forefather

Changing political and economic circumstances have always influenced the size and status of family groups. Although this applied in particular to the nobility, groups of commoners too, underwent such fluctuations. Powerful families commanding respect, would usually introduce an exalted forefather as a justification of their position. Such families often had great attraction for outsiders who wanted to belong to them. Thus, powerful families increased in size and actually turned into some kind of alliance. On the other hand, such a family could also dwindle if it lost its power. Thus the Balinese was actually not so rigidly linked to one particular forefather. Depending on the vicissitudes of political fortune, he tried his luck with a different *kawitan*.

In old Bali, power and status were hard-won. This changed when, at the beginning of this century, the island came under colonial rule. Dutch Administration officials could hardly make head or tail of the maze of class differences they encountered on their arrival. So they tried to create some order by accomodating the multitude of family groups in one uniform 'caste system'. The result was a rather rigid system highly protective of the old nobility. Once a family had been assigned to a particular caste, it was stuck with it. And, once excluded from a higher caste, one could never hope for a better position and a higher status. At the beginning of the fifties this strict caste system became the subject of debate. Bali was now part of

▲ *Only after it is set free from its mortal frame, can the soul of the deceased return to its origin, the world of the gods. Hence to the next of kin it is a sacred duty to carry out a cremation.*

▲ *Gunung Agung slumbers, shrouded in mist. Heaven and Earth seem to touch above the temple complex at Besakih.*

▲ *In a festive procession the gods of a village temple are borne to the sea for a cleansing ritual. In the background the mountains, the lofty seats of gods and ancestors. To the left is Gunung Batukau (2276 metres), the westernmost of Bali's three great volcanoes.*

the Republic of Indonesia, and a strong movement arose that wanted to get rid of the 'feudal' era. Class or caste barriers had to be razed, for henceforth differences in status were a thing of the past. Turbulent times began. Political parties appeared on the scene, and party-political conflicts deeply penetrated society. Identification with a political party became more important than the orientation towards a forefather. After all, unlike political leaders he offered no political shelter and did not bestow favours. Temporarily, the *kawitan* had to make way for the party membership card.

A turning-point followed in the first half of the sixties, when after the eruption of Gunung Agung, the escalating social conflicts also erupted, and old feuds between families (and often also conflicts within families) were settled at the same time. After 1965, under the new rule of General Suharto, a peaceful period set in. Party-political differences were pushed into the background and the people reorientated themselves toward the *kawitan*. There was a run on 'forgotten' forefathers, and entirely new 'family' contexts were formed and given a basis in newly written chronicles. The renewed identification with the *kawitan* seemed entirely a-political.

Power presupposes a forefather

Yet the following example shows that ancestor worship may sometimes be of a political nature. In one of Bali's villages lived a wealthy man who together with his family had a considerable say in local matters. He owned quite a lot of land, and was involved in various trade activities. In addition, in town he was a high official.

At the beginning of this century his grandfather was still rather poor and his family belonged to the anonymous and marginal nobility. However, this changed. The family's wealth increased with its local power, so they wanted a status to match. And they succeeded: nowadays the family members adorn

◄ *After the cremation, in procession, the next of kin take the ashes to the sea or to a river. There, by scattering the ashes over the water, they see to it that nothing of the mortal remains is left on Earth. Only then is the soul completely free, and can it return to the world of the gods.* ▼

*Part of a **merajan gede**, the house temple of a noble family.* ►

themselves with exuberant noble titles, and the family possesses a fine chronicle to prove that they actually are of the blood.

Ironically, the measure taken in the fifties to raze caste barriers and limit the privileges of the nobility, has now resulted in an increasing number of wealthy families, especially in town, regarding themselves as belonging to the higher nobility. In doing so, they refer to a lofty forefather and pretend they have always belonged to the high nobility.

"The other day one of the newcomers addressed me as an equal, just like that!", complained the impoverished heir of an old, noble family, adding with a sigh: "but what can you do? They are rich and I no longer am."

In Bali, the relationship between the living and the dead, between families and their *kawitan*, is subject to constant change. New political and economic circumstances force the Balinese to redefine their identity time and again, and subsequently to express this surrounded with sacrifices.

*A **tukang banten**, a woman who prepares offerings, has finished her work.* ▼

A 'ground' offering, meant to appease the demons. ▼

Offerings

In Bali, preparing offerings or **banten** *is a typical woman's job. At a very tender age, girls are initiated into this art by the adult women in their household. Out of palm-leaf strips the women and the girls make all kinds of constructions,* **jejaitan**, *that serve as a basis, but also as an ingenious decoration of the offerings. But their preparation also includes the moulding of biscuits out of rice dough,* **sesamuhan**. *These multi-coloured biscuits may have abstract shapes or may represent plants, animals or people. Time and again the sacrifice makers manage to create exceedingly beautiful tableaus. Flowers, fruit, rice, sugar-cane, coconuts, eggs or meat, are used for the finishing touch.*

The balian taksu: link between the visible and the invisible

An ancestor returns

"Who is this who was born anew?"
"It is I, your grandmother. Now I am your grandchild. Do you believe this?"
"Yes, I do".

"Father, father!"
"Yes, here I am."
"It's me, I Kadek, your second child. Actually I did not want to be reborn. But I obey the will of the gods. Now I have returned home."
"But we possess nothing at all!"
"Just do your best, and the gods will favour you. Then I Kadek will become a human being. But if you don't do that, I Kadek will have been born in vain."

Though the living and the dead reside in two different worlds, in Bali they are closely linked. How close, is evident from the ideas of the Balinese about the reincarnation of the souls of the dead. What is so characteristic about this, is the belief that rebirth always takes place within the family circle. For a Balinese family, the birth of a child does not only mean extension of the kingroup with a new descendant, but also the return of one of the ancestors to his descendants.
The position the soul occupies in the body of the newborn baby has not yet stabilized, though: just returned from the realm of the gods, the soul is still so close to the divine sphere that it could easily return to it. That is why the family will do their utmost to bind the soul to its earthly existence. For a start, they will have to know which ancestor has crossed the boundary between the visible and the invisible worlds. Who is this ancestor who wants to start a new life on earth: a grandparent, a great-grandparent, or possibly even a great-great-grandparent?
More important even than finding out the identity of the ancestor, is to know his possible wishes for the ceremony to be held on the baby's 105th day. At that moment the child may enter the ancestral shrine for the first time; an event officially confirming his status as a descendant, belonging to the living kingroup. The ancestor may wish that special sacrifices be made, or that a certain musical or dance performance be given. In the interest of the child the family must know and grant these wishes. Otherwise, the soul, dissatisfied and disappointed with its earthly existence, might decide to return to where s/he came from, which would result in the child's death.
To get an answer to such questions, the family will turn to someone who can function as a contact between the living and the dead. Such a person is the *balian taksu*, sometimes a man but usually a woman, who, when in trance, voices the ancestors' wishes and their words of advice to the mortals.

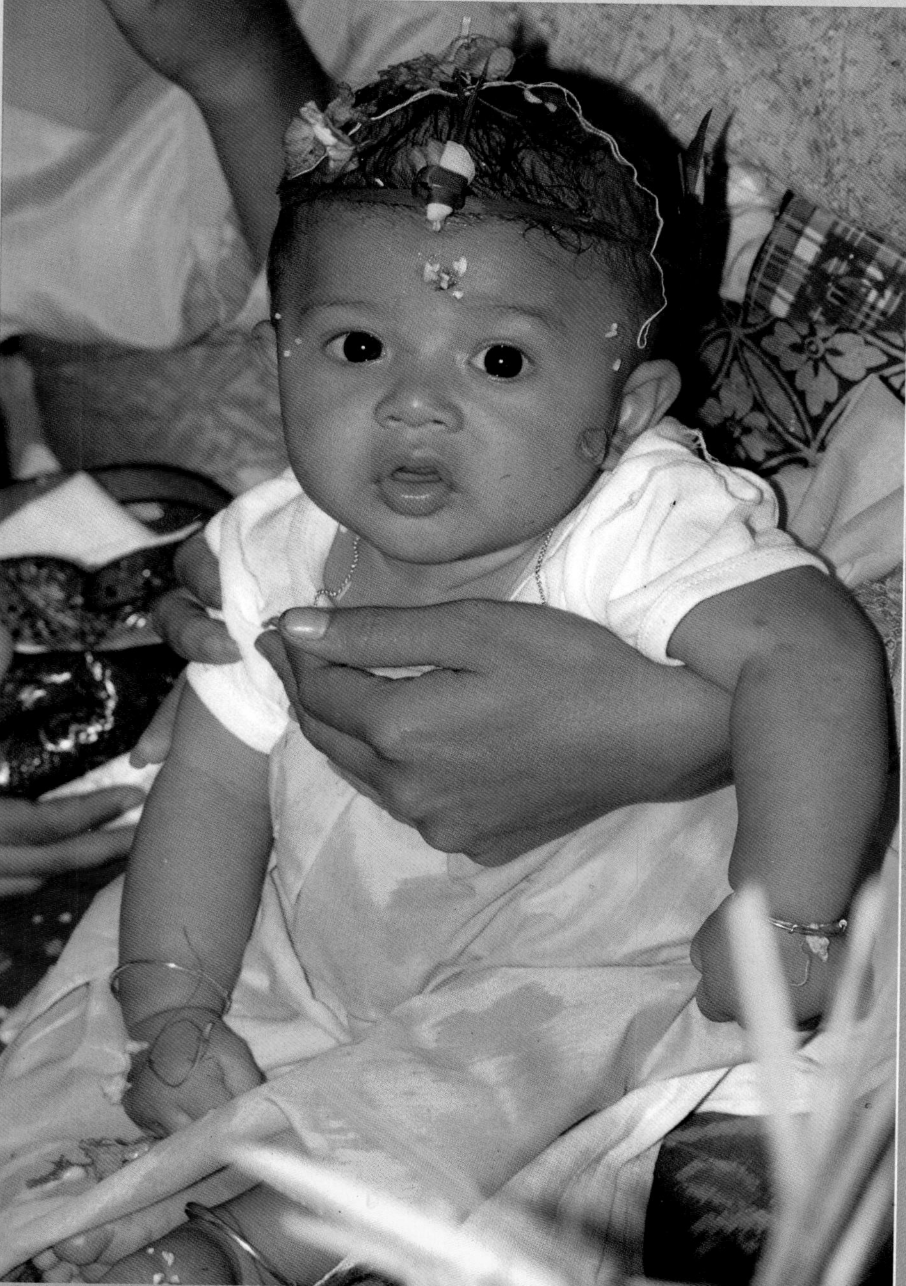

▲ *Seated on mother's lap during the three months' ceremony (when the child is 105 days old), the baby is sprinkled with holy water by the Brahman priest, the* ***pedanda****.*

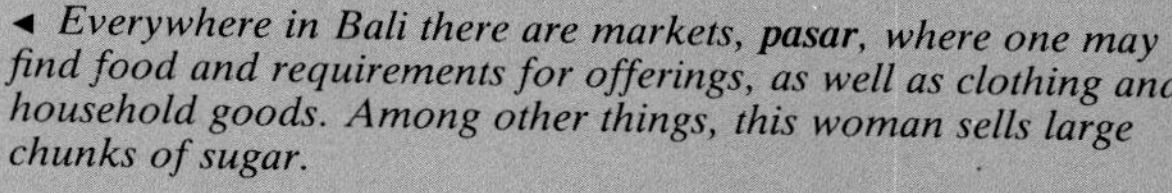

◄ *Everywhere in Bali there are markets,* ***pasar****, where one may find food and requirements for offerings, as well as clothing and household goods. Among other things, this woman sells large chunks of sugar.*

▲ *A daily ritual at the home of Made Suti, a well-known trance medium often consulted: early in the morning, before starting her consultations, she loudly invokes the gods.*

A pure soul

Trance is a common and generally accepted phenomenon in Bali. There are various kinds of trance, which differ in their external form, but all trance is seen as a sign that a supernatural being has penetrated the body of a human. This being may be a god or an ancestor, but it could also be a demon. Whereas in Bali, being possessed by a demon is considered unfavourable, being possessed by a divine being has a favourable meaning. Thus it is not surprising that the *balian taksu* occupies a special position in Balinese society and is approached respectfully by most Balinese. After all, the gods and ancestors, perfect beings par excellence, would not use just any mortal as their instrument. Of course they select somebody whose soul is utterly pure, and who for this reason is, so to speak, very close to the divine beings.

The *balian taksu*'s being a medium is not an occupation one can choose of one's own free will, or that during a certain period one can study or train for. It is a vocation. Those who practise it, became mediums more or less from one day to the next, by divine calling. The will of the gods reveals itself to them in various ways: for instance, by means of a dream or a vision in which the chosen one meets a god or an ancestor. Usually, though, a *balian taksu*'s confrontation with being a medium doesn't come as a total surprise. In most cases, during a shorter or longer period, events occur in his or her life, which can be seen as omens. For instance, a period of physical and/or mental illness, sometimes striking not only the medium but also the next of kin. Others suddenly, find themselves in possession of particular objects, *barang suci*, that they regard as gifts from the gods. They find these 'sacred objects', perhaps a stone of striking shape or colour, or a ring or an old Chinese coin, in their house temple for instance, sometimes after this was predicted in a dream.

The *balian taksu* does not belong to a special ethnic or age group. Both caste members and non-caste members may become *balian taksu* and their age varies from very young, about sixteen, to extremely old. Often they have hardly any formal education, or none at all.

Becoming a balian: obeying the will of the gods

Though the omens leave no doubt that one is soon to become a medium, it may take a long time before the chosen one resigns to the will of the gods. With all the consequences this may have. The story of I Wayan Serdaka, a teacher, testifies to this:

"I have been a **balian taksu** *since 1980, but the first signs date from 1969. Every time I prayed to the gods in a temple, I found sacred objects,* **barang suci***. But I didn't understand their purpose. So I put them away and didn't worry about them. But after a while I was struck by disaster: between 1976 and 1980 I was seriously ill. I tried various doctors, but to no avail. Then my entire family became possessed by an evil spirit. Finally, I went to a* **balian taksu***. He advised me to become a medium too. He said: 'You have some* **barang suci** *at home: stones and a kris (a dagger with a wavy blade). If you wish, you will prosper. But if you do not obey the gods, I dare not vouch for your life.' Now my family and I are doing well. Since I became a* **balian taksu** *in 1980, illness has interrupted my teaching job only once."*

In many ceremonies the services of the Brahman priest, the **pedanda***, are indispensable. For with the right chants and formulae he can bring about a temporary unity with Shiva, the supreme deity. And preparing holy water also is one of his tasks.* ►

▲ *Demons, the* ***buta*** *and* ***kala****, who dwell in the underworld, form a relentless threat to mortals. But even more dangerous are the* ***leyak****, women with the appearance of a witch, who do not belong in the underworld but do disturb the order of life with their black magic. For that matter, not all representatives of the underworld are evil. No, on the contrary, it is the task of the snakes Antaboga and Basuki, to balance the turtle Bedawang who carries the island of Bali – and thus to prevent earthquakes.*

Fear and insecurity

The birth of a child is not the only reason to consult a trance medium. There are other matters, too, in which the Balinese feel the need to know the wishes of their ancestors. Thus the cremation of a relative may be a reason to consult a *balian taksu*, to ask the deceased about his or her wishes with regard to the cremation ritual. In Bali the dead are cremated to free the soul of its earthly frame (the body), thus enabling it to return to the realm of the gods. If consultation were to reveal that the deceased still owes the gods something, the next of kin can arrange for this debt to be paid, thus preventing that the soul need begin a later life with a debt, or, due to the unpaid debt, even be denied full deification.
The *balian taksu* can act as a contact between mortals and their ancestors, but also as an intermediary between humans and gods. This may be important after an unfortunate event has disturbed the order of existence, an event for which those involved have no solution. For instance, a serious row among relatives, that threatens to break up the family.
Another frequent reason for consulting a trance medium is a relative's disease for which no cure can be found (in some cases, after both traditional and modern medicine failed). A *balian taksu* is also consulted in case of a violent or premature death in the family.
The Balinese are strongly aware of a person's own responsibility for a safe course through life. Anyone who neglects his or her religious duties or misbehaves in some other way, runs the risk of losing the protection of the gods and exposing him- or herself to all kinds of disaster. Therefore, the Balinese constantly strive to keep at bay the evil forces surrounding them (embodied in demons), and to hold on to the good forces (the gods and ancestors). But, however devoted one may be in his efforts not to displease the divine beings, one does not always manage to stay out of trouble. Anyone struck by disaster knows he has been punished for a slip, even though he is unaware of his wrongdoing. After all, isn't Man an imperfect being who easily strays from the straight and narrow path?
To be freed from such evil, the bond with the gods must be restored as fast as possible. However, this can be done only if one knows both the cause of the disaster and how to deal with it. But how does one find out what it was that brought down the wrath of the gods on oneself? And more in particular: what is to be done to regain their favour? Only the gods themselves can answer these questions, so the Balinese will resort to a *balian taksu* to come into contact with these invisible beings.

The use of barang suci

Often the objects a ***balian taksu*** *receives from the gods have a particular function. Thus, stones and rings may be used to cure the sick. For instance, people stung by a scorpion or bitten by a snake, are given water to drink that derives its healing power from a ring lying in it: one of the* ***barang suci****. Sacred objects may also be used to establish contact with a divine being. An example is the white stone that looks exactly like a chicken egg, and that a* ***balian taksu*** *once found in a temple and now uses to communicate with a goddess. After having chanted to her, the medium can hear the divine voice addressing him via the stone.*

The consultation

A Balinese wishing to consult a *balian taksu*, is usually accompanied by at least one relative. Mostly, a group of relatives visiting a trance medium will consist of several generations. In connection with the cremation of a parent or grandparent, often both the children and grandchildren of the deceased will come, as well as the husband or wife. If a birth is the occasion for consulting a medium, both the parents and the grandparents will be present if possible.
How many customers a *balian taksu* has, depends mainly on his or her reputation, but also on the range of skills s/he masters. Some mediums deal exclusively with illness, while others may be consulted for just about anything. There are trance mediums who are so well-known that people come flocking to them (often from far and near). In some cases the clients must even take a number off a hook to avoid confusion as to whose turn it is.
A consultation of a *balian taksu* proceeds according to a fixed ritual that may differ from one medium to another. The course of events at a well-known *balian taksu*'s in Tabanan may serve as an example. Having arrived at the medium's house, the vistors sit down in the yard and wait for their turn to enter. The *balian taksu* grants the audience in a special room, often small: the *kamar suci*. In this 'sacred room' there is an altar on which a motley collection of attributes is

found: statuettes of the gods, jars of holy water, small stacks of white and yellow cloths, all kinds of sacred objects, incense and flowers.

Prior to the consultation, the trance medium, dressed in white and seated on a dais in front of the altar, accepts the offerings and presents brought by the customers. Usually, these are small offerings meant for the gods: little palm-leaf boxes holding some flowers, rice, biscuits and money. And usually in addition: some fruit, a few eggs or coconuts. After everything has been placed on the altar, the *balian taksu* sprinkles her customers with holy water so that, cleansed and unsullied, they may approach the gods or ancestors.

Now the *balian taksu* begins to invoke the gods. She closes her eyes holding a bowl of smouldering wood in her right hand. She informs the divine beings that people have come to offer them sacrifices. Then she addresses her *taksu*, the deity who usually animates her. He is requested to enter the body of his servant and make his presence known. The *taksu* acts as a spokesman of the gods, but he may also have an ancestor's soul take possession of the medium to speak by way of her mouth.

From the moment the *balian taksu* is possessed, a dialogue develops between the visitors and the deity or ancestor; a quiz, in which the customers will often get dressed down for their neglect in religious matters or other reprehensible behaviour. And it may get very emotional, for instance when an old man hears his recently deceased wife speak to him, or a child is told by her deceased mother that she mustn't be so cheeky to her father. But things are not always so serious in the *kamar suci*: now and then people have a good laugh. After all, ancestors do crack a joke sometimes. Since the door to the *kamar suci* is usually left open during a consultation, nothing said is secret. So those waiting outside can listen in and possibly benefit from the lessons in social and moral values given here.

When the *taksu* or the ancestor withdraws, the *balian taksu* wakes up from her trance and the consultation is over. The trance medium then asks her visitors whether they have found what they were looking for. Because during her state of being possessed, the *balian taksu* is aware of nothing, she won't remember anything said. Hence it is important for the customers to keep well in mind the advice and wishes of the gods and ancestors, so that they can later follow these or carry them out to the letter. Nowadays, this problem is often solved with the help of modern technology: several trance mediums record their utterances on cassette tape. For a small consideration customers may take this tape home to listen to it at leisure within their family circle.

After the *balian taksu* has given her customers some more holy water, they will ask her permission to leave. The trance-medium's husband then invites the next visitors to enter the *kamar suci*. Again offerings are presented: a new consultation can begin.

▲ *So as to be freed of evil influences, a young married couple undergoes a cleansing ritual at a* ***balian taksu****'s, in which the trance medium uses a* ***lis****, a holy-water sprinkler made of palm leaf. On the altar lie* ***barang suci****, sacred objects, and other attributes needed during the seance.*

A simple offering ▸ *in return for a consultation with a* ***balian taksu****.*

Trance

If at a temple feast in Bali one of those present goes into a trance, the Balinese use the term ***tedun****, meaning 'descent'. Thus they wish to express that the deity of this temple has descended into the body of one of the believers to make his presence known. Such an event won't scare the bystanders. On the contrary, they will take good care of the person possessed by the deity, and bring him or her incense and holy water. Sometimes the temple priests will take the opportunity to ask the deity questions concerning religious matters.*

A side effect of some kinds of trance is physical invulnerability. For instance the so-called ***Sanghyang Jaran****, in which a boy or temple priest is sent into a trance by means of incense and chanting. In this drowsy state he dances barefoot through a fire, riding a hobby horse made of bamboo and palm leaf, and without getting hurt in any way.*

Barong

On the occasion of a temple feast or other religious ceremony, it often happens that two male dancers stage the Barong, a mythical being. The Barong looks like a fabulous fairy-tale animal, but to the Balinese its appearance means far more. To them the Barong represents all that is good, protecting Man against the destructive force of evil, personified by the witch Rangda.

The struggle between these two is acted out in the Calon Arang tragedy. At its height a few spectators will usually intervene in the fight, to help the Barong. They attack Rangda with krisses, but she wards them off with her magic weapon, the ***anteng***, a white cloth. Bereft of their senses, the attackers direct their weapons at their own bodies, the so-called ***ngurek***. But thanks to the protection of the Barong who has made them invulnerable, they cannot hurt themselves.

The struggle always ends undecided: neither Rangda nor the Barong is defeated. Good and evil continue to exist side by side, the one cannot exist without the other. The Balinese regard both beings as very sacred. In the temple their masks are kept in special shrines, and the temple priest worships them with sacrifices. By no means everyone may wear the masks; this privilege is often reserved for the Brahmans.

In addition to the Barong who appears in the Calon Arang tragedy as Rangda's opponent, the Barong Keket, there are various other Barong in Bali. For instance, the Barong Macan (the tiger-Barong), the Barong Bangkung (the swine-Barong), the Barong Gajah (the elephant-Barong), and the Barong Landung, two gigantic human figures (one male, one female) regarded as the pre-eminent protectors against disease and epidemics.

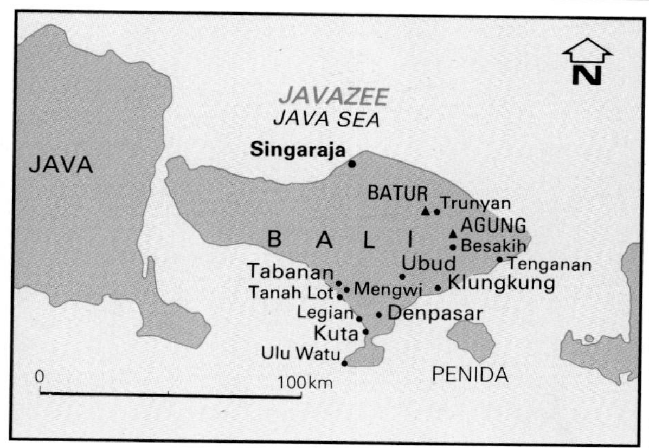

In Bali, thousands of sacrifices are made every day. This will instantly strike the tourist landing at Denpasar Airport. The taxi driving him into town will have a little offering on its dashboard. The drive will take him along rice fields with offerings in little stone columns or on top of bamboo structures. Once in town, the taxi will have to brake frequently for dogs eating the remainders of offerings laid down that morning on intersections. Sometimes a visitor may come across a colourful procession of women on their way to a temple, carrying beautiful offerings on their heads. At the entrance of each hotel small niches are found in which small offerings are put every morning. Finally, anyone going down to the beach, shouldn't be surprised to find a procession has just arrived there. Accompanied by the shrill sound of percussion instruments, the offerings brought along are entrusted to the sea.

Offerings shape the constant dialogue the Balinese have with the invisible world around them. Gods, ancestors and demons are worshipped with care, and people try and stay on good terms with them. After all, anyone who forgets his obligations, runs the risk of bringing down disaster on himself. So time and again, one may see ceremonies performed in various, often ancient temples in the island (Bangli, Tampaksiring). At an elevation of 1,000 metres, on the slopes of Gunung Agung (erupted in 1963), stands the greatest and most sacred mountain temple of Bali: the ***pura*** Besakih. The sea temples may be mentioned as counterparts of the mountain temples. Famous examples are the ***pura*** Ulu Watu and the ***pura*** Tanah Lot. The location of both kinds of temples reflects the difference in their functions: while in Besakih, in the mountains near the gods, divine favours are asked, in Ulu Watu and Tanah Lot the Balinese seeks protection against the evil of the demons in the sea. Between the mountains and the sea live about 2.5 million Balinese. In the villages, the walled yards are built close together. Here, to some extent, life seems to proceed in seclusion. And yet, collective forms of entertainment especially, are extremely popular. The many immovable feast-days present occasions for the performance of all kinds of plays and dances. These often act out the struggle between good and evil. Well-known are the Calon Arang tragedy with the Barong, the modern Kebyar dance, the Kecak, the Legong and the Baris, a war-dance.

Nowadays, special tourist performances are a nice source of income for many Balinese. For the same reason, traditional crafts have boomed. Painters (in Ubud), wood-carvers (in Mas), silver smiths (in Celuk), and stone-masons (in Batululan), are real tourist magnets. Enjoying their products, far removed from the hard work in the fields, and unaware of the fragile cosmic balance, the traveller wanders around in these villages as if in a paradise on earth.

▼ *The **pura** Tanah Lot.*

4 Kalimantan

Hardly anywhere in the world is the rainfall more plentiful and are the trees taller. Borneo. Once an island without any roads where the water level in the river determined one's range of action. Where, upstream, in its green heart, isolated tribes were living. Due to commercial deforestation its leafy roof now has gaping holes, hardly offering shelter any longer. Soon Borneo's last forest nomads will be heading for home.

Unlike the sedentary Dayak, the Punan, hunters and gatherers deep in Borneo's forests, have been on the move for centuries. Contrary to what is generally assumed, virgin rain-forest floor can be negotiated without much difficulty. High above, the upper layer of tree tops screens off the sunlight, and instead of finding one's way blocked by a curtain of vegetation, a carpet of fallen leaves covers the ground. Here Jenne de Beer followed the Punan in their tracks. He introduces us to their trekking existence, describes their strained relations with the Dayak, and warns against the consequences of a further disturbance of the balance between man and nature in Kalimantan.

The rain forest as storehouse

Endless rain forests once dominated the landscape of the island of Borneo. The population lived and worked in perfect harmony with nature. Until over twenty years ago. Timber-felling companies took possession of the island, initiating the destruction of its natural splendour. The first giants of the forest were axed, bringing down with them a rich and varied cultural life.

Nature

At least three quarters of the island is still covered in tropical rain forest. Such eternally green forests are the richest eco systems in the world: real treasure-houses of genetic material, with a unique wealth of plants and animals.

Nearly half of all known kinds of plants and animals can be found in these forests: a total of five million species. And yet, rain forests cover only two percent of the Earth's entire surface. The combined result of these two factors is that any hectare contains only few specimens of each species. Most species are highly specialised and have a very limited area of distribution. Hence they are often rare.

An important cause of the enormous diversity of life forms, is the great age of the South-East Asian rain forests. For tens of millions of years the climate has

◂ *Removing tropical hardwood from the forest. Trucks take the logs to the rivers where they are assembled into rafts that float to the coastal ports, from where the timber finds its way all over the world.*

Sago island

Borneo is the third largest island in the world. Only Greenland and New Guinea exceed it in size. About two thirds of Borneo is Indonesian territory, and usually only this south-eastern region, with its population of eight million, is called Kalimantan. Perhaps this name was derived from the old, indigenous term for newly harvested sago, ***lamanta***. Sabah and Sarawak to the north are part of the Federation of Malaysia. Also north of Kalimantan lies Brunei, the small but immensely wealthy oil sultanate.

▾ *In Borneo sago is often washed in a brook.*

remained stable and favourable to living organisms, that is: warm and humid. In Borneo alone the evolution of the forest has resulted in over two thousand tree varieties.

Contrary to what the exuberant vegetation would suggest, the soil of tropical rain forest is thin and very poor. Most nutrients are not found in the soil but in the so-called biomass, the whole of living plants and animals. This is a closed system in which the nutrients are constantly recycled. This cycle functions so efficiently that hardly anything is lost.

High above the forest floor, the dense leaf cover breaks the force of even the heaviest of tropical showers. But this changes radically if human intervention has thinned out the forest. Then the rain soon washes away the thin layer of humus. In addition, such downpours make the soil far more compact: the air is squeezed out of the earth, thus further diminishing its fertility.

The rain forest not only protects its own soil, it also creates an equable climate. During the abundant rains the leaves and root mat store part of the moisture, to release it gradually during drier periods. But where the forest disappears, dry and wet periods grow more extreme. This has already led to severe flooding, among other things.

The Sumatran rhinoceros

At the moment, the survival of the Sumatran rhinoceros (Dicerorhinus Sumatrensis), the smallest of its kind, is seriously at risk. In Sumatra there are a few hundred; in Borneo an estimated few dozen survive – in Sabah, Sarawak, and possibly in a few remote regions of East Kalimantan. Around the turn of the century the rhinoceros was fairly common in these areas. But intensive hunting with fire-arms in the twenties and thirties rapidly reduced their numbers. Rhinoceros horn still is sought after in the traditional Chinese pharmacy. Finely ground into powder or mixed into pills and potions, it supposedly reduces fever and cures impotence. Other parts of this rhinoceros, such as its hide and toe-nails, are also used for this purpose. Horn is worth more than gold.

The people on the coast

The small coast towns and the villages along the great rivers connecting the coast and the interior, are inhabited by Malay, Buginese and Chinese. With their flat-bottomed boats, *tempel*, and 'longboats' equipped with powerful outboard engines, they control trade in this part of the world. They transport salt, petrol, tools and other necessities upstream. Once beyond the rapids in a river such as the Mahakam, these goods fetch fabulous prices. On their way back to the coast the traders take along forest produce, such as rattan, sandalwood and swallows' nests.

Trade in these products has been going on for centuries; trade relations with India and China may even date back to the era before Christ. In a Chinese text of the late Ming period, at the end of the fifteenth century, the following merchandise from Brunei is mentioned: rhino horn, parrot feathers, gold-dust, hornbill ivory, rattan mats, red peppers and dragon's blood (a kind of resin).

Over the centuries, in various strategic locations along the coast, small independent states developed. Here Muslim traders introduced Islam, and at the beginning of the sixteenth century, everywhere the local princes presented themselves as Sultans. Although their influence did not reach far inland, some sultanates managed to prosper tremendously thanks to a trade monopoly in forest produce. Even then, Brunei enjoyed great prosperity, as did for instance, Kutai on the upper Mahakam and Banjarmasin in the deep south.

As for the earliest history of human presence in Borneo, much is still obscure. In the Niah caves, in Sarawak, in 1958, a skull of Homo Sapiens was found. Its estimated age: forty thousand years. Perhaps the skull belonged to an ancestor of one of the ethnic groups living in Borneo today. But probably it stems from a member of the Negrito population that disappeared from Indonesia some time ago. The Introduction already paid attention to these dark-skinned hunters and gatherers.

The people in the interior

The present inhabitants of the interior are the Dayak and the Punan. Dayak is a collective name for a great number of peoples, including the Kenya, the Kayan, the Iban, the Ngaju, the Ot Danum and the Kelabit. They differ particularly in language and social organization. Thus the Kenya and the Kayan have a highly stratified society with classes of aristocrats, freemen and slaves, whereas the Iban have a more egalitarian society. But the Dayak also have a number of things in common. They all practise dry rice cultivation, live in their typical 'longhouses', preferably on a river bank, and have largely similar world views. Their method of agriculture is shifting cultivation, usually called *ladang* cultivation in Indonesia. The Dayak farmer clears not too large a part of the forest, leaving some big trees within the clearing and some at its edges. These serve to inhibit the growth of weeds, to help control burning operations, and to stimulate the recovery of the forest vegetation after the period of cultivation. Next he burns the felled trees and

▲ *Pictures used in spreading the gospel in Kalimantan. Left: pursued by a tiger, a non-Christian runs for his life. Right next to him, a perpendicular cliff face, in front of him a chasm. Centre: the terrified man lowers himself on a rope, but in the chasm a crocodile awaits him with wide-open jaws. From above, the tiger is a patient observer. Right: the man on the rope seems lost when two rodents also close in on him. But then, suddenly a red, burning cross appears out of the blue. The evil animals all slink off, and the man is saved.*

The Mission

In Kalimantan a federation of fundamentalist missionary societies is operating under the.name of KINGMI. In certain regions, such as Apoh Kayan, this federation with its fleet of small aircraft practically has a monopoly on transport. The conversion activities of the missionaries are aimed in particular at the sedentary Dayak.

Though the traditional world view of these **ladang** *farmers differs from one group to another, there are some essential similarities. The best developed theme of all Dayak religions is the adventurous journey that the soul of the deceased must make to the realm of the souls, usually a mountain that is hard to reach, and situated in the region of origin of the people concerned. Here the soul of the deceased lives and works until the time is ripe to be reborn as a human being. Mostly during important ceremonial gatherings, the shamans, called* **belian**, *tell compelling stories about the dangerous journey, and about life after death. In addition, all Dayak generally recognize a supreme being, although in their crowded pantheon lesser gods also play an important part. It is the KINGMI missionaries' premise that the Dayak's polytheistic faiths are not true religions. With much diligence and dedication the missionaries direct their energies primarily against the* **belian**. *These religious specialists and traditional healers are usually women whom the missionaries regard as representatives of the devil.*

Another target of their interest are the **hampatong**, *frightening sculptures, a number of which usually stand around any Dayak community. These roughly hewn wooden images represent human figures endowed with greatly enlarged sex characteristics. The purpose of this latter feature is to scare off evil spirits, who themselves are sexless. The missionaries regard them as signs of immorality, and induce the people to burn the carvings or, in a final ritual, to throw them into the river. After their conversion, all traditional songs and dances connected with the old religion are equally taboo.*

Usually the nomadic Punan are less easily accessible to the KINGMI missionaries. That's why so far, relatively few of them have been christianised.

scatters the ashes over the *ladang* to enrich its acid soil.

Once or twice a Dayak will plant his field cleared in this way. Then he will leave it to lie fallow, and somewhere else he will clear another part of the forest. In due course, after a *ladang* has reverted to forest, he will return. This regeneration period takes some ten to twenty years.

There is a widespread and stubborn misconception that shifting cultivation is a destructive form of agriculture. But recent research has shown that the traditional *ladang* cycle, as carried out by expert farmers such as the Dayak, is ecologically fully justified. As long as the population pressure does not increase, allowing for brief periods of cultivation, and long fallow periods, the natural environment will not be harmed at all.

▲ *Dayak community along a river; these modern 'longhouses' with corrugated zinc roofing, form a relatively large settlement.*

▲ *Striped kingfisher.*

Omen birds

All Borneo tribes attach great importance to the omens to be inferred from the behaviour of certain animals. These may be insects or reptiles, but far more important is the flight (and the call) of certain birds, regarded as divine messengers who will never show themselves to people without good reason.

The Punan will let the direction in which to hunt, depend partly on the omens they infer from the flight of an omen bird they encounter on the way. The Dayak will look for favourable signs to start the successive stages of the rice cycle. Such a sign will give the Dayak farmer confidence in the future, and urge him on to devote himself fully to his task.

In observing the flight, it is noted whether the bird flies from left to right or from right to left. Another significant movement is: away from the observer or towards him. Movements such as diving and hovering have a special meaning, too.

Well-known omen birds are the hawk (Haliastur Indusintermedius), the brown woodpecker (Blythipicus rubiginosus) and the striped kingfisher (Lacedo Pulchella).

Blow-pipe and dart-poison

The blow-pipe the Punan use for hunting is a long, hollow hardwood tube usually fitted at one end with an iron lance head. From this blow-pipe, small, poisonous darts are shot. The poison, ***ipoh***, comes from plant species such as the Antiaris Toxicaria and Derris Elliptica. From the stem of the former and from the roots of the latter, a milky juice is extracted. By mixing it with water and other ingredients, and thickening this mixture, the right concentration and viscosity is attained.

The hunter always carries two quivers: one for his dart-shafts about twenty centimetres long, and the other for his dart-heads, with varying doses of poison. The choice of dart-head depends on size and weight of the prey. The shaft will break off on impact, so that the wounded animal cannot rid itself of the dart-head. Within a few minutes the ***ipoh*** paralyzes the victim's central nervous system. The flesh surrounding the dart-head is cut away. The rest is edible.

For birds, one uses blunt, unpoisoned darts.

The Punan

Deep in Borneo's forests live the Punan, a people of hunters and gatherers. There are about twenty thousand of them, spread out over a large area in Kalimantan, Sarawak and Brunei. They wander around in groups of thirty to forty people.

A group will stay in one spot for a few weeks, preferably on a hill near a stream. When the natural food sources in the vicinity approach depletion, they will break up camp, so as to set up a new one elsewhere. Within a day the huts are finished. They are built on piles, high above the ground, to keep out moisture, crawling vermin and dogs.

Material possessions are kept to a minimum, as everything must be carried. The Punan hardly keep any stocks either; the forest is their storehouse. Here are the leaves of the *nipah* palm, out of which to make cutlery and roofing. Here as well are rattan, bamboo and other building materials, and finally, a great variety of food. The forest provides everything.

The Punan hunt with blowpipe and darts dipped in *ipoh*, a vegetable poison related to strychnine. In addition, the hunters use a great variety of traps; a few merely use a lance. A pack of hounds always accompanies the hunters. It is their task to corner the game. Almost everything that flies, walks, climbs or crawls is a possible catch.

A general exception is made for a few kinds of birds. Nobody will ever shoot a so-called 'bird of omen'. The flight of this bird tells a Punan whether the time is favourable for an undertaking, e.g. a journey. To kill such a messenger might bring disaster. In addition, every Punan has a special bond with one particular species, whose flesh s/he is not allowed to eat.

Wild swine are their favourite food. But these animals behave in whimsical and unpredictable ways, and especially before or after the fruit season they are not easily caught. When the trees bear fruit, the hunt is a cinch. The pigs grow round and fat, hardly moving around. For the Punan this is a time of plenty. In the off-season when fruit is scarce, the animals get restless. In search of food they cover great distances, and cross rivers, making difficult targets for any hunter.

Although some Punan women are very good at it, hunting is done in particular by the men. When a successful hunter returns with his prey, the meat is distributed among all households, without delay or discussion. Then they have a feast and everybody eats as much as s/he can. Ancient stories are told, and memorable events recalled, children and adults sing songs or play the Jew's harp and nose-flute. After the feast the skulls of the game are put up on stakes around the huts, so as to lure their friends and relatives to the camp. After a few days, when all that remains of the catch are a few bits of *krotong* – blackened hide –, the first team of hunters set out, long before daybreak.

Gathering forest produce is just as important to the Punan's existence as the hunt. Sago, the marrow from the trunk of the wild sago-palm, is the main ingredient of their fare. It is used to make *noah*, a gelatinous mash that provides the necessary carbohydrates. In

To the Punan, sago is the most important ▶ *source of carbohydrates. They prefer to pitch camp near a brook and some wild sago palms.*

The proboscis-monkey

A conspicuous presence in the forests of Kalimantan is the proboscis-monkey. This animal possesses an olfactory organ of extraordinary proportions, and somewhat human features. Its Latin name is Nasalis Larvatus, but the Indonesians call him ***Orang Belanda****, Dutchman ...*

addition, they look for mushrooms and all kinds of fruit; honey is a special delicacy.

Some forest products are not gathered for home consumption, but for barter. Along the upper reaches of a river, in a neighbouring Dayak settlement, in exchange for their forest produce, rattan baskets and mats, the Punan get some salt, tobacco, iron and textiles. From the Dayak village the goods then find their way to the coast, where they fetch a price many times higher than what the gatherer got.

Though in principle, both parties benefit from their trading relations, the Punan and Dayak are not always on friendly terms. A Dayak usually feels superior to his nomad trading partner, and a Punan has the often correct impression that he is being fobbed off with a bad price for his goods. Moreover, it is still fresh in many a Punan memory that until the beginning of this century, the Dayak on their head-hunting expeditions liked to pick the Punan in their small groups, as victims.

◄ The Punan are famous for their beautiful rattan baskets. The plaiting is done mainly by the women, while the children watch and lend a hand. Thus they learn the necessary skills without effort. Most plaiting is meant for the exchange trade.

The rhythm of hunters and gatherers

The Punan are perfectly adapted to surrounding nature. They use their natural environment without harming it. Even in regions where the Punan have been living for centuries, there are few signs that the forest has been degraded. And usually nothing indicates human presence.

That the Punan manage to support themselves so well, is due mainly to their knowledge of the flora and fauna of the different micro-zones in the tropical rain forest. Thus among other things, they know a great deal about the healing properties of many of the wild plant species.

Besides, they limit the number of children per household. The women use a contraceptive, the juice of the *lengsat* root, which renders them infertile. This remedy is often taken after the birth of the fifth child. Too large a brood of children would hamper the parents' mobility, a freedom essential to them.

The way in which the Punan deal with death, also corresponds with their nomadic existence. When a member of the group dies, the camp is broken up and the deceased is left behind. Far away a new camp will be set up; never again will they return to the old huts. There is a fear that the spirit of the deceased will stay near the dwelling in which s/he died. Overpowered by loneliness it will try to persuade a second soul to join it on its journey to the realm of the dead.

Over the past few decades, Indonesian government policy was aimed at keeping the itinerant Punan in one place, and urging them to take up agriculture. The point of departure is that they need an incentive to reach a higher level of civilization. Officially most Punan now have a permanent address, but rarely can anyone be found there...

As rice farmers the Punan are only moderately successful. A year's harvest barely suffices for three months. Hunters and gatherers do not feel comfortable in the heat of an open *ladang*; in many cases they won't start work in the fields until late in the day. The rhythm of the Punan does not fit in with a farmer's life, and they cannot easily master the long-term planning required in farming. Even the few sedentary Punan still get much of their food from the forest.

▲ *The forest provides the Punan with almost everything.* ***Nipah-*** *palm leaves not only serve as roofing or eating utensils, but also as an umbrella.*

During the harvest feast of the Iban Dayak, which they named 'Hornbill Feast' after their most important ritual animal, they give thanks to their supreme deity. All adorn themselves as beautifully as they can, with hornbill feathers, or, like this man, ▼ *with the hide of a panther.*

The hornbill

Of all Borneo birds, the hornbill (Bucerotidae) most readily stirs the imagination, with its typical disproportionate bill. On top of it, one species, the Helmeted Hornbill, has a massive horn protrusion which used to provide the so-called hornbill ivory, with its peculiar ruddy sheen. For centuries this was exported to China, as a material for fine carvings. It was more precious than jade.

The hen lays her eggs in a hollow tree. While brooding, she plasters the entrance to the nest from within, while her mate seals it from the other side. When the job is done, only a small slit remains, just big enough for the bill. The hen is now a prisoner throughout her breeding period. Her mate feeds her. During her confinement the hen grows very fat and filthy, and so stiff that she can hardly fly. Not until the chicks are big enough is the entrance to the nest broken open. Not without reason, in Dayak mythology the hornbill is the symbol of death and resurrection.

▲ *In Kalimantan, change is not merely imposed on the natural environment. Due to the conversion work of the Mission, these roughly hewn frightening statues* **(hampatong)** *have survived only around a few Dayak communities.*

A threatening disaster

At this moment the rain forests of Kalimantan with their unique flora and fauna, their economic significance for the native population and their function of climate regulator, are at risk. This is due on the one hand to commercial timber-felling companies, and on the other hand to large-scale transmigration programmes. As a result, over the past twenty years large forest areas have been razed at an alarming rate. If this destruction continues at the present pace, the rain forests of Kalimantan will vanish before the end of this century. This would be an ecological disaster of the first magnitude.

Every year the timber companies fell at least 423,000 hectares of virgin forest. A figure that merely represents the official concessions. In addition, every year an unknown acreage of woodland disappears illegally, even in a nature reserve such as Kutai.

The timber companies apply the system of selective felling: for a few trees of a valuable kind of wood, many are devastated. The damage is largely inflicted by the violence of bulldozers and other heavy rolling-stock used in building the roads for transporting the felled giants of the forest. Tropical hardwood is exported mainly to Japan and the European Community, ending up as newspapers, chopsticks, doors and door and window frames.

The present transmigration programmes resulted from experiments initiated under Dutch colonial rule. However, since 1953 these programmes have escalated, and in independent Indonesia a massive relocation has been set in motion. Now, from overpopulated Java, large numbers of landless farmers but also homeless people from the cities, have been resettled in sparsely populated islands such as Borneo. By now the Indonesian authorities have become aware of the environmental problems in Kalimantan, and are trying to achieve a careful management of the scarce remaining rain forest (Indonesia still has 144 million hectares – 575,000 square miles – of primary forest). In the policy developed for the future, one third is destined for commercial timber felling (hand in hand with a stringent reafforestation policy), one third is set aside for nature reserves, and one third will be cultivated for transmigration purposes.

But with this latter intention a great problem remains. In regions now still covered in tropical rain forest, the new inhabitants are supposed to practise permanent farming, a form of agriculture that on poor soil usually won't produce the desired results. Therefore, in many cases the migrants soon turn to a kind of *ladang* cultivation which may justly be called 'slash and burn'. Contrary to the Dayak, the newcomers have no experience with shifting cultivation that offers the forest a chance to recover. Due to this lack of knowledge the soil is soon utterly depleted, and what remains is a useless kind of grassland. All the farmer can do, is to clear another patch of forest, where the process repeats itself. New nomads inhabit Kalimantan.

Bulldozers clear the way for the removal of the felled woodland giants. ▼

Anyone flying over Borneo in the sixties, would see one green expanse in hundreds of hues. Nowadays the island, and especially East Kalimantan, looks more like a patchwork quilt. Instead of finding primeval jungle, the tourist stumbles on lumberjacks' camps. And yet, a journey into the heart of Borneo still has the nature of an expedition. Although the interior is very mountainous, there are no prominent peaks or active volcanoes. Central mountain formations are the Kapuas Range, separating Sarawak from Kalimantan, and the Müller Range named after George Müller, the European who on his way to the centre of Borneo in 1825, was murdered by the Dayak.

In many cases the water level in the rivers still determines how far one gets: renting an aircraft is expensive. Fortunately, rainfall is abundant: between 2,500 and 4,500 millimetres annually. The rainy season differs from one region to the next, but nowhere is there a really dry season. Roughly speaking, most rain falls between September and May.

In this period, taking a boat up the Mahakam from Tenggarong on the east coast of Kalimantan, one can penetrate to a point very close to the Sarawak border. Now and again the virgin forest opens up along the banks where Dayak have built a 'longhouse', a great elongated pile-dwelling parallel to the river, in which the whole community lives. After a laborious hike to the upper reaches of the Kayan, one can return to the coast by taking a boat to Tarakan.

Wild animals are hardly ever seen on the way. Usually, one catches only a fleeting glimpse of a shadow darting away amid loud cracks. Kalimantan's nature reserves offer better chances. The Kutai wildlife reserve, for instance, which can be reached from Samarinda on the east coast, still shelters many orang-utans, in spite of timber felling.

But in 1982/83 the original population of monkeys and apes was vastly reduced by the blaze that ravaged East Kalimantan for months. An area almost seven times the size of Bali was left charred. In the autumn of 1987 persistent forest fires raged once more in the same region. And again, an irreplaceable stretch of rain forest went up in flames; even fewer animals survived this latter catastrophe.

The cause of these fires may well lie in the large-scale decrease of wooded area. Rain forests are said to 'perspire', holding the moisture for a long time; their destruction inevitably leads to a process of dehydration. Anyhow, the primary forest has withstood the fires considerably better than the parts thinned out by timber felling, where the remaining trees only served to boost the fire.

South and West Kalimantan are far less important for the timber industry. Here, stretches of marshland and mangrove woods dominate the landscape, and valuable tropical hardwood is dispersed. Via the Kapuas, the longest river in Indonesia, or the Barito, the daring may visit the old trading posts in the interior. Beyond the last mission post one reaches the heart of Borneo.

Iban Dayak with characteristic tattoos. The cap is part of daily attire. ▲

At the Iban Dayak's harvest feast in June, hornbill feathers often make a magnificent headdress. ▼

5 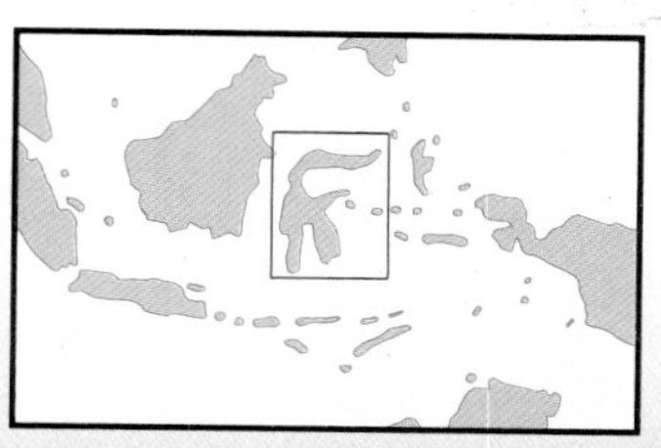 Sulawesi

Sulawesi – once an island from which notorious pirates made their forays, now the domain of respected traders. Business acumen inspired the Toraja to grow coffee, the Minahasa to grow cloves, and the Bugis to build cargo sailers, swarming out to all corners of the archipelago. At home each people displayed the accumulated wealth differently: everywhere in Sulawesi cultures broke adrift.

As trading partners of the Toraja, the Bugis soon managed to find their way to the plateaus in the interior of Sulawesi. Here, with their profits from the coffee trade, the Toraja laid the foundation for spectacular funeral rites, to the greater glory of the families organizing the feasts. Hetty Nooy-Palm describes how one particular traditional funeral proceeds, and indicates how this ceremonial richness is financed, nowadays.

Many Bugi traders settled in Kendari, home of the Tolaki in South-East Sulawesi. On its assimilation into a 'wider world', the *adat* of the original inhabitants was exposed to pressure. On the basis of the 'marriage by elopement' Dinah Bergink shows how among the Tolaki old traditions are now being broken down. Whereas among the Toraja, trading activities led to status feasts for family groups, among the Minahasa financial success resulted in a display of wealth with very individual aims. Mieke Schouten lays bare the roots of society in North-East Sulawesi, and points out that the rivalry in their life on Earth continues after death.

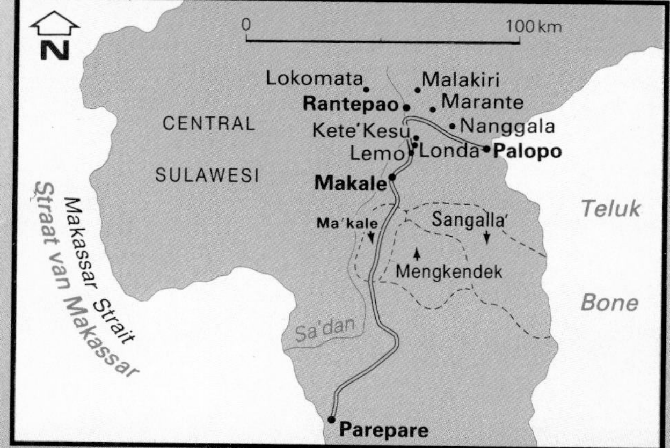

At the ***pasar*** *in Rantepao, Toraja women offer their ▼ merchandise.*

A rock grave as the Sa'dan Toraja's final resting-place

Toraja is a general name for the ethnical groups living in the mountainous interior of Sulawesi. In the south-west part of this region, in the district of Tana Toraja, live the Sa'dan Toraja. Their area (3,500 kms^2) is only two thirds of Bali's, but due to the hilly terrain it looks bigger. The river Sa'dan intersects the plain from north to south, and the steep limestone cliffs rising as if from a canyon, lend an un-Indonesian appearance to the landscape, reminiscent of the work of Chinese painters.

The scattered villages are connected by narrow mountain paths; a tarmac road links the two towns of Makale and Rantepao. On market days all roads are crowded: the *pasar* in Rantepao is one of the biggest markets in all Indonesia. Women with wide-rimmed bamboo hats on their heads and heavy baskets on their backs, bring in their market goods. Men carry

◄ Though Toraja fear the souls of their ancestors, they are not afraid of their skulls. Coffins, such as these in an old place of interment in Marante, fell into disuse over ten generations ago; ever since, the Toraja bury their dead in niches they cut into the cliff face – presumably to combat the violation of graves.

▲ *To earn some extra money, Toraja farmers make decorated bamboo containers; some motifs, such as 'the sun with rays', are cosmological.*

their goods on a pole over their shoulder. With the exception of a few horses, pack animals are rarely used. Though minibuses are growing more popular, people still do most of the carrying themselves. Up and down the mountains they go, hurrying after each other. The Toraja pay little attention to the scenery. Tourists do. In increasing numbers they visit Sulawesi's interior. Their attention is drawn to the *adat* houses, *tongkonan*, decorated with wood carvings, and beautifully situated in the landscape. They also come to look at the unusual graves cut out in the cliffs. The impressive funeral festivities are a great tourist attraction.

The conquest

There are about three hundred and forty thousand Toraja, and their chief livelihood is agriculture. Some ten percent make their living in government service, holding an ecclesiastical office, or as a shopkeeper in the tourist trade. In various villages farmers earn some extra money as artisans, chiefly making wood carvings, and in certain districts farmers' wives weave cloths for the tourist market. Rice, the status food, is grown most. Poor people eat corn, cassava and tubers. Although the export of cloves and pepper is steadily increasing, coffee is the Toraja's main commercial crop. This shrub has been grown here since the end of the last century, when the Toraja were as yet utterly unknown to the Dutch oppressors. But by then the Bugis living south of Tana Toraja, had been trading with the Dutch for centuries. Like Arab traders they transported the coffee meant for the world market, from Tana Toraja to the coastal ports of Sulawesi. Until the beginning of this century, another main source of income was the slave-trade. Among the Toraja, slaves used to form the lowest class. One class above them were the freemen, followed by the nobility, and finally by the highest class, the princes (Puang) of the three mini states in the south of Tana Toraja. In 1906 the Dutch colonial Administration found cause in the slave-trade to subject this region. The new rulers prohibited traditional headhunting, and the education they introduced soon became popular. The introduction of Christianity was a far more laborious process. Certain measures on the part of the Church, such as the abolition of cock fights, ran into a lot of resistance. In 1950 less than ten percent of the Toraja had been converted. A situation that rapidly changed, as a result of the political unrest in independent Indonesia. In the early sixties Islamic groups entered Tana Toraja, and this confronted the population with the need to choose between Islam and Christianity. Many chose the latter; nowadays, some twenty-five percent of the Sa'dan Toraja still profess the old religion.

The main street in Rantepao. A man takes his merchandise, palm wine in bamboo containers, to the busy ***pasar***. ▼

For the appropriate celebration of a feast, the necessary pigs have been assembled on the outskirts of Rantepao. ▶

Aluk To Dolo

The Toraja call their religion *Aluk To Dolo*, the 'Rites of the People of the Old Days', or the ancestral religion. Ancestors are important. From on high they look after the community's well-being and the fertility of the fields. The first human being was created in the upper world by the supreme god Puang Matua (The Old Gentleman), at the same time as the buffalo, the chicken, the pig and some plants. A descendant of this ancestor was getting bored in the upper world: he opened heaven's window and saw the ocean below. He found this very interesting, and asked Puang Matua to throw down a lump of earth onto which he could be lowered (with a house, family, buffaloes, slaves and so on). His wish was granted. This descended man became the first To Manurun, 'He who descended on Earth'. Afterwards more To Manurun followed. They 'landed' on the rocks and mountains in Tana Toraja, and it was here that they built their first house, a *tongkonan*. The rituals that were customary in heaven were maintained on Earth, thus preserving the cosmic balance.

The Toraja cosmos consists of three strata: the upper world, the Earth, i.e. the world of the human beings, and the underworld. The upper world is the domain of Puang Matua, who, together with a few other important gods and goddesses and the deified ancestors, is enthroned in the zenith. The Earth is held aloft on the head and palms of Pong Tulakpadang, 'Supporter of the Earth'. When she's in a bad mood, his wife can cause earthquakes. A tunnel connects the underworld with the realm of the dead, called Puya. The way through is guarded by Pong Lalondong, 'Lord Rooster', the judge of Puya who cuts off people's thread of life. For that matter, the realm of the dead lies on Earth, somewhere south of Tana Toraja. Therefore, both this point of the compass and the west, the direction of the setting sun, are associated with death. North and east, the direction of the rising sun, are associated with life. Likewise, the Toraja classify their ceremonies: all rituals involving the living lie in the eastern sphere, and ceremonies having to do with death, are 'west'.

Tongkonan: lofty seats

Some of the Toraja houses have a very special status. These are the ***tongkonan***, or 'seats'. They form the centre, the 'seat', of a family group, called ***pa'rapuan*** or ***rapu*** for short. Genealogical experts among the Toraja can exactly identify the ancestors who founded the ***tongkonan***, and can also say how many generations ago this took place. Thus the founding mother of the families in the village of Kesu', whose name was Lai' Ambun ri Kesu' ('Lady Morning Mist of Kesu'), together with her husband, built the ***tongkonan*** Kesu' on the mountain of the same name. Reputedly, some ***tongkonan*** were brought down from heaven by the ancestors.

Most ***tongkonan*** used to be situated on a mountain summit, which befitted their lofty status. Later, after the arrival of the Dutch, many were moved to the plains. However, a few ***tongkonan*** are still to be found in the mountains.

▲ *View of Ke'te' Kesu', a Toraja settlement that has now been proclaimed a monument.*

The funeral festivals

Within the Toraja culture the current focal point of interest is the ritual of the dead. Of all ceremonies this has been the most resistant to modern influences, and thus, comparatively, gained increasing importance: great funeral festivals are now a pre-eminent cultural manifestation. In the last century the disposal of the dead was far less spectacular. As a result of coffee-growing and its profits, it was only towards the turn of the century that people began to surround family funerals with more ritual. Next, the Pax Neerlandica that provided a certain measure of peace, stimulated this development, and nowadays, in a peaceful atmosphere, all possible attention is paid to the funerals of loved ones.

The rites of the dead now performed for christianised Toraja, are often quite as pompous as those for 'heathens'. The Christians, too, sacrifice buffaloes, and sing the old funeral songs (if sometimes with different lyrics). A controversial issue is the use of the *tau-tau*, a wooden dummy representing the deceased, and placed by his grave. Some church functionaries say this dummy 'reeks of an idol'. According to others the *tau-tau* is no more than a memorial statue. As to the presence of the traditional funeral priest, the Christians are less divided: his involvement is not appreciated.

The rituals surrounding the 'heathen' interments, demonstrate a certain hierarchy. Those for babies and young children, for the poor and (formerly) for slaves, are very simple. The more complicated interments are categorized according to the number of nights they take; depending on the status of the deceased they vary from *sang bongi*, the one-night festival, to *pitung bongi* lasting seven nights. One counts the nights (and not the days), because darkness is associated with death: black is the non-colour of mourning, and 'black as the night' are the mourning clothes and bands. Many rites take place at night. Only when the deceased is someone of the blood (a Puang), the non-colour of mourning during the final stage of the funeral festival is white, reputedly the same as that of princely blood. Princes' entombments too, proceed in a special way. A deceased Puang is given a ceremony of an even higher order than *pitung bongi*, the seven-nights' feast. A prince is entitled to an interment in two stages, a *dirapa'i*, the funeral feast that includes a rest period.

▲ *This shows a tragic development. Between 1981 and 1987 most* ***tau-tau*** *disappeared from the once so important gallery in Lemo. Malafide art dealers offer fortunes for the funeral effigies, artefacts that play an important part in Toraja culture. How inappropriate a* ***tau-tau*** ◄ *looks in a museum.*

Dirapa'i in Sangalla'

When in 1968 the last prince of Sangalla', Puang Lasok Rinding, had died, a *dirapa'i*, a ritual of the highest order took place, as befitted his position. An extremely expensive funeral feast that could only be celebrated after the prince had lain in state for two years in the southern room of a distinguished *tongkonan* in his tiny realm.

Puang Lasok Rinding, whose official title was Palodang the Twelfth, had ruled over Sangalla' for many years. By virtue of his personality he exercised real power, and enjoyed considerable respect among his subjects. He was a great expert on the *adat*. In contrast to the two other princes in Tana Toraja (of the mini states of Mengkendek and Ma'kale), Puang Lasok Rinding had not yet become a Christian, hence his interment was also to be the last ever held according to the old ritual for a Puang.

Even before the start of the first stage, *aluk pia*, or 'childhood ritual', all kinds of time- and money-consuming preparations had to be made, such as furnishing the guest-houses and getting two feasting grounds ready. The first of these two was the yard around the home of the deceased, and the second was the slaughtering ground of the buffaloes. On this latter field also stood the 'menhirs', the memorials to Puang who had died previously. Guest-houses were built around this spot, and arranged in such a way that the complex gave the impression of a village with a village square; hence the Toraja speak of a 'village of the dead'.

From the start of the first ritual, the widow, who remained at the deceased's side day and night, was no longer allowed to eat any rice. Important decorations were prepared and on the feasting ground near the house of mourning, two buffaloes were killed. One is called 'the Appendix to the Soul', and is supposed to accompany the soul of the deceased to the hereafter. The death of the other buffalo is compared to the actual death of the person for whom the ritual is performed. For till the very moment that this second buffalo is killed, the deceased is said to be 'ill'. Only after the animal's death is the sick man considered to have died and is his corpse turned north to south, instead of the east-to-west position it had previously occupied (for two years, in the case of Puang Lasok Rinding).

For seven days the rites for the dead Puang were continued. Mourning dances and songs for the dead were performed, and buffaloes and pigs were slaughtered. During this period guests came flocking to the village of the dead, and were put up in the guest-houses. Finally, on the seventh day the Puang was temporarily 're-buried', i.e. the deceased, whom the funeral priest had wrapped in strips of fabric until the whole thing looked like an oversized bolster, was screened off from the outside world by a mosquito net. The funeral songs stopped, and those who wished to do so, could now eat rice again. Puang Lasok Rinding was allowed to rest until he would be woken up again at the start of the second part of the funeral festival: *mantunu*, 'the slaughter of the buffaloes'.

▲ *The horns of all buffaloes slaughtered during a funeral festival, have been attached to a stake in front of a* **tongkonan**. *Such a display lends status both to the house and to its* **pa'rapuan**.

The buffalo

The buffalo is the most important animal of the Toraja: it is a sacrificial animal, a status symbol, and it plays a part in many a myth. The horns of this animal were (and still are) the emblem of headhunters. Warriors used to look upon the strong, brave bulls as their examples; headhunting served as proof of virility and increased the fertility of the rice-fields.

A buffalo is judged by posture and size, by the shape of his horns (preferably pointed and sickle-shaped like the new moon, or, for oxen, very long), and by colour. Pitch-black is highly praised, but spotted buffaloes, in Indonesia virtually found only in Tana Toraja, usually cost more. Most expensive are the white buffaloes, speckled like a plover's egg. These spots are associated with abundance: the many grains of rice, the stars in the sky. And all-white buffaloes? Those are worth nothing at all. They were born blind, so the Toraja say.

The Puang is woken up

It was mainly for financial reasons that the second stage of the funeral ritual had to be postponed for two years, till 1972. Very early in the morning of the first day a gong was sounded and two drums, meant especially for this ritual, were beaten to signal the end of the rest period. The Toraja call this *matundan*, 'being woken from sleep'. That same morning a pig was killed, and some time during the afternoon a buffalo. The funeral priest presented the deceased with bits of meat from these sacrificial animals, and the singing of the mourning songs was resumed.

The next important rite, in which another pig was sacrificed, consisted in wrapping the body all over again. Now a special artist started making the *tau-tau*, the wooden dummy representing the deceased, which was later to be placed among the other dummies in front of the family grave.

At the same time people were working on the *saringan*, the bier on which the swaddled deceased was to be carried in procession, first to the feasting ground in the village of the dead, and then to the family tomb complex. The princely graves are in Suaya, a steep

During a funeral ritual, a Toraja in funeral attire ▶ *brings in a black buffalo. Kin or friends of the deceased who are staying at the 'village of the dead', often contribute such a buffalo.*

▲ *The decorated façade of a* **tongkonan**. *The chicken represents the mythical Lando Kollong, 'She with the Long Neck'; the buffalo head represents an earthly buffalo, slaughtered during a funeral feast.*

rock in the principality of Sangalla'. Here, in a few perpendicular cliff faces, dozens of tombs have been hewn, next to each other, and one above the other. The higher the grave, the greater the status of the deceased interred there. The 'undertaker' does the job at his own risk, and risk there is: someone's interment may cause the death of daring undertakers; to take the corpse to its grave sometimes demands bold feats of mountain-climbing.

The ceremonies were continued by transporting the remains from the *tongkonan* to the opposite rice-storehouse. The female relatives resumed their weeping and the *tau-tau* was placed in front of the rice-shed. Every evening a pig was slaughtered and every time small bits of meat were sacrificed to the deceased and to the *tau-tau*. Those present shared the remaining meat in accordance with their social status. The roll in which the deceased was wrapped, was now decorated with a covering of red fabric onto which gold-leaf cut-outs had been glued. Each of these figures has a meaning of its own: for instance, to both ends of the roll the *pa'barre allo* motif is glued, the 'sun with rays', a motif from the upper world.

After three days the body was taken in procession from the rice-storehouse to the village of the dead. Such a procession has its own fixed order. The war-dancers in front, adorned with (fake) buffalo horns, followed by men carrying the 'buffalo's ornament'. This is a beautifully decorated, triangular bamboo construction, probably representing the front gable of a *tongkonan*. The remains of a distinguished deceased used to leave the *adat* house through this part of the façade: thus on the way to Puya, the realm of the dead, the soul of the deceased would as it were, mount

The buffaloes taken to the 'village of the dead' by friends and kin, are slaughtered. For status reasons, during every funeral festival tabs are accurately kept on the number of buffaloes killed. ▼

The **tau-tau** *representing the deceased prince of Sangalla', Puang Lasok Rinding. The dummy is dressed as a dignitary; at his feet* ▼ *lie offerings.*

a buffalo. In the procession the buffalo bearing 'the soul of the dead', its back draped with a sacred cloth, leads the way for the other buffaloes. Next comes the sedan chair with the widow, completely hidden from view by a tent-like construction, as she is considered to be tainted by the atmosphere of death. This also applies to the other women who kept watch near the deceased: they too, are brought along screened from sight. Then comes the *tau-tau* in full regalia, seated in a splendidly decorated sedan chair. The dummy is indeed visible to all: after all, its official name is *bombo dikita*, 'the soul of the deceased that is seen'. And finally, the deceased himself.

The swaddled body of Puang Lasok Rinding, adorned with krisses (double-edged, wavy-bladed daggers), lay on an ornate couch, fitted with a roof like that of a Toraja house, and was covered with a sacred cloth – one of the holy objects of Sangalla'. Relatives, friends, dignitaries, villagers and other residents of Sangalla' all joined the procession. As usual, the bier of the dead was jostled about a lot. Several explanations have been proposed. One is that this tossing and shaking confuses the soul of the deceased so that he can't find his way back to the village again. Others think that this prevents evil spirits from pursuing the deceased. Sometimes the action around the bier even looks like fighting.

On the feasting ground in the village of the dead, the Puang was taken to a special house-like structure, the *lakkean*. The widow and the other women with tasks in the mourning ritual, got out of their sedan chairs and joined the deceased. To do this, they had to climb a high ladder to the top platform. The decorated *tau-tau* was placed on the floor below. Here the mourners danced and sang, well into the night. At the break of

A cosmic symbol

A Toraja house looks bigger than it really is. Often there are no more than three rooms. As among many other Indonesian peoples, among the Toraja too, the traditional house is more than just a shelter. It is the visible symbol of the family group, the ***rapu***, and at the same time its spatial structure refers to the cosmic order: the space under the house represents the underworld, the living area represents the Earth (the world in-between), and the roof the upper world. The place of sacrifice to the gods in this upper world, is the triangular front gable; this is also the place where the soul of a noble deceased Toraja supposedly leaves the house. The living area itself is also arranged according to the cosmic orientation. The room facing south is associated with the funeral rites, as Puya, the realm of the dead, lies south of Tana Toraja. The west, the direction of the setting sun, is identified with death. When the funeral festival commences, the dead are laid in state in the western part of the central room. Like the north, the eastern part of the central room, the sunrise side, is associated with life: here we find the provisions and the kitchen. The northern part of the living area is used as a reception room.

◄ *The rice shed is as it were a scale model of the house, and like the* ***tongkonan*** *it is a status symbol. Often, as in this case, the façade is beautifully decorated.*

▲ *The roll containing the remains, is carried into the rock grave. Because the deceased was a man, the ends of the body roll are decorated with the* **pa'barre allo** *motif, 'the sun with rays'.*

day buffalo fights were organized, and all buffaloes present were eventually slaughtered.

Finally the moment had arrived for the actual interment of the Puang of Sangalla' in the ancestral cliff grave. For generations now, rulers had been entombed here. In the same order as it had come, the procession headed for the family graves in Suaya. Within ten minutes after arrival, via bamboo ladders the heavy red roll containing the deceased, was hoisted into the burial chamber, over forty metres above the ground. Tense moments for the spectators, for as already mentioned, the interment of a distinguished deceased is a heavy and perilous task. Next, the *tau-tau*, the statue of Puang Palodang the Twelfth, was placed in the ancestral gallery of the eleven deceased Palodangs. As in the first part of the funeral festival, the ceremonies were concluded with cock fights. According to the ancient belief, the hundreds of buffaloes slaughtered during the rituals, have accompanied the Puang on the rest of his journey to the hereafter. For there too, the rule applies: the more buffaloes, the higher one's status. With this, the funeral rites drew to an end. They had been grander and costlier than all ceremonies that had ever befallen this unpretentious prince during his lifetime.

Sacrifices for Tana Toraja

Funeral rites of such pomp and circumstance as performed for Puang Lasok Rinding are an exception, even for the Toraja. Yet festivals for less lofty dead often are of a splendour that surprises every outsider. Christian and *Aluk To Dolo* rituals alike, enhance the reputation of the host family. But the expenses involved often far exceed the financial capacity of simple farmers. In many cases, the festivals can only be organized with the help of relatives who have moved out of the area.

There are now some seventy thousand Sa'dan Toraja outside Tana Toraja. Many of them live in the capital of South Sulawesi, Ujung Pandang, in the nickel-mining districts of Central Sulawesi, in the oil-fields of Kalimantan, in Irian Jaya, and in the capital of Indonesia, Jakarta. In the big city they will usually be put up first by relatives, friends or former fellow villagers; hence Toraja usually live together in certain neighbourhoods, with people from their native village or region.

In spite of this solidarity and the great prosperity many of them have achieved in their new locations, many in the 'diaspora' are left with feelings of insecurity. Tana Toraja remains their familiar environment, the place where they feel at home, and where they will seek refuge in an emergency. In the same way that migrant Toba Batak shape the link with their native region in Sumatra, by contributing to grave monuments such as the *tugu* (see Chapter One), a migrant Toraja will rarely refuse a request for financial help from kin in the region of origin. Thus he will frequently contribute to the cost of a relative's funeral rites. Not only does this participation enhance his status, it also gives him a sense of ethnic security, and guarantees him life-long solidarity with Tana Toraja.

▲ *At house-inauguration feasts, girls and young women often dance the* ***ma'gellu'****. The dancers are adorned with precious ornaments belonging to the* ***pa'rapuan****, such as the sacred krisses stuck in their belts, and* ***kandaure****, fyke-shaped beaded ornaments worn on their backs.* ▼

Costly family ties

As the status-enhancing funeral feasts show, a sense of family is highly developed among the Toraja. But to maintain all family ties is no simple matter for them. The kinship system is not unilateral, but bilateral: one is a member both of one's father's and of one's mother's ***pa'rapuan****, and consequently linked to both* ***tongkonan****. But the grandparents'* ***tongkonan*** *are also important, and so are the great-grandparents', and so on... Standing is gained by bonds with many, preferably distinguished,* ***tongkonan****. Genealogical experts help the Toraja find their way in this maze of houses and families. But nowadays the 'membership' of several* ***tongkonan*** *requires a lot of time and money, and often too much of it. Thus for every ceremony in which a house is the focus of the festivities, one has to make a contribution in the form of, for instance, a pig or a buffalo. For the rice-fields and other farm-land belonging to the* ***tongkonan*** *don't yield enough to pay for the upkeep of the house and the initiation rites this entails. And festivals in honour of the* ***tongkonan****, the domain of the* ***pa'rapuan****, at which the house built by the ancestor is the sacred centre, must be held to ensure good fortune for family group and village.*

The Tolaki marriage by elopement

Smoothly Garuda's F-28 lands on the Wolter Monginsidi airport near Kendari, the capital of South-East Sulawesi. Like most Indonesian airports it was named after a national hero: Wolter Monginsidi fought for independence against the Dutch captain Westerling in the late forties. Once a day a plane flies in from the big city of Ujung Pandang (formerly called Makassar), returning the same day. That city is the transit port linking Sulawesi, the Moluccas and Irian Jaya with the rest of Indonesia. At such moments it gets very crowded, the incoming and outgoing passengers meet each other here.
In many cases you can get a ride to Kendari in an official car of a provincial department, or in someone's private jeep. If not, there will always be a seat in one of the minibuses, vans with two benches along the sides. A forty-kilometre drive down a road that is safe and wide, takes you to the capital. At the end of the trip the traveller catches a glimpse of the splendid bay, compared by some to Lake Toba in North Sumatra.
In fact Kendari consists of a line of villages along the coast, a ribbon some fifteen kilometres long.
Until recently, the harbour was the most important trade centre of the town. Here lived the Buginese, seafaring tradesmen, as well as many Manadonese and Moluccans, veterans of the Royal Netherlands East-Indies Army. Recently the steady influx of migrants from all over Indonesia has created a new centre further inland, around the administrative buildings and houses for officials. Many Chinese still running shops in the old harbour district, have already leased land so that in due time they can move their businesses to this new part of town.

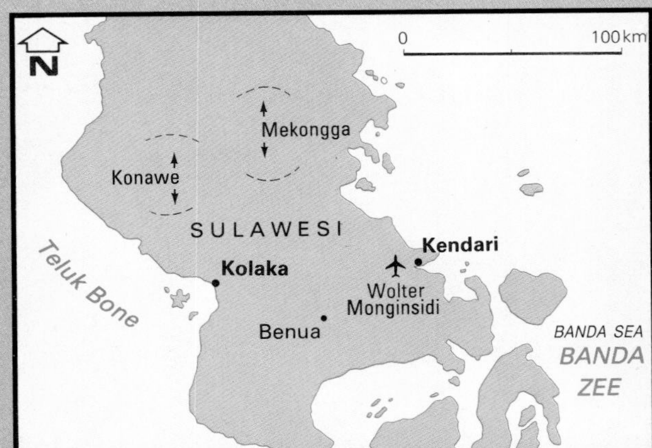

Brave people

The Tolaki belong to the indigenous inhabitants of the peninsula of South-East Sulawesi. Their name means 'Brave people'. For a number of years now this region has been flooded with migrants from all over the Indonesian archipelago. In the districts of Kendari and Kolaka, the Tolaki, now estimated at 250,000, make up only half of the total population.
The unity of their culture has suffered from this, and numerous traditions are threatened with extinction. In many places the lack of any feeling of ethnic pride accelerates this process. In the cities many youngsters are now ashamed of being Tolaki; they hardly understand their own language, let alone speak it.

▲ *Tolaki girls are considered mature enough for marriage after their first menstruation. And marriage used to follow soon (around their fourteenth year), but nowadays they usually first complete a lengthy school career.*

Hardly any of the indigenous people of this part of Sulawesi, the Tolaki, are to be found in trade. They usually prefer office jobs in the Administration or beyond. This preference is inherent in the class structure of traditional Tolaki society. As residents of what used to be the realms of Konawe and Mekongga, the Tolaki nobility had slaves to cultivate their swiddens. The freemen, too, worked in the fields, while the noblemen busied themselves with politics and the like. Nowadays, the descendants of the slaves are no longer regarded as such, and the Tolaki only distinguish between nobility and commoners. The first category is subdivided into noblemen with political functions, and those without. The Tolaki nobles working at Administration level, still have the highest status.

In Kendari the talk of the town turns out to be the elopement of a highplaced government official's daughter. This noble Tolaki's child was said to have run away with a Bugis boy, the son of a member of the South-East Sulawesi Provincial Council. The girl's parents do not tolerate her marrying a Buginese: he is neither a Tolaki nor of noble birth. As the girl decided to follow her heart's desire, she resisted the will of her parents, and took the bus to Kolaka with her brother and a female friend of hers. From there they were to take the night ferry to BajoE, and the following morning the bus to Ujung Pandang. Here the girl will meet her Bugis lover. Next they are to fly to Jakarta, where they will hide in the anonymity of the big city. Nobody will know their whereabouts. The modern marriage by elopement is now a fact: the Tolaki *adat* has been brushed aside.

Broken boundaries

Among the Tolaki, marriage by elopement in itself is nothing new. The *adat* has always offered the possibility to evade payment of a high bride-price, or to avoid marrying someone chosen by parents and kin. *Adat* law provides for an arrangement aimed at neutralizing as soon as possible the tension an elopement creates in the community; thus the problems that have arisen, are solved in a way acceptable to all.

Over the past few decades, 'the big world', modern Indonesia, has tightened its grip on the peninsula community, and these traditional *adat* guidelines geared to local society, have come under pressure.

The attraction of Indonesia's big cities for today's runaways who ignore local boundaries, causes problems that no one is prepared for: suddenly the old, familiar *adat* procedures for settling a marriage by elopement, seem useless – and this often has far-reaching consequences for the local community.

In particular among young people of noble birth, this modern marriage by elopement is gaining popularity. In order to forge a strong unity, the highest class always preferred to arrange marriages within their own kin group. In both former Tolaki kingdoms, the administration was in the hands of the nobility, a unity that was highly appreciated. However, in due course South-East Sulawesi came to be populated by many people from other parts of Indonesia, and today it increasingly occurs that a Tolaki wishes an outsider as partner, and that someone of noble birth wants to marry a commoner. So as to gain status and influence at the local level, nowadays non-Tolaki officials even consciously look for a wife within the local nobility, as these circles still play an important part in numerous Administrative affairs.

If no objections are raised, a Tolaki and an outsider will usually get married according to local traditions, sometimes complemented with modern customs, such as sending wedding invitations and giving a reception. An important element of the traditional marriage arrangements is the bride-price. Even today the future husband has to pay this to the parents and kin of his future bride. It comprises several objects and a sum of money, the size of which has to do with the bride's social status. If she is of noble birth, this could lead to astronomical amounts – particularly in the city – and hence to many couples such a price is reason for

Town and country united in Kendari: a rooster hanging from the handlebars of a ▾ *modern motorcycle.*

a marriage by elopement after all.
In society's view the girl thus breaks an old *adat* rule: the initiative for a marriage should be taken by the man (and his kin), not by the woman. Therefore, her parents will put the blame on him: after all, if he had respected them and the *adat*, they wouldn't have lost their daughter. They feel gravely insulted. If the eloped couple stayed within the community, and thus decided on a traditional marriage by elopement, the procedure prescribed by *adat* is then initiated as soon as possible. This procedure offers both parties a chance of reconciliation. The following description shows how this comes about; at the same time the consequences of the modern version and the lack of such an arrangement, become clear. This marriage by elopement took place in the early eighties in the Kendari hinterland.

The kalo

An object that occupies a central position in Tolaki culture, is a simple ring, the *kalo sara*, or *kalo* for short. The ring is made of three pieces of rattan, intertwined as in a rope, their ends tied together. The knot symbolizes Man's head; the three intertwined parts symbolize the people's unity. Some compare the pieces of rattan to the three classes; according to others they refer to the *adat*, the administration and the religion.
There are several sizes of *kalo*, but only two are still in use: for the nobility 'one that fits round the shoulders', and for the commoners, 'one that fits round the head'. Which kind is used depends on the social status of the person to whom the ring is offered.
The *kalo* is used in many situations; it is indispensable for weddings, for negotiations to settle conflicts, for an invitation to a meeting, and for the announcement of a death. The *kalo* should be offered on a dish of plaited rattan or of pandanus leaves, but nowadays a modern tray serves equally well. Covered with a white cloth as a symbol of purity, the dish shows the honest and sincere intentions of the Tolaki bringing the *kalo*.
In offering the ring, money is sometimes put inside it. In that case one says 'The *kalo* contains something'. The money is a sign that serious discussions are intended.
During a wedding ceremony the unity of husband and wife is symbolized by putting a *pinang* nut and a *sirih* leaf inside the ring. The 'head of the *kalo*', the rattan knot, must always point to the person being addressed, so during negotiations the dish has to be turned around frequently.
By no means everyone is allowed to use the *kalo*; its guardianship is vested in the hereditary function of the *paabitara*. No one would ever dare refuse a *kalo* offered by the *paabitara*: to every Tolaki this ring forms the foundation of *adat* law.

Labio and Mburi

Because Labio fears that Mburi's parents will demand a bride-price that his family can't raise, he decides to run away with her. Very early in the morning, at first light, the couple leaves quietly. For hours they walk from village to village, until at last they reach the house of Labio's elder brother. As soon as they tell him they have eloped, he informs the village head, for it is important that delicate matters such as these be dispelled as soon as possible. The village head listens to Labio's brother, and instructs him to bring the couple back that same day, to the village they left that morning, where Mburi lives. Here, according to the *adat*, in the village of the woman involved, a marriage by elopement ought to be settled.
Late in the afternoon, Labio and Mburi return to the village they had left so secretly. Without delay they are taken to the house of an uncle of Labio's, for his father is deceased. Here, giving all the details, Labio's brother tells what has happened, and soon after, a family delegation prepares to go and break the news to Mburi's parents. They ask the village *paabitara* (the pre-eminent expert on *adat* jurisdiction) to accompany Labio's kin. The *paabitara* brings the *kalo*, a ring of plaited rattan, to ensure a polite reception by Mburi's family – in spite of everything. For the *kalo* symbolizes the *adat*, and this must be respected. Nonetheless, Mburi's parents are furious: they regard the event as a kind of kidnapping of their daughter. It is decided to settle the matter in a week's time.

Around the kalo

In the evening of the day agreed upon, sixty to seventy people, kin of both parties, assemble in the house of an uncle of Mburi's. Feelings are still running high. The women are sitting in the bedroom, the men in the living room. Experts on the *adat* (the *adat* elders) and members of the village administration are also present. Mburi is represented by her elder brother, Labio by his uncle. In addition, the *paabitara* is here again, with the *kalo*; it is he who will open the discussions, and try to lead them in the right direction. In order to ask permission to settle the matter, the *paabitara* first addresses the village head, in the way prescribed by *adat*. Opposite to him, he sits down on the floor; between them he places a tray covered with a white cloth. On this spotless surface he places the rattan ring, with its knot, the 'head of the *kalo*', pointing towards himself. Next he puts five hundred *rupiah* inside the ring (about 50 cents in American money), and turns the tray so that the head of the *kalo* points to the village head. Then for an instant, he holds the tray first on his right knee, then on his left knee, next with both hands he raises the tray to stomach level, then to head level, holds it in the direction of the village head, and finally puts it down in front of the latter, whom he now addresses. In elaborate detail he explains the situation that has arisen, and asks his permission to bring the matter to a good conclusion. The village head responds by touching the tray with two fingers, answering in the affirmative, and turning the tray so that once again the head of the *kalo* points to the *paabitara*. He tucks the 500 *rupiah* under the white cloth. Again the *paabitara* puts money inside the rattan ring, now 100 *rupiah*, and carefully repeats the manipulations with the *kalo* and the tray. This time he offers the *kalo* to an *adat* elder; before further negotiations can even be considered, Labio's lack of respect for the *adat* has to be compensated for by penance to this *adat* elder. Labio's representative pays the elder five thousand *rupiah*. It is the fine that has been set for Labio's kidnapping of Mburi, based on the number of villages the couple passed on their flight: nine. The more, the higher the fine.

So as to enable actual discussions about a marriage, the *paabitara* repeats the ritual with the *kalo* another two times. To dispel feelings of anger, Labio's representative first pays fifteen hundred *rupiah* to Mburi's family, and then an additional one thousand *rupiah* and a sarong are handed over, to restore her parents' reputation. These payments are considered essential to improve the disturbed relationship between both parties to such an extent that no obstacles to the bride-price negotiations remain.

Now, in a less heated atmosphere, the size of the bride-price is discussed, and the place and time of its payment. These discussions as well, are led by the *paabitara*, and again the *kalo* plays its mediating and linking part. After extensive argumentation, the spokesmen of both parties agree on an amount that is only a quarter of a 'normal' bride-price. The *paabitara*, the village head and the *adat* elder conclude the official part of the meeting, by sharing the money that the speakers tucked under the white cloth on the tray.

Now the young lovers who during the negotiations kept a low profile elsewhere in the house, come forward. To apologize for his offense against the *adat*, Labio first shakes hands with Mburi's brother, then with the village head, and finally with all others present. Mburi follows his example, but is soon sent to the kitchen to serve tea and biscuits to the guests. Finally, a relative of Labio's removes the *kalo* from the tray: the unity within the community has been restored, the rattan ring has served its purpose. On the tray the *kalo* is replaced by the IOUs written by Labio's family to restore the relationship with Mburi's kin. Four times the tray is lifted, to ensure that the burdened relationship is finally rid of evil influences. After the snacks, everyone goes home with relief. The attempt at reconciliation has succeeded.

▲ *Tolaki bride and groom in traditional attire.*

Bride-price

The bridegroom and his family are obliged to pay a bride-price to the bride and her kin. Part of this compensation is still quoted in the old Spanish currency unit, the **real***; nowadays the rest is paid in* **rupiah***, rather than in buffaloes, gongs and rice as was customary in the old days. The amount depends on the bride's class: among the nobility, amounts that for Indonesian standards are inconceivable, are no exception.*

Apart from raising the bride-price, the bridegroom has to collect some objects, meant for the mother of his bride. Thus she is to receive a sarong from her son-in-law to compensate for her daughter's wetting her lap when she was still a little child. She must be given a little lamp, because she used to keep one lit to watch over her child. And she is to get a washbasin and ladle to bathe her future grandchildren.

In addition, the groom and his kin pay for all wedding expenses.

▲ *Handing over the bride-price. Beside the* **kalo** *lies a pile of sarongs and a washbasin, meant for the mother of the bride.*

Between Kendari and Jakarta

Nowadays, fewer and fewer elopements turn out this way. Over the past few decades, the Tolaki's horizon has widened considerably, and frequently lovers who wish to evade a high bride-price or an arranged marriage, escape to areas beyond the reach of the local *adat*; Indonesia's big cities are ideal places of refuge. This means that the reputation of the girl and her parents remains harmed, and that social relations between the two families involved cannot be restored. An insufferable situation, particularly in the hinterland of Kendari where within the farming communities everyone is related to each other. But even in the town itself contact between members of parties that are at variance with each other, cannot be avoided. However, the feelings of hostility can't be dispelled, and the lost stability in society cannot be restored. Those left behind have been deprived of a chance of reconciliation, the *kalo* cannot be rotated. The Tolaki *adat* has yet to find the right answer to this contemporary form of interaction with modern Indonesia. Its survival is severely put to the test, but its toughness is well-known. As long as the *adat* is not reshaped and adapted, the parents of the Tolaki girl of noble birth who eloped to Jakarta, probably cannot shake hands with their 'son-in-law'. This Bugis youth would undoubtedly find the traditional arrangement too expensive: the road from Kendari to Indonesia's capital passes through many, many villages!

Only in the farming communities can one or two traditional Tolaki pile-dwellings still be found. Not a single nail was used in building them. By now, bamboo and coconut frond have been ▾ supplanted by brick and corrugated sheet material, and the earth is used as a floor.

At weddings and other festive occasions, the Tolaki form a circle and dance shoulder to shoulder. Like the ***kalo****, the circle – such as this one during the* ***lulo-ngganda*** *danced at the annual feast – symbolizes the unity of the people: everything that separates the participants – class, wealth, age – is forgotten, and room ▾ is made only for those approaching the dancers 'from within'.*

The annual festival

To conclude and re-open the agricultural cycle, all Tolaki used to celebrate the ***monahu-ndau****, the annual festival. Today only a few villages still perform this once so important ritual.*

In Benua, one of these villages, the ***kanda****, a sacred drum stemming from heaven, plays an important part in the ceremony. Just before full moon in September, the guardian takes the* ***kanda*** *from his attic and brings it to a small, specially built* ***kanda*** *house. It is only here that this drum may be played. For three nights the villagers dance the* ***lulo-ngganda*** *near this little house. These dances, linked to agriculture, may be performed only once a year.*

After the third night of dancing, the actual agricultural ritual takes place at the crack of dawn. All villagers bring their sowing-seed to the ***kanda*** *house to have it blessed. In front of the house, they place seven bowls of cooked rice and seven bamboo pipes containing rice-wine. A priest invokes the gods and ancestors with prayers, offering them a sacrifice of* ***sirih*** *(Piper betle) and* ***pinang*** *(Areca catechu). Thus the Tolaki hope to placate the invisible forces so that the coming year will bring a rich harvest, good health and prosperity to the community. The priest also offers an egg in the hope that all sins the villagers committed over the past year, will be forgiven. Finally, the* ***lulo-ngganda*** *are danced again.*

After the ceremony young and old take part in popular traditional games, and the ***umoara*** *is presented, a war-dance that used to be performed by brave Tolaki just before leaving on a headhunting trip.*

In front of the little ***kanda*** *house*
▼ one places seven bamboo containers filled with rice wine.

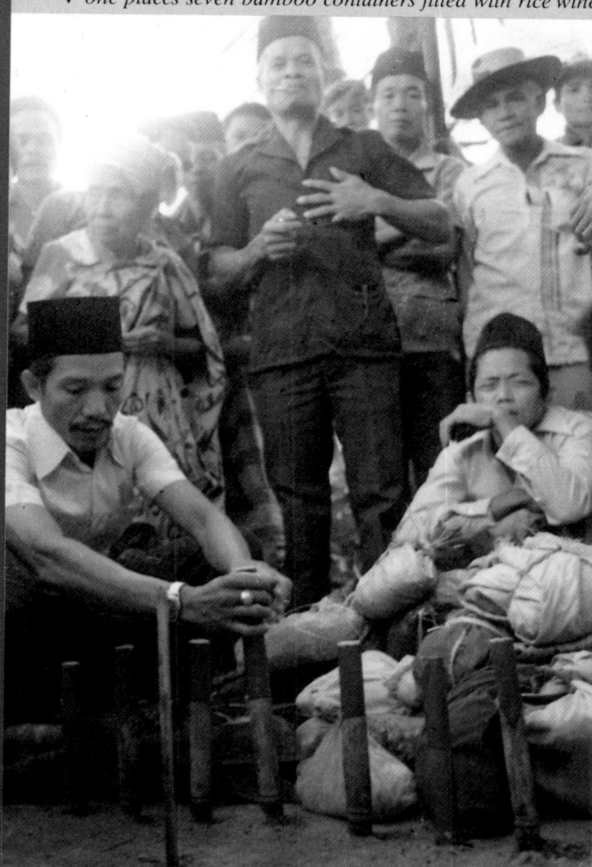

▲ Beside the ***kanda*** *hanging from a post, the villagers' sowing-seed awaits the blessing of gods and ancestors. After the annual feast, the young train themselves in performing the* ***umoara****, the Tolaki war dance. ▼*

▲ Epitaph for a Minahasan famed for, among other things, his bravery in the Java War (1825-1830).

▲ The ornaments indicate that the man buried here, made his fortune in clove cultivation.

▲ Mausoleum for a married couple; the husband was the first in his village to found a transport company.

▲ Many Minahasans tried to find well-being and prosperity beyond their native country.

▲ A **waruga** lid decorated with human figures.

The Minahasans: eternal rivalry

Wandering around in a Minahasa cemetery is a fascinating experience. Most Christian names on the gravestones ring familiar to a Dutchman: Drikus, Jans, Deetje,... The Dutch inscriptions on the older tombstones, often quoted from the Bible, testify just as silently to the Dutch influence, once so powerful. And what to think of the details sometimes mentioned about the position of the deceased, for instance 'teacher of the indigenous', and 'clerk first class with the Royal Packet Steamship Company'.
Even so, what is most striking about any Minahasa graveyard is a number of – often fairly recent – pompous monuments. Their design often reveals the source of their opulence. Some are decorated with plaster cloves, others are shaped like a lorry. Obviously the deceased had made a lot of money in the trades depicted and wanted to boast about it for all time. The tomb may also be the final resting-place for a wife, a brother or a sister. But it certainly is no real family grave; it rarely holds the remains of more than three people. Unlike the Toba Batak in North Sumatra, whose special tombs (the *tugu* and *tambak*) serve to emphasize the fame of a whole clan (see Chapter One), the Minahasans erect monuments to glorify one individual's status based on special merit.

Waruga: pre-colonial status

In or near older villages one may often find mausoleums of an entirely different nature, clearly dating from ancient times. Their size and design catch the eye: a great, rectangular sandstone urn bearing a second, sloping stone. The whole thing reminds one of a small house with a gabled roof.
These *waruga*, as they are called in the Minahasa, usually pre-date the first contacts with Europeans, hence were erected before the sixteenth century. The

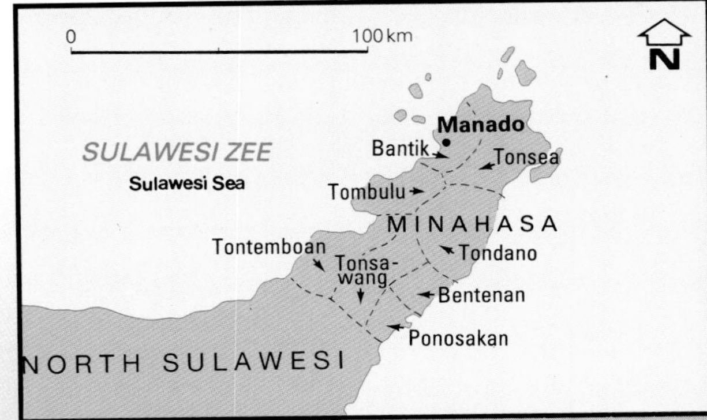

Orang Minahasa

Minahasa is the extreme north-eastern part of the northern peninsula of Sulawesi. This region is also named Manado, after the capital of the province of North Sulawesi; in that case, the people living in Minahasa are referred to as 'Manadonese' or '*orang* Manado'. It is better, though, to speak of 'Minahasans', *orang* Minahasa.
Yet even this latter term is somewhat misleading, for it suggests a homogeneous ethnic group. But this 'people' consists of eight different ethnic groups, each with its own language: the Tontemboan, Tombulu, Tondano, Tonsea, Tonsawang, Bantik, Bentenan and the Ponosakan. The first five do show similarities in language and traditions, yet each group has its own original culture.
True, in recent times migration, marriage relations and external cultural influences have diminished the differences, but anyone visiting the villages will find that the old languages are still really spoken. Usually they are mixed with phrases and expressions from 'Manado Malay', a common Minahasa variant of ***bahasa Indonesia***, the official Indonesian language. This variant has many typical expressions and a wealth of terms borrowed from Dutch, Portuguese, Spanish and the eight local Minahasa languages.

▲ The Minahasan mausoleums are surrounded by many less pompous grave monuments. In the foreground the grave of two brothers who died on the same day in 1961, during the 'Permesta', the civil war that aimed for, among other things, a more independent Minahasa.

slightly more recent ones, from the time of the Dutch East India Company, are sometimes decorated with depictions of human figures in Western dress: half-long coats with lots of buttons, big hats and holding long Gouda (earthenware) pipes.

The last *waruga* were made in the second half of the nineteenth century. In the meantime, the Dutch Administration and the Mission had decided that henceforth the dead could only be buried in wooden coffins. Moreover, in that same period these oppressors put an end to most ways of expressing the old Minahasan religion and to the tribal way of life, which were closely linked to erecting *waruga*. In pre-colonial times the *waruga* (unlike the simpler graves such as dug-out tree-trunk) had the same purpose as today's mausoleums: they emphasized the excellent qualities of the deceased.

The tribal Minahasans did not have a rigid class structure, and descent was of little importance in determining someone's position and status in the community. This egalitarian nature of society, and the fact that the Minahasans lived with and amidst a luxuriant vegetation, almost evokes an idyllic vision. But reality was forbidding.

The prevailing system of shifting cultivation meant hard work, in particular when breaking new ground, while the yields were as variable as the weather. And the constant state of war was another obstacle to a peaceful existence. Continuously there were tensions between the small political groups in which Minahasan society was organized. In such circumstances it is no surprise that qualities such as courage, physical strength and the ability to recruit and command fellow-warriors, were highly regarded. Success in agriculture was also appreciated, as proof of bodily strength and divine blessing.

There was a chronic state of tension, not only between the different groups, but also within each separate community. Precisely because leadership was not hereditary but resulted from preferences expressed by other group members, candidates had to go to great lengths to display their qualities in order to gain followers. This was done by means of the so-called festivals of merit. But even for those who finally rose to the important positions within a community, the coast was never clear. With unrelenting zeal opponents tried to push the privileged off their pedestals, and not least through intrigue. Only leaders who had managed adequately to ward off such attacks, and Minahasans who had gained exclusive status by organizing festivals of merit, were given a special grave: a *waruga*.

▲ *The **waruga** used to lie scattered in various village yards. Nowadays they have often been brought together in one location, as was done here, in the Tonsea area.*

The strength of a head

*To the Minahasans human skulls had intrinsic value: they represented strength, and were considered a guarantee of fertility and prosperity. For instance, when founding a new village, usually a few heads were hunted first. These were buried by the **watu tumotowa**, the 'sacred stones of the village'. In Tontemboan, one of the Minahasa languages, this spot was called **keter in do'ong**, 'the strength and well-being of the village'.*

To some extent, anybody could acquire the strength of hunted heads, by boiling them, and then eating part of them, or drinking the broth. This also happened in 1829, when Minahasa soldiers who were to take part in the Java war (to fight Diponegoro in the principalities – see Chapter Two), were waiting for a ship near Manado. Suddenly a few of them had disappeared. Afterwards it turned out that they had killed two people from nearby villages, had cut off their heads, and had ensured themselves of some extra strength, the Minahasa way.

The heads were not only sacral objects, but also proof of courage. Anyone returning from the war with a skull, was allowed to display it in the front porch of his house; the pots in which the heads were boiled, were sometimes used to decorate the house.

Karate is a sport that is very attractive to Minahasan youngsters. May one cautiously assume a ▼ *link with the value Minahasans have always attached to physical strength?*

Festivals of merit

There is a rare eye-witness account of a festival of merit dating from 1835, written by the missionary J.G. Schwarz. This sacrificial feast was organised by the household of a man who had gained a reputation of bravery in the Java war, the struggle that broke out in the Central-Javanese principalities after a conflict between a Dutch Resident and Diponegoro, uncle and guardian of the Sultan of Yogyakarta (see Chapter Two). They had first waited for a good harvest to be able to offer this feast.

During the first stage the host and his wife sat motionless in front of their house. He was wearing a white robe and a red-and-white turban, decorated with bird-of-paradise feathers; his cheeks had been rubbed with pig's blood. Under a shelter a big drum had been placed, and over this, two crossed swords and a tuft of human hair. After numerous, elaborate procedures and an extensive study of the omens of the gods, finally a great feast took place that lasted for days. All the villagers could eat and drink to their hearts' content. Thus, the wealth accumulated by one individual was redistributed among the community.

Actually a feast of merit was part of a series of nine feasts. If somebody managed to perform the whole cycle – usually by then he would be an old man – this person achieved the ritual degree of perfection, and earned the title of ***wa'ilan****, 'the blessed one'.* ***Wa'ilan*** *enjoyed special privileges; and they were buried in a* ***waruga****.*

Though Minahasa is a relatively small region, the communication problems are considerable ▼ which is largely due to the jagged landscape with its wide rivers.

Mission and colonial authority

Hence prior to Dutch interference, Minahasan society had a great deal of mobility, due to its changing leadership. But according to prevailing opinion, social dynamics reputedly resulted from external influences in particular. This is not entirely incomprehensible. In the colonial era, which in Minahasa started around 1820, utterly new phenomena and possibilities were introduced that changed the character of society. Both the Christian religion and the introduction of Western schooling changed the culture. In addition, the latter brought privileged positions within reach of the few who were better educated. Moreover, administrative and economic changes opened up new prospects for a small part of the population.

At the same time, Dutch measures severely limited the possibilities of change that had always existed in Minahasa society. Thus it was forbidden to wage war and to organize festivals of merit, activities which until then had offered the opportunity of proving oneself. And the religious foundation of these cultural expressions was undermined by missionaries propagating the gospel. Whereas in the past, wealth used to provide much status, now very little room was left for individual development. Colonial measures such as forced coffee-cultivation and statute labour, radically changed daily life. Men, women, and sometimes even children spent most of their time on such work, and got very little in return.

An important consequence of all this, was a more or less sudden consolidation of the existing élites' positions, and a concentration of wealth among them. They were supported by the Dutch Administration, the overpowering factor in this context. Of course the traditional tensions in society inevitably remained, but under the repressive colonial rule of the last century these could hardly erupt. After the turn of the century, when the forced supplying of coffee had been abolished, and the Dutch Administration and the Mission showed more flexibility, those tensions once again had the chance to surface. And after Indonesia had gained independence, these chances increased.

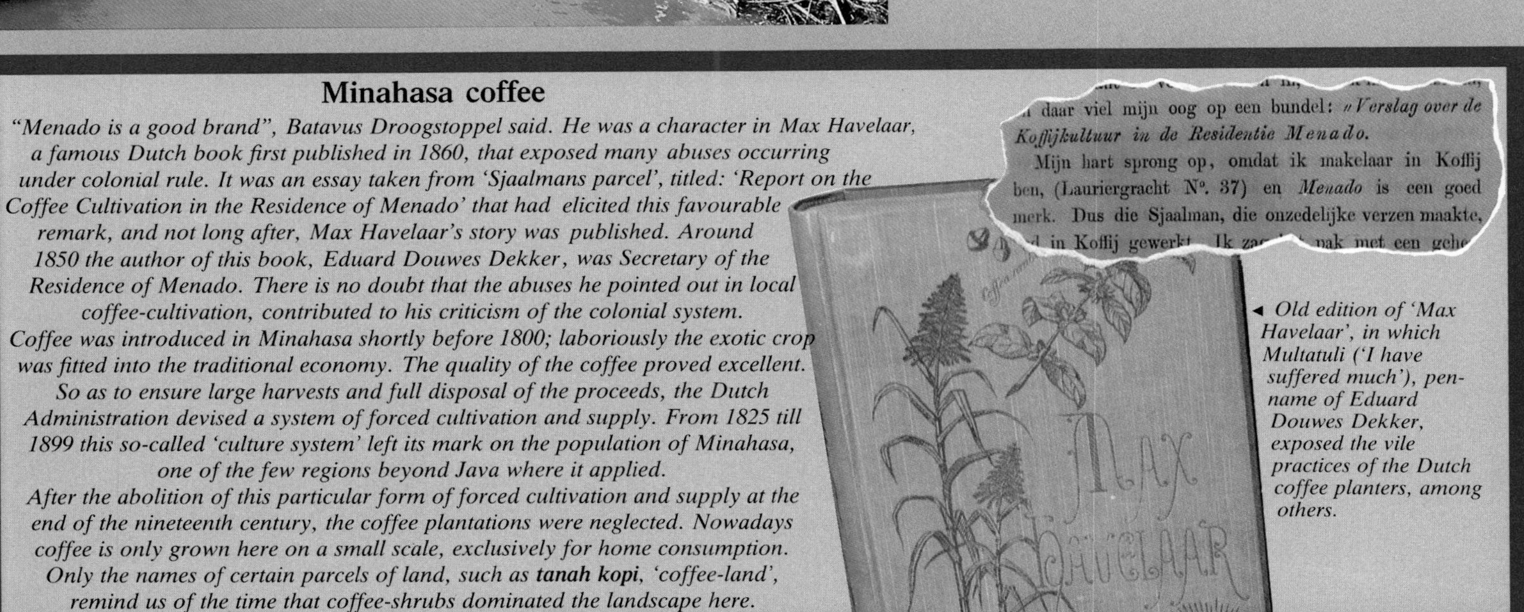

Minahasa coffee

"Menado is a good brand", Batavus Droogstoppel said. He was a character in Max Havelaar, a famous Dutch book first published in 1860, that exposed many abuses occurring under colonial rule. It was an essay taken from 'Sjaalmans parcel', titled: 'Report on the Coffee Cultivation in the Residence of Menado' that had elicited this favourable remark, and not long after, Max Havelaar's story was published. Around 1850 the author of this book, Eduard Douwes Dekker, was Secretary of the Residence of Menado. There is no doubt that the abuses he pointed out in local coffee-cultivation, contributed to his criticism of the colonial system.

Coffee was introduced in Minahasa shortly before 1800; laboriously the exotic crop was fitted into the traditional economy. The quality of the coffee proved excellent. So as to ensure large harvests and full disposal of the proceeds, the Dutch Administration devised a system of forced cultivation and supply. From 1825 till 1899 this so-called 'culture system' left its mark on the population of Minahasa, one of the few regions beyond Java where it applied.

After the abolition of this particular form of forced cultivation and supply at the end of the nineteenth century, the coffee plantations were neglected. Nowadays coffee is only grown here on a small scale, exclusively for home consumption. Only the names of certain parcels of land, such as ***tanah kopi****, 'coffee-land', remind us of the time that coffee-shrubs dominated the landscape here.*

daar viel mijn oog op een bundel: »*Verslag over de Koffijkultuur in de Residentie Menado.*

Mijn hart sprong op, omdat ik makelaar in Koffij ben, (Lauriergracht N°. 37) en *Menado* is een goed merk. Dus die Sjaalman, die onzedelijke verzen maakte, in Koffij gewerkt. Ik za... pak met een gehe...

◄ Old edition of 'Max Havelaar', in which Multatuli ('I have suffered much'), pen-name of Eduard Douwes Dekker, exposed the vile practices of the Dutch coffee planters, among others.

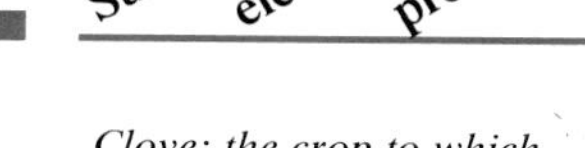

Contemporary rivalry

In particular in village-head elections, involving an office rooted in tradition, the internal differences are unmistakable. Often for months prior to the elections, the village is in turmoil. Even villagers living and working far away (as far out as Java), return to their native village especially for the elections. The candidates' kin groups try to outbid each other by offering sumptuous meals to possible supporters. At the same time this shows how wealthy, hence how excellent, their candidate is. Usually, election time is a period of great unrest, in which all tensions bottled up over the past few years, are let out. Manipulation, intimidation and lobbying are the order of the day, and the support of the traditional priests (the *tonaas*), is frequently sought.

When the names on the ballot-papers are read out, the atmosphere is tense. Losers may take the result very badly. Famous is the story of the candidate who, on the announcement of his crushing defeat, mounted his horse, and riding recklessly, plunged down a ravine. More often, losers will show their feelings of resentment and disappointment in a less spectacular way, yet to such an extent that the new village head cannot always feel quite secure about his position. In many cases the supporters of a defeated candidate will stoop to gossip to make it impossible for the winner to do his job.

Thus in a Minahasan village in the seventies, the candidate of the wealthiest family was defeated. Subsequently his family twice managed to have the elected village head suspended. The first time, the help of an influential member of the family, the wife of a high Administration official, was sought in spreading the insinuations. When after a few months these accusations proved unfounded, the village head was reinstated. But the atmosphere remained restless and finally, the village administration was sabotaged. Soon after, the village head was dismissed.

At the subsequent elections the family got what they

*The office of the village head (**hukum tua**) in a*
▼ *prosperous clove village.*

wanted: one of theirs was chosen as village head. But rumour had it that this time as well, the triumph had been rigged with the help of the related Administration official. When reading out the names on the ballot-papers, this official's subordinates seem to have made frequent mistakes...

Such goings-on will probably soon be a thing of the past. A recent law has given the village head in Minahasa the status of 'official', and he is now under the direct authority of the Indonesian government. Hence from now on, rivalry between local groups will have to take a different shape. No doubt an important way to express it, lies in the display of material wealth which from time immemorial has been a significant Minahasan criterion of someone's qualities and the extent to which he is the gods' chosen one. Financially, some families have the good fortune of being head and shoulders above the rest of the community, thanks to profits from the cultivation of cloves or coconuts, or from trade. This provides them with a basis for outbidding others, for instance by organizing large-scale and exuberant feasts, but also by means of more permanent signs of wealth: stone houses like fairy-tale palaces, cars (even though the road to the village is almost impassable) and ...mausoleums.

Clove: the crop to which some families now owe fabulous wealth. ▼

▲ *An enormous nervous bustle surrounds the village-head elections. The blackboard lists the names of the candidates.*

Tonaas

Under Christian influence, many aspects of the old Minahasa religion have vanished, but the practices of the *tonaas*, the traditional priest, have been preserved. In general, his involvement is not considered to be in conflict with Christian doctrine. Although the *tonaas* performs ceremonies in which the ancestors play a central part, he recognizes only the one Christian God. In contrast to what one might expect, within the community the *tonaas* is by no means a marginal figure. Some priests have important functions on village, church or school councils, and it is not at all unusual or improper for a good, Christian family to call in the *tonaas* for help on special occasions.

If one considers this necessary, one may have the future predicted from an animal's gall-bladder, or as an electoral candidate one can ask advice on the best strategy, or, in case of illness, one may ask the priest for help in bringing about a quick recovery of the patient. During the healing procedure the priest mumbles mysterious spells, and often the patient has to drink water to which special stones, herbs or bits of wood have been added. The *tonaas* provides amulets for protection against future ailments.

The priest acquires such objects on the instruction of the ancestors who often appear to him in some sacred spot. Before the *tonaas*, supported by his helpers, invokes the ancestors, he will make a sacrifice to them here: nine eggs, nine ***pinang*** nuts (Areca catechu), nine mugs of palm wine, cigarettes, rice and other treats. Then he will fall into a trance: his eyes start rolling, his facial expression changes, he begins to tremble, cannot remain standing without support and starts uttering sounds, in a seemingly uncoordinated way. Now, in a vision, the ancestors will reveal the spot where the necessary objects can be found. Coming to himself, the priest goes to this place, collects the objects and returns home.

▲ *Under the supervision of the* **tonaas**, *two assistants prepare the offering to the ancestors.*

The **tonaas** *in trance.* ▼

Looking like a strange sea creature, Sulawesi lies between Kalimantan and the Moluccas. Four jagged peninsulas meet in a central highland with peaks several kilometres high. Until the turn of the century, the Toraja lived here in the seclusion of a mountain world, nowadays their villages are the greatest tourist attraction of the island.

Actually the term Toraja derives from the Buginese language, and means no more than 'inhabitants of the interior' or 'mountain dwellers'; the people themselves have a different interpretation: ***to*** is said to mean 'human(s)' and ***raja***, so they claim, comes from the Indonesian word for king. A people of kings, hence a regal people.

By now, many Toraja have descended from their lofty world to look for a living in the southern city of Ujung Pandang, at whose airport many tourists arrive in the island. However, if a mountain dweller should die here, then if at all possible, his mortal remains are taken back aloft in a taxi, to be buried there in a rock grave. A Toraja funeral in bustling Ujung Pandang stops the traffic absolutely. Whereas in the highland about a hundred buffaloes and pigs take part in the funeral procession, in the city formerly called Makassar it comprises more than a hundred taxis loudly honking their horns. And not one of the nearly one million inhabitants will dare to interrupt the procession.

Even in the old days the port sheltered members of various ethnic groups. Makassar was a free port offering safe anchorage in all seasons. In addition to the Makassarese and Buginese of South Sulawesi (the island was then called Celebes), numerous merchants from the Asian mainland lived there, and later, Europeans as well. The old Dutch fort Rotterdam still looms near the harbour. Here Diponegoro, the Javanese folk hero who fought the colonial government in the Java War (1825-1830), died in prison.

In the port itself one can often find the unique ***pinisi***, impressive seagoing wooden sailing ships built by Buginese. An estimated eight hundred of these cargo sailers are involved in transporting the heavy logs from the interior of Kalimantan to Java. These ***pinisi*** help to make Indonesia's fleet of cargo sailers the largest in the world. New ***pinisi*** are usually built of timber that also comes from Kalimantan. In the two southern peninsulas of Sulawesi that are quite densely populated, only a sparse natural vegetation remains. In the central highland and in the northern peninsulas, the traveller may enjoy an environment hardly violated and truly miraculous.

In particular the Tangkoko-Dua Saudara Reserve in Minahasa, shelters a unique flora and fauna. Like the rest of the peninsula, this area is famous for its constant volcanic activity. A more appropriate setting for the special character of Minahasa society hardly seems imaginable!

▲ *The volcanic landscape of Minahasa has fascinating surprises in store for the traveller: the sulphate lake of Linow.*

Every ***adat*** *house in the mountain world of the Toraja has at least one rice shed; the space between the houses and storehouses serves as feasting-ground and work space.* ▼

6 Moluccas

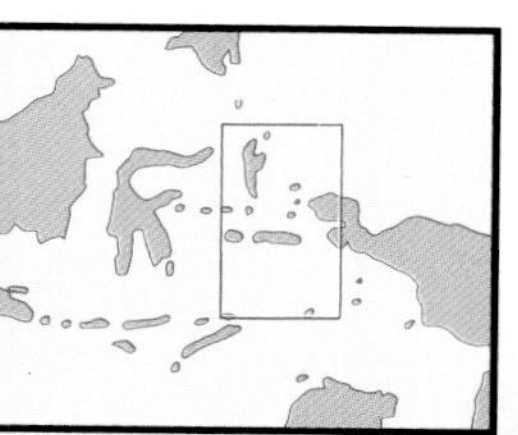

Once, the pungent smell of spices drew all the world's attention to them: the Moluccas. Tiny islands with a golden lustre attracting tradesmen from far away, like flies to honey. And on the heels of the merchants came the world reformers, bringing their religious message. The traders have long since turned their attention elsewhere; the messengers have remained.

▲ *Mass tourism has not yet discovered the white sandy beaches of the* **pasisir**. *The government hopes that this will soon change; in regional development policy the promotion of tourism has been given priority.*

With the arrival of Dutch traders in the Moluccas, the Protestant Mission also came into action, training locals in Ambon to become clergymen long before this was done in other parts of Indonesia. In the Ambonese *pasisir*, Protestantism developed into an essential part of the ethnic identity, yet relations between the ancient *adat* and Christianity always remained strained. According to Anneke Wessels the clergy now has the upper hand.

What seems to be far less fraught with tension, is the relation between another world religion, Islam, and the system of traditions honoured by the Giman in Halmahera. Though this ethnic group only recently adopted Islam, Dik Teljeur already observes such a profound and harmonious interweaving of traditional and Islamic opinions that they can hardly be distinguished.

In Maluku Tenggara the difference between old and new is easier to establish. Though conversion to Christianity was started early by clergymen working for the Dutch East India Company, on these southern islands ancient forms of ritual symbolism have been preserved. Nico de Jonge illustrates this with a striking example from the remote Babar archipelago.

Adat and Church in the Ambonese pasisir

In the Moluccas trade dates back at least to the beginning of the Christian era. Even then merchants from Java, Sulawesi and far-off China were attracted by the cloves that were originally found only in the string of islands along the west coast of Halmahera. There was also intensive trade with the Banda archipelago, south of Ambon, where nutmeg and mace were bought. With Asian and Arab tradesmen as intermediaries, the spices reached the Western world. The increasing European demand in the fourteenth century further stimulated Moluccan trade. Sailing routes followed the coasts of West Seram and the small islands of Ambon-Lease (Ambon, Saparua, Haruku and Nusa Laut). Immigrants from all over Indonesia settled in and around the market towns that developed here. Later this region came to be called the Ambonese *pasisir*, and its inhabitants Ambonese. The word *pasisir* means coastal region, and in Indonesia it is used

Genesis in the pasisir

Originally, the geographical name Maluku (Moluccas) refers to the islands around Ternate in what is now the district of Maluku Utara (North Moluccas). For centuries the name has been linked to this centre of clove cultivation. Today's province of Maluku now extends far beyond that area. Not only do the northern islands belong to it, but also the southern district of Maluku Tenggara (South-East Moluccas) and the Ambonese *pasisir*.

The descendants of the Ambonese who came to settle in this trading region hundreds of years ago, are still called ***orang pendatang***, immigrants. The origin of the forefathers of these families is usually known, and there are many myths about them, full of miraculous events. As ***moyang sakti***, holy ancestors, these forbears wield great power.

The members of the indigenous families in the ***pasisir*** are called ***orang asli***. Tradition has it that they come from Mount Nunusaku in West Seram. In the world view of the Christian Ambonese, the old myths of origin set on this mountain, have merged with the story of Genesis. The first people lived on the slopes of Nunusaku in peace and abundance. When they were made to leave paradise after the Fall, they scattered over Seram and the islands of Ambon-Lease.

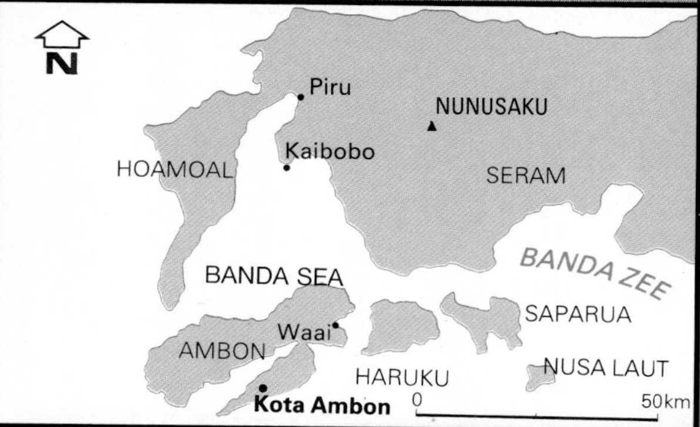

◄ *The province of Maluku covers an enormous area, and in many respects the Moluccan cultures differ from one another. The traditions of Maluku Tenggara closely resemble those of the Lesser Sundas. Material expressions of culture, such as the headdress of this South-East Moluccan woman, also indicate this.*

to refer to areas with a long-standing tradition of trade and a population of mixed origin.
When cloves, nutmeg and mace became more expensive in the West, and the very name of 'Spice Islands' even gained a magical sound to it, the Europeans started a feverish quest for the regions of origin: the era of the great voyages of discovery had started. Portuguese sailors were the first to trace the coveted sailing route to the Moluccas. In 1512 they set foot on Ambonese soil. From that moment on they made frantic attempts to control the lucrative spice trade. After about a century these efforts came to an end when in 1605 the Dutch appeared on the scene and drove out the Portuguese.

*A **dukun** looks into the future. Over a glass of water he phrases a question that ▼ can be answered by a simple 'yes' or 'no'.*

Then he breaks a chicken's egg in the water ... and mumbles a secret formula.

Now he can read the answer to his question in the glass: if the yoke floats on ▲ top, it is 'yes', otherwise 'no'.

Dukun

*Ancestors are a major support to their descendants. They protect the possessions and rights of the family group, and at the request of their progeny, they will assist them in case of emergency. Every family saves its own secret spells with which to invoke the ancestors' assistance. Every village also has its own **dukun**: specialists distinguished by their extensive knowledge of magic rituals. Though they can also predict the future, influence fate, and identify a thief, in particular the **dukun** work as healers.*

*According to the Ambonese, serious diseases always have a specific cause. This may be a violation of the **adat**, a sin against God's commandments, a broken promise, an evil spirit or witchcraft. A **dukun** knows certain methods of divination with which he can find out the cause of the patient's illness, and he knows exactly what to do about such cases. True, the pills, powders and especially the injections administered by Kota Ambon doctors are highly appreciated, but at the same time people here are convinced that Western medicine can merely strengthen the patient's body. The **dukun's** treatment is aimed primarily at removing the cause, which is a necessary condition for recovery.*

*Every **dukun** has his own techniques which he will only reveal to his successor, usually his son. He may never use his knowledge to his own advantage nor to harm others. His powers are regarded as a gift of God, that will be taken away when abused.*

Dutch attempts to monopolize trade were more successful than their predecessors' had been. After several bloody battles that wiped out the whole population of Banda and the Seram peninsula of Hoamoal, they managed to utterly subject the coast people. The empire of the Dutch East India Company was established, and the heart of clove cultivation was moved to Ambon-Lease. Under Western rule the small island of Ambon was to develop into the pre-eminent economic and political centre of the Moluccas.

The Ambonese pasisir

Where the Portuguese built their fort, over four centuries ago, now lies Kota Ambon, capital both of the Maluku Tengah district (Central Moluccas) and of the province of Maluku. The town is wedged in between hills on the one side and an inner bay on the other: over a hundred and thirty thousand people work and live here, packed together in an area of less than six square kilometres.
At first glance there is little in this overcrowded Kota Ambon to remind us of its long colonial past. The stately government buildings and shady trees that used to determine the appearance of its streets, have been destroyed by heavy bombings during World War II. Instead, now there are banks, schools, university buildings, army barracks, government offices and hospitals. Small Kota Ambon can hardly stand comparison to the bigger towns of Java, Sumatra and Sulawesi, but as the Moluccas' centre of trade and administration, its regional importance is greater than ever.
The developments that have changed the appearance of Kota Ambon over the last decades, have not left the neighbouring villages untouched. With the extension of the road network and of the shipping services between the islands of the *pasisir*, traffic between town and hinterland has increased tremendously over the past few years. Sports shoes and jeans sold at the big Kota Ambon market have found their way to all villages in the region, and so have plastic utensils and imported foodstuffs. More and more young Moluccans abandon their home villages to seek education or work in town. Kota Ambon beckons; the countryside has little more to offer but a farmer's existence.
In the *pasisir* villages the people live traditionally off small-scale agriculture and fishing. A lot of time is spent in the fields and at sea, so that villages often even seem deserted. And this picture is hardly affected by the latest Indonesian top hits blaring almost non-stop through the empty, dusty streets.

▲ *Kota Ambon's attraction has a wide radius. With its tricycle taxis it has the atmosphere of a big city, and the* ***pasar*** *is a real commercial junction. Here farmers and fishermen can sell their produce, and all kinds of modern consumer goods are on sale that are not only of practical use to the Ambonese, but also offer a certain status.* ▼

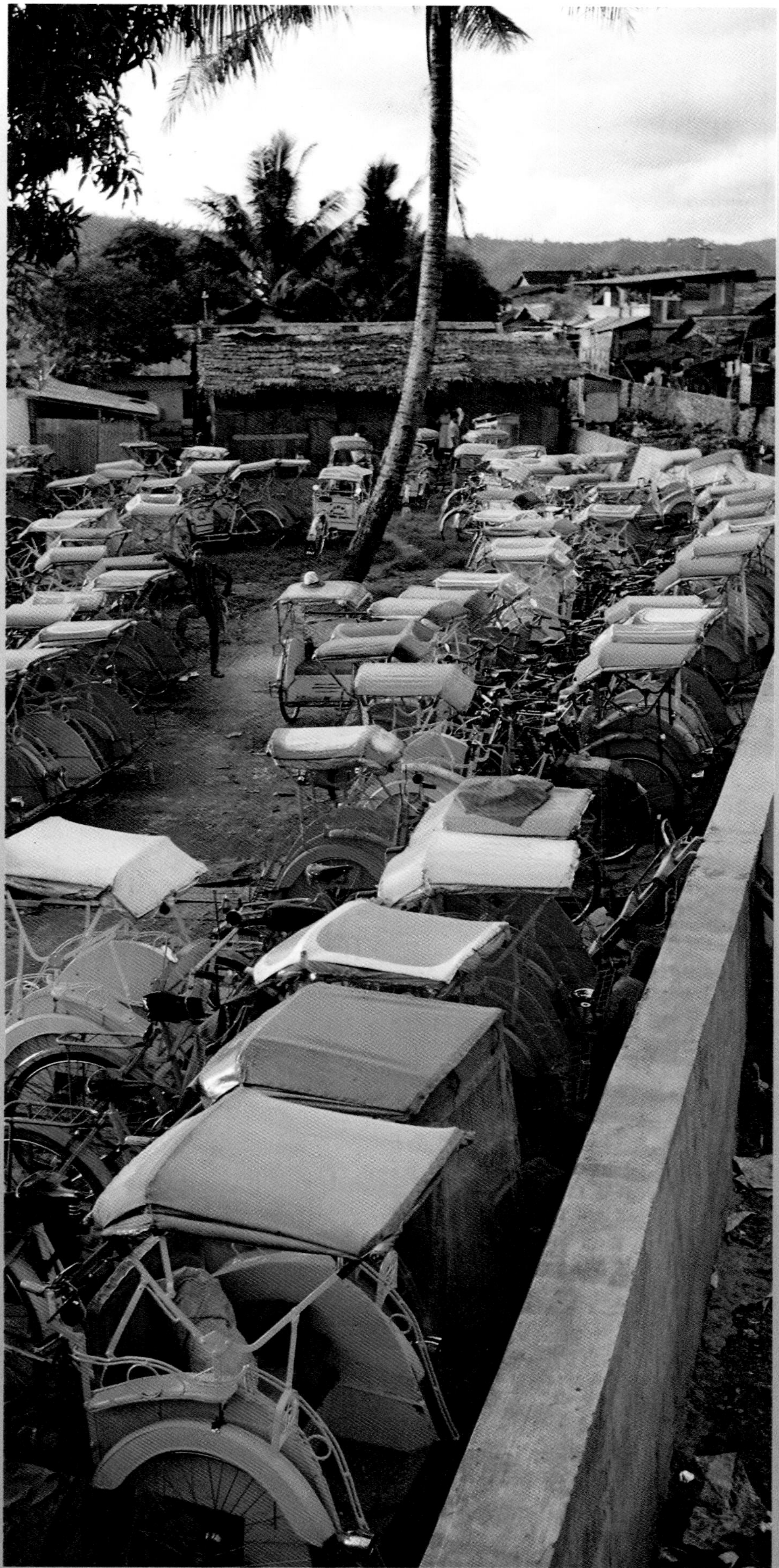

▲ *The church of Kaibobo in West Seram has just been restored: the new zinc roof sparkles in the sunlight.*

▲ *A black sarong and smock are the women's traditional church attire. The sash worn over the shoulder, is often decorated with hundreds of little beads, a precious possession.*

▲ *Since a Dutch minister introduced the flute around 1840, church singing is accompanied by a bamboo-flute orchestra.*

Agama Ambon

About half of the *pasisir* population is Muslim, the other half is Protestant. Any Christian village is recognized from afar by its steeple rising from the foliage of shady fruit trees, like a beacon plastered white. Surrounded by simple houses of stone or *gaba-gaba* (sago-palmleaf ribs), the modern style of recently built churches strikes one as futuristic, almost. Quite often these structures are the result of competition between neighbouring villages trying to outdo each other in the size and architecture of their places of worship. A religious community will make great sacrifices for the church and for village prestige. And relatives in Jakarta or the Netherlands, as well as Christian or Islamic villages with which there is a brotherhood relation (*pela*), usually make contributions to emphasize their solidarity with the village.

A Sunday morning in a Christian village: after the church-bells have rung, the villagers go to church with appropriate modesty. Accompanied by the legato sounds of a bamboo-flute orchestra, they will sit down on the long, low benches on either side of the aisle. The younger women are dressed in the leading Kota Ambon fashion. Their Western dresses in exuberant pink, yellow and blue, light up brightly among the black of the traditional church attire of their elders. When the minister enters, everyone rises respectfully. From his high pulpit he admonishes the congregation, sometimes in a softly penetrating voice, then in loud and passionate tones. Sermons and prayers are alternated with wistful-sounding songs, sung melodically and with dedication by various small choirs and the congregation.

The Protestants in the *pasisir* are very conservative. Any change the minister wants to introduce, inevitably meets with resistance from the elder parishioners. These people are strongly aware of deep-rooted church traditions and do not appreciate a break with the past; their idea is that any change in the tried and tested rituals will diminish their mystical power. Some villages in the *pasisir* have been Christian for nearly five hundred years, and Protestant for over three and a half centuries. Over all that time Protestantism has developed into an essential part of the ethnic identity. The Ambonese in the *pasisir* even speak with pride of their *agama* Ambon: the Ambonese religion.

The adat: marriage

For centuries now the Church has exerted its influence on the community here, at the expense of many local traditions: the old *adat* has lost terrain. Earlier village rituals have given way to Sunday services, Holy Communion and the Protestant holidays, and the transition from one stage of life to the next is no longer marked by the original ceremonies but by baptism, confirmation or Christian funeral.

A number of *adat* rules have always been honoured, though; especially those regarding kinship and village organization are still strictly adhered to. For example, fishing grounds and farmland are still divided according to the *adat*, and the positions in the village council may only be held by members of certain patrilineal family groups. Neither have the *pela*, the brotherhood relations between villages, ever been debated. In accordance with the sacred oath sworn by their ancestors, *pela* members will always help each other and never refuse each other anything. In the *pasisir*, marriage too, is still subject to *adat* procedures. But in contrast to the other remaining *adat* rules, these marriage customs have their Protestant counterparts. Hence it is especially in this area that the two traditions collide.

The *adat* distinguishes two ways of marrying. One is *kawin minta*, the 'marriage by proposal': the boy's parents formally ask for the girl's hand in marriage, and the other is *kawin lari*, the 'marriage by elopement': the girl runs away with the boy. In practice, for various reasons the latter is the most frequent by far. Sometimes it is clear beforehand that a proposal would be rather useless, as the parents will not agree with their daughter's choice. In other cases the proposal has been made, but negotiations have reached a deadlock, for instance due to mutual accusations of impolite behaviour, or disagreement about the size of the bride-price. But in contrast to the Tolaki in South-East Sulawesi, among whom inflated bride-price demands are the pre-eminent cause of marriage by elopement (see Chapter 5), in the *pasisir* pregnancy is the most common cause: this avoids the time-consuming negotiations involved in a marriage by proposal. The boy's parents often co-operate if their son wants to run away with his beloved. True, a marriage by proposal will add to their status, but because of the elaborate feasts they are supposed to finance, it is also very expensive. So the prestigious *kawin minta* usually remains a dream, cherished by fathers of nubile daughters.

If an elopement is decided on, the couple will set a time. In the chosen night the young man steals to the house of his beloved with a few bachelor friends. There may be some danger here: the father may be so set against his daughter's will that he will use force in trying to prevent her escape. If the abduction succeeds nonetheless, the friends of the bridegroom-to-be will announce this at the top of their voices. Triumphantly they will shout "*putus bujang-e*", words that indicate the end to a bachelor's existence. When this cry disturbs the nocturnal silence, the villagers, startled out of their sleep, will know a girl has been abducted. An anxious father will see his suspicions confirmed and find his daughter's bed empty: instead there will be a bottle of *sopi* (the locally distilled liquor) and a letter telling him in poetic phrases that he need not worry: his daughter is in good hands. The letter and the *sopi* have been left by the boy, as the *adat* prescribes.

When his parents think the time has come, they will let the girl's parents know that they would like to visit them to ask their forgiveness for what has happened. If the 'bride-givers' agree, and accept the 'bride-takers'' humble apologies, the size of the bride-price is discussed. Only when this *adat* payment has been settled, can the union be blessed in church. For the *pasisir* people the church ceremony is the finishing touch: the solemn conclusion of the marriage negotiations prescribed by *adat*.

All this may take a long time. The girl's father may be so mad about the 'kidnapping' of his daughter that he refuses to receive the bride-takers' delegation. Public

▲ *Off the coast of Waai in Ambon, travellers await the departure of their boat to Seram.*

Pela: advantage and security

Nearly all villages in the ***pasisir*** maintain one or more brotherhood relationships, ***pela***. Some of these pacts go back a long time. It is assumed that the first ***pela*** were a kind of peace treaties. The Ambonese used to be headhunters, and at the time life in the ***pasisir*** was far from safe. So as to limit the dangers to some extent, neighbouring villages often concluded a pact, so that at least they would have nothing to fear from each other. Endless village feuds too, would be resolved by vowing brotherhood to each other. A few old ***pela*** date from the tumultuous wars during the reign of the Dutch East India Company.

More recently, ***pela*** have been concluded after one village had helped another in times of economic crisis or in building a church or mosque. Such pacts are mainly found between the coastal villages of Seram and villages in the densely populated islands of Ambon-Lease, where food and raw materials are more scarce.

Misfortune also underlay the ***pela*** between the Seram village of Kaibobo, on the coast, and some quite elevated mountain villages. But in this case it was not so much a matter of economic motives, but of religious ones. In the years after World War II the mountain villages were hit by disease and scarcity. A minister established that this was God's punishment for the villagers' past sins: they had only recently been converted to Christianity, and previously they had often gone head-hunting among the people of Kaibobo, which was Christian. It was decided that the inhabitants of Kaibobo would be asked for forgiveness, and on this occasion the ***pela*** was concluded. Though many of the elderly in Kaibobo attended this ceremony, they no longer remember the names of the mountain villages. Far more important to them is the link with the little village of Waai in Ambon. This ***pela*** relationship guarantees travellers from Kaibobo a good reception and a seat in the often overcrowded mini buses to Kota Ambon. In turn, people from Waai benefit from the pact by being allowed to beat sago on Kaibobo territory, and to fish off the coast as much as they like. Thus practical considerations play a part both in concluding a ***pela***, and in maintaining it.

In Kaibobo in Seram a simple but effective construction makes meal out of sago marrow. ▼

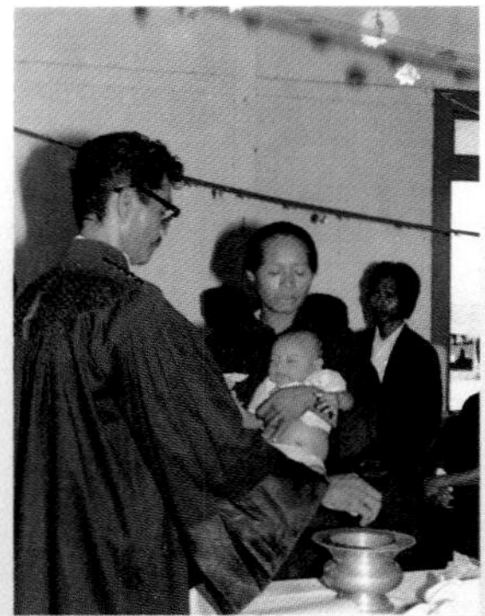

▲ *In the* ***pasisir*** *the christening of every child is a festive occasion.*

opinion will turn against him in this case: his pride is an obstacle both to a proper procedure and to his daughter's happiness. The marriage by elopement may not be the ideal form of marriage, but it is a well-accepted one. In the end the offended father will nearly always give in, though occasionally by that time the couple will have produced one or even more children.

The Church is extremely unhappy about the number of children born out of wedlock in this way. That is why the synod has decided that the first of a series of illegal children may not be baptized before the parents have been married in church. Thus one hopes to accelerate the confirmation of marriage in church, that is before payment of the bride-price prescribed by the *adat*. By turning around the sequence that emphasizes the *adat*, the couple is tempted to take a step that relegates the *adat* to second place. Though in the community's view, to pass up baptism is a heavy sanction (the high infant mortality rate carries the serious risk that a child dies without being baptized, and consequently does not go to heaven), this strategy is not very successful: obviously the Church has stumbled on a hard core in the Ambonese society.

The explanation of this indomitability can be found in the traditional village and kinship organization. Every Ambonese village consists of a number of family groups. To every villager, membership of one of these groups secures his or her existence. It gives them the right to catch fish off the coast, or to grow sago on certain patches of land. These rights are protected by the ancestors. They see to it that only their descendants and the in-laws use that land; outsiders will pay for violation with disease and death. Hence it is of vital importance that it be clear to which family group one belongs.

As long as the bride-price has not yet been paid, the *adat* decrees that the children belong to the mother's group. But if under the minister's pressure the parents were to marry in church before the bride-price is paid, the children would get the father's name. This is an unthinkable situation: not only would the ancestors strike the nuclear family with disease, but due to this half-hearted status the children would have no rightful place in either family group – a position that would make life in the village community virtually impossible for them.

This girl eloped a few days ago. Now, with her partner and his family, she is visiting her parents to ask their forgiveness. Reluctantly, her father has received ▼ *them: furiously he dwells at length on some careless behaviour of the 'bride-takers'. According to the* ***adat*** *he has a right to do so, and he demands satisfaction.*

Adat and agama

The *adat* marriage rules concern the relationship between two groups, whereas the church ceremony seals the personal link between bride and groom. Instead of *adat* and Church being alternatives, they complement each other.

Christian Ambonese occasionally compare the *adat* to the Jews' Torah. They believe that God has given their ancestors the *adat*, as a guideline for their lives and those of their descendants. These prescriptions have to do with the relations between people in this temporary life on earth. In contrast, in the Church the Ambonese focus their attention on the eternal: the heavenly deliverance from earthly sufferings. This division of tasks between the *adat* and the Church is embodied in two important village authorities: the *raja* (village head) and the minister. They are called the father and mother of the village. The minister is the female half of the couple; he always comes from another village and has moved in, so to speak.

The dualism apparent in this view of the relation between the *adat* and religion fits in with ancient symbolism. Thinking in dichotomies, such as heaven and earth, man and woman or father and mother, is an ever recurring ordering principle in the Indonesian cultures. Each pair forms a unity, but at the same time there is a certain tension between the two components. That there is tension between the *adat* and *agama*, is quite certain – as the vicissitudes of marriage clearly show. And in practice, the symbolic marriage of *raja* and minister isn't harmonious either. A minister is never appointed in his home village, so that he will not be tied to the local *adat* and the *raja's* authority. By interfering in 'worldly' matters, he will increasingly trespass on the domain of the village head, and this frequently leads to conflicts. Occasionally, the whole village gets involved in a quarrel between the minister and the *raja*, but usually no one takes sides, as everyone has to live *menurut agama dan menurut adat*: according to religion and according to the *adat*.

Even now, after over three hundred and fifty years of Protestantism, the ancestors still occupy a vitally important position in the lives of their progeny. But it is uncertain whether they will be able to maintain this position. Increasing government influence, radio and television, education and urbanization: these all encroach on the sheltered village life, and lead to a more individualistic society. The *adat* in the *pasisir* is increasingly undermined: times seem to favour the minister.

▲ *In villages far from the administrative centre, ten or more couples will often marry simultaneously, to make the official's long voyage worthwhile. Thus the civil confirmation can directly precede the church wedding – as it should.*

▲ *Nowadays most Christian couples prefer Western wedding attire.*

The money collected during the church service, is counted. Some coins are wrapped in white paper; to such an offering a special wish is attached. ►

▼ *A typical scene in the Ambonese* **pasisir**: *cloves are dried in the sun.*

▲ *Out of bamboo, a* **dukun** *makes a* **matakau**. *Anyone who ignores this warning, will get a swollen belly, as the Chinese lantern-like shape indicates.*

Matakau and sasi

If somebody wants to protect his crop from thieves, he can have a **matakau** *placed near his field. A* **matakau** *is a warning sign that has been cursed. It often graphically depicts the fate that will strike a thief. Thus there are* **matakau** *shaped like grass-hoppers. In case of theft this insect will 'hop about' in the thief's stomach and cause terrible cramps there. Other* **matakau** *are more abstract, like the bamboo sticks crossed diagonally, causing deafness.*
To combat the theft of young coconuts, **matakau** *are rarely used. Instead, the owner will ask the minister to place his coconut palms under the protection,* **sasi**, *of the Church for a certain period of time. If this request is granted, the Church Council will pray to God to keep the coconuts from theft. During a church service this is publicly announced, so that every villager will know that anybody violating the* **sasi** *by taking the nuts off the tree or picking them up, will be punished by God.*

A **matakau** *in the shape of a locust keeps watch. The bit of red cloth around his neck indicates that magic* ▼ *powers are involved.*

Seafood

The Moluccan waters are good fishing grounds; in all islands seafood is the daily fare. Now that foreign fishing companies have discovered this wealth, ships from Japan and Taiwan with modern equipment prey on tuna and shrimp on a large scale, thus exhausting the Moluccan seas.
With the stock of fish, the indigenous population's livelihood is also at risk. The simple fishing techniques of the local fishermen still provide enough, but every year they see their catches diminishing.
For the time being, ***laor*** fishing is not threatened. On March evenings, during the Palola seaworm's mating season, by the light of torches or lamps, the coast people scoop up from the dark seawater great numbers of the sexually mature parts of these animals. Fried or grilled a real treat.

*◂ The **laor**, the wriggling mass that people have been looking forward to so eagerly, is scooped from the sea.*

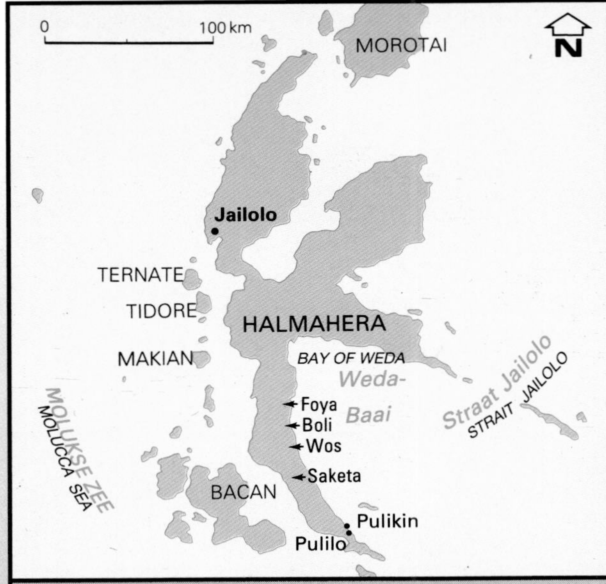

Malo Plim

Together with Morotai, Ternate, Tidore, Makian and Bacan, the island of Halmahera belongs to the group that used to be known as the 'Spice Islands'. Its flora and fauna closely resemble those of Irian Jaya, and the southern peninsula has some 20,000 inhabitants. Most of these are migrants. The indigenous ethnic groups are jointly called ***Malo Plim***, the 'Five Regions'. These include the Foya, the Boli and the Wos on the east coast of the peninsula, the Saketa on the west coast, and the Giman on both sides of the southern tip, in the villages of Pulikin and Pulilo.

The Giman version of Islam

Unlike the population of the Ambonese *pasisir*, the majority in Maluku Utara consider themselves Muslims. Long before the arrival of the first Christians, Islamic merchants brought a tolerant version of Islam to these northern islands, a version marked by West-Indonesian influences. This helped to blend the old and new religious beliefs in this region into one harmonious whole: a striking difference from the *pasisir*, where European Christianity and the local *adat* came to oppose one another far more sharply.

The arrival of Islam

The North-Moluccan islands used to be subordinated to the princes of Ternate, Tidore, Bacan and Jailolo. The islands had always been the centre of clove cultivation, and foreign merchant ships had called at them from times immemorial. Islamic merchants too, discovered the 'golden fruit''s region of origin. Some of them settled in Ternate and introduced their religion here. By the end of the fifteenth century they managed to win over the four local princes to Islam; after their conversion these called themselves 'Sultans'. The first Europeans to arrive at the 'Spice Islands' shortly afterwards, were quite surprised to be greeted here by 'Sultans'.

Though the political centres were islamized fairly early, the vast regions under the reign of the Sultans, came under the influence of the new religion only gradually. It was merely the local leaders who were pressured into becoming Muslims. The really massive conversions took place centuries later. In Halmahera

In any Moluccan village the arrival or departure of a boat interrupts the day-to-day worries. Elated, the young flock to the beach, the travellers are greeted or seen off; soon after, the murmur of the sea is all that ▾ remains.

for instance, the largest island in Maluku Utara, a substantial part of the population was persuaded to convert to Islam as late as the nineteenth century. The image in which the new religion manifested itself here, was characterized by a decidedly Indonesian streak; hence it fitted in easily with the indigenous culture. Together with the long period of introduction, among the local cultures this led to syncretism: such a thorough blending of traditional and Islamic customs that they are hardly distinguishable now.

The Giman

A visit to the Giman, a small ethnic group living in relative isolation in South Halmahera, provides a fascinating picture of the way in which Islamic customs have been fitted into a local culture. In a dug-out equipped with an outboard engine, one can cross from Ternate to Halmahera, which largely consists of four peninsulas, their shapes all long and jagged. For some 24 hours the boat will follow the coastline until it reaches the extreme southern tip of the island. Here lie Pulikin and Pulilo, the two villages of the Giman, a group of some fourteen hundred people with a language of their own. Their livelihood is agriculture, sago, fishing and deer-hunting.

After centuries of domination by the Sultan of Ternate, it was only in the last century that the Giman actually and collectively adopted the religion that this prince propagated. But prior to this step, in many respects Islamic ideas must have 'tooled' their culture. This may be deduced from the way in which an originally Islamic custom has been incorporated in the local *adat*: the circumcision of boys and girls.

Circumcision as initiation

The transition to Islam meant that henceforth all new-born babies were to be circumcised. According to Islamic principles circumcision is not compulsory, but *sunat*, 'advisable'. The doctrine indicates that circumcision is a deserving deed: "Mohammed was born circumcised. We must follow Mohammed and be circumcised too".

Of course the operation differs according to sex. Like other peoples who have accepted Islam, the Giman make a small cut in the girl's clitoris; the tip of the boy's foreskin is placed in a bamboo clamp and cut off with a razor. Unlike girls, who are circumcised at a very early age – in many cases when they are forty days old – boys wait till they are between five and nine; prior to which it is considered too great a risk.

Contrary to Islamic rules, the Giman thoroughly regard following the circumcised Mohammed as an obligation. In their view, a child gains the status of Muslim only through this operation, and for boys there even is a more compelling reason: for a man circumcision is a necessary preparation for marriage. The Giman consider a non-circumcised man unfit to fulfil his duties as a husband, since he is said to be still 'unclean'.

The reason for this uncleanliness dates from the moment of his birth, when he comes into contact with his mother's vagina. The Giman regard this as a form of incest, which makes the relationship between mother and son unclean. And whoever is unclean, may neither touch the Koran, nor join in prayers and fasting. And in Pulikin and Pulilo a non-circumcised man is not allowed to attend ritual meals, ceremonies at which a good husband and father is supposed to represent his family.

Clearly, the Giman see circumcision as an important condition for marriage. This cleansing of the man by removing his foreskin is phrased in a simple metaphor: "To be able to eat a banana, it must first be peeled. Thus a man, in order to 'eat' (marry), must also be peeled, his uncleanliness must be removed". It is clear to which extent an originally Islamic custom like the circumcision has been fitted into the Giman world view. The 'Gimanizing' of circumcision has transformed it into a full-fledged initiation ritual.

An 'old' taboo

The interior of South Halmahera is devoid of human life, but teems with swine. For religious reasons the Islamic Giman do not consider these animals fit for consumption. This is one of the reasons why the pigs have constantly grown in number, and have become a real pest. Continuously harvests are destroyed, and apparently many kinds of fruit are true delicacies to them. The story goes that one swine stood on top of another in order to reach a bunch of bananas!

One might think that Islam, in banning the consumption of pork, had presented the Giman with a serious problem here, and that after conversion to this religion it must have been very difficult for them to leave this high-protein food untouched. Not at all, in the view of today's inhabitants of Pulikin and Pulilo. They point out that even before the conversion to Islam, pork had always been 'taboo'. Pigs and humans are said to have the same kind of skin, hence to eat pork would be a form of cannibalism. The Giman are convinced that on eating pork, one's hair will fall out and one's skin will erupt in such gaping wounds that death is inevitable. Probably, the ban on eating pork was adopted from Islam at a very early date. Nobody remembers that it is not originally a Giman custom – which is not surprising when we see how completely this taboo has become embedded in the local culture.

Mounting and descending

The ceremonial celebration that accompanies a circumcision, beautifully illustrates the initiation character of this operation. Because of the financial sacrifices it demands, mainly due to the quantities of rice needed, the feast usually takes place at a later date than the actual circumcision. To cut costs, ceremonies are often postponed until there is an opportunity to celebrate several occasions at the same time. It is far from unusual to combine it with the ritual cutting of a baby's hair, or with a ceremony performed to conclude the older children's Koran education. If financial problems are really pressing, the celebrations are sometimes held 'secretly': after prayers in the mosque the father will whisper his invitation to only a few men.

Usually, though, a circumcision feast is celebrated with great ostentation and guests are openly invited. In front of the house a temporary shelter is built, and a long feasting table is placed underneath. At nightfall all the male guests sit down here. For this occasion, instead of their daily sarong, they will wear a shirt and trousers. When everybody is seated, all will join in reciting a prayer from the Koran, a *doa salamat*, to lighten their ancestors' burden in the hereafter. Finally, tea and biscuits are served and the men

▲ *The mosque of Pulilo with a view of the bay.*

Hakim sara

Islam has deep roots among the Giman, although the actual conversion only dates from the nineteenth century. Following this transition a mosque was built both in Pulikin and in Pulilo, and 'mosque staff' were appointed: an ***imam***, a ***modin*** and a ***hatib***. The ***imam*** leads in prayer five times a day, the ***hatib*** reads the Friday sermon, and the ***modin*** summons the believers for the ritual prayers.
But to the Giman these three religious functionaries are far more than just mosque staff. This is apparent from, among other things, the fact that these functions are hereditary, and reserved for members of certain family groups. In addition, the joint name for the three religious tasks is revealing: ***hakim sara***, 'Judge of Islamic Law'. Within the community the ***imam***, the ***modin*** and the ***hatib*** first of all supervise strict compliance with Islamic law.

At the head of the festive table two candidates are seated, ready for the ceremony that is to conclude their Koran instruction; the sacred book lies before them on the table. ▼

prepare for the night of feasting ahead.
While everything outside proceeds according to 'orthodox' Islamic rules, inside something of the *adat* is visible. Here the festivities begin with the so-called 'mounting' of a ceremonial bed. Surrounded by the women guests, the boys and girls at the centre of this ceremony lie down on a beautifully decorated bed fitted with a mosquito net and thus prepare, as it were, for the circumcision (which many of them will have already undergone, as was observed above). Sitting on the bed that is covered with colourful cushions, an old woman rubs them with white powder from head to toe. Powdered white and screened off from the outside world, here they are to await the new day. Under no circumstances may they leave the ceremonial bed; they must have their evening meal here as well. (Though of course they are allowed to get off in response to nature's call.)
In the meantime there is a constant stream of visitors; youngsters amuse themselves with music and dancing, while outside at the table dominoes is a popular game. It is only when the cocks crow and the day dawns, that the children are allowed to 'descend' from the bed to be circumcised, if this has not yet been done. Over time, the period spent on the ceremonial bed has diminished substantially. Instead of one single night, the children formerly had to stay there for up to two or three whole days.
In the afternoon, after their descent and possibly their circumcision, and after the final *doa salamat*, interest focusses on the children. Hence they are allowed to sit down at the head of the table, now laden with yellow and white rice, the latter in the shape of *jaha*: rice bars heated in bamboo stalks and boiled in coconut milk. After the men have recited another part from the Koran, one of them will take some strikingly shaped biscuits from a bowl on the table. These are the so-called *saro-saro*, small biscuits baked in the shape of a ring, a frog, a snake, or a human being. These are swung slowly in front of the children's faces, while a wish is expressed: "*saro-saro*, may you learn well, and become a teacher", or "*saro-saro*, may you go on a pilgrimage to Mecca when you are older". And, especially for the girls: "*saro-saro*, may you marry a pilgrim". These wishes exemplify that to the children a door has been opened on a new phase in their lives.

The ceremonial bed as womb

Mounting and descending are also part of other rituals that mark the life cycle of the Giman. For instance, on the eve of their wedding, bride and groom, each in their own home, must sit down on a bed and they too, must be rubbed with white powder. Only in the evening of the next day may they descend to be married.
This gives both ceremonies, of circumcision and wedding, the characteristics of a classical rite of passage, the ritual ensuring the transition to a new status in life. Just as the unmarried person gains the status of adult through marriage, the non-circumcised person becomes a true Muslim through circumcision, and in addition a boy thus becomes a potential marriage partner. The white powder that makes the skin 'soft' and 'light' serves to boost the health of the person going through the critical transition. Among the Giman, a fair skin is more than just an epitome of

After the marriage has been solemnized, bride and groom appear in public, 'enthroned' on their beautifully decorated seat. ▼

beauty, it is also a sign of vitality and success in life. The night of isolation on the bed may be compared to a new stay in the womb. The 'descent' from the bed and the ensuing circumcision or wedding ceremony may then be taken to be a symbolic rebirth into a following stage of life.

Mohammed's broken tooth

In addition to 'Gimanization' of Islamic customs, the reverse is also found: islamization of traditional Giman customs and views. Thus in Pulikin and Pulilo, filing the incisors is no doubt an ancient, pre-Islamic custom. During their puberty most boys and girls have these teeth filed to beautify them. With a small grindstone the upper and lower teeth are polished until they are beautifully even. The type of Islam the Giman were converted to, embraced the same custom; here old and new joined almost seamlessly.

But nowadays the Giman, like the Javanese Muslims, base the custom on an incident that reputedly took place at the battle of Uhud in Arabia (in 625). "Mohammed", the story goes, "fought the heathens. When his enemies approached, he hid in a cave. Here a *cicak* (house lizard) lived, and because of the noises it made, the enemies threw a stone into the cave. The stone broke one of Mohammed's teeth and that is why the prophet had them all evenly polished." This legend enables the Giman to see the filing of teeth as a good deed, for, as they argue once again, it is an imitation of the prophet.

Thus in many different ways the local *adat* and Islam are intertwined. Everywhere in South Halmahera this interweaving is intense, and in some cases old traditions and Islamic cultural expressions have given each other new meaning. The attraction of the special fruits of the Spice Islands has led to special cultures.

The wopal

Though in the course of many years the Giman have managed to reconcile many of their own customs with the Islamic points of departure, not all new ideas fit in with the old. Thus in performing the ceremony for certain marriages, one makes do with a unique compromise.

According to the Giman **adat**, *the bride-price that a groom hands to his in-laws, should really be responded to with a gift in return, from those 'bride-givers'. This gift is called* **wopal**. *But in Pulikin this return gift has been abolished, as it is believed to conflict with the Islamic view that grants the husband an exclusive right to his wife. The argument is that he obtains this right by handing over the bride-price; henceforth the daughter is no longer at her parents' disposal.*

But were the bridegroom to accept the traditional return gift from the bride's family, the rights to her would remain with his parents-in-law. Thus the **wopal** *custom was believed to conflict with Islam, which is why this return gift passed into disuse.*

But in Pulilo, the other Giman village, people are far more conservative, and though the villagers feel themselves to be true Muslims, they have maintained the **wopal** *in spite of Pulikin's changed opinions.*

So what happens if a Pulikin boy marries a Pulilo girl? For such a situation the following expensive compromise was contrived: the bridegroom pays the (normal) bride-price twice! The first time, to the satisfaction of the Pulilo people so true to the **adat**, *he duly receives a return gift from his in-laws. The second time round he will not get a* **wopal** *in return, thus satisfying the Pulikin people.*

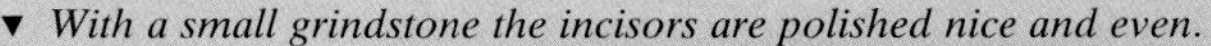

▼ *With a small grindstone the incisors are polished nice and even.*

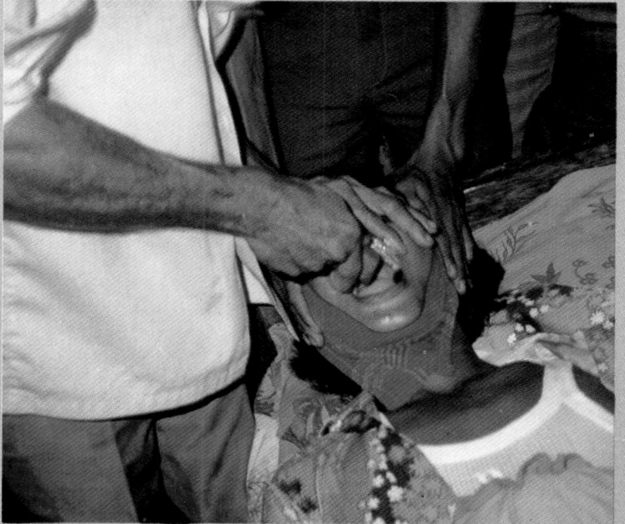

Aboard in Babar

In the deep south, far from market towns such as Ternate and Ambon, lie dozens of islands that came into contact with world economy only recently. Most of these emerge from the waters of the Banda Sea with hardly any vegetation. Nowhere near is the luxuriant flora of the northern Moluccas, the landscape is savannah-like, the soil unsuitable for cloves. Actually many islands in Maluku Tenggara are known mainly for the fact that economically there is nothing to be gained from them. Only during the rule of the Dutch East India Company (V.O.C.) was there a temporary interest in Aru and Kai: at the time the monoculture in the nutmeg centre of Banda necessitated the supply of sago from these islands. Christian and Islamic influences in the South-East Moluccas are quite recent, certainly if we compare them to the Ambonese *pasisir* and the surroundings of Ternate. Apart from a few Arab merchants, there are hardly any Muslims, and only in the course of this century did the Catholic and Protestant missions gain a foothold in these islands. The population of Aru, Kai and Tanimbar calls itself mainly Roman Catholic, while the islands between Timor and Tanimbar form a Protestant mission field.
Unfortunately for the population of Maluku Tenggara, their joining a world religion has not improved their communication with the rest of the world. Transport facilities to the provincial capital of Ambon are extremely limited, and during the east monsoon (from April to October) and the west monsoon (from December to March) rough waters render many islands in the southern Banda Sea hardly accessible.
A few times a month a coaster scrapped in Europe, leaves the port of Ambon for a tour of several weeks of the South-East Moluccas. The packed deck, with an awning of plastic sheets, is like a sailing market place. Traders and other passengers swarm everywhere, and unrolled sleeping mats truly are territories. Only the crew members smile: they have just pocketed the money for berths sold to military men and civil officials.
On the way the ship calls at towns and villages where administration officials reside, to unload rice as part of the salaries. Wind and weather permitting, the ship will sometimes anchor in more remote areas. Dozens of dug-out canoes dart for the ship, and at the stalls the paddlers quickly do their shopping. Usually they buy no more than a few articles of clothing, or batteries for their radios – which in many villages, for lack of television and cars, are the pre-eminent status symbols. Money, mainly used for church collections, is scarce; during the months before the monsoons break, when the sea is calm, the traditional barter trade flourishes everywhere. But most months of the year, big waves and small proas force many islanders into isolation.

The image of the boat

The great distance to Ambon is not merely geographical, it is also cultural. As in fact the islands of Maluku Tenggara form the end of the arch that runs from Bali to Irian Jaya, a cultural link with the Lesser Sunda Islands is more obvious; and the close relationship with this area has been proven many

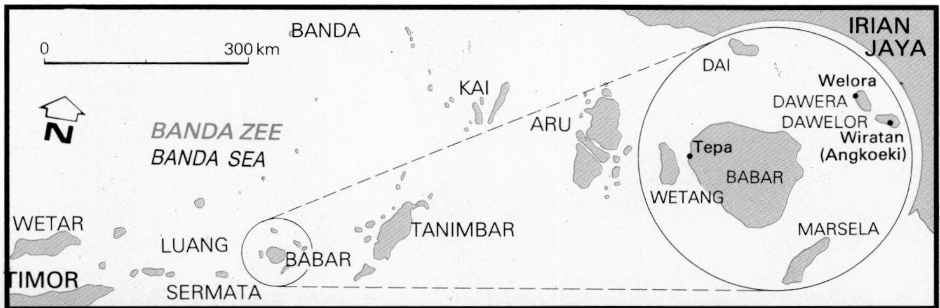

Babar: the kitchen of an archipelago

Halfway between Ambon and Australia, as a few inconspicuous specks in the Banda Sea, lie six islands forming the Babar archipelago. The group is named after the largest island, Babar. This fertile, densely wooded island is surrounded by five coral islands with hardly any vegetation: Marsela, Wetang, Dai, Dawera and Dawelor. Around 15,000 people live in the archipelago, more than half of them in Babar.
Due to the poor soil and the frequent lack of rain, the yield of the gardens in the smaller islands – which islands total about 50 square miles (125 kms^2) – is often insufficient to span the period between two harvests. So in order to survive, many turn to barter trade. Men set extra fish-traps or distill ***sopi*** for 'export'; women make all kinds of plaiting. In Babar these products are traded for vegetables and corn, the staple food.
But a number of families have tackled the recurrent problem in a different way: they have asked for and obtained garden land in Babar. Wind and weather permitting, they are at sea for hours to fetch new supplies, or as the islanders themselves put it, "just going to get something from the kitchen".

Maluku Tenggara as a transition area

The plant and animal life of the Moluccas form a meeting ground between the western part of Indonesia and Irian Jaya, or in a wider sense, between South-East Asia and Australia. The Moluccan animal life is sometimes characterized as a (relatively) impoverished Indonesian fauna, lacking for instance the large mammals of western Indonesia, and scantily complemented with specifically Moluccan species and some that represent Irian Jaya and Australia.
As early as the mid-nineteenth century research showed that western and eastern Indonesia do not form a coherent fauna region. Thus, on the basis of data he gathered during a stay in Indonesia from 1854 to 1862, the British naturalist Alfred Russel Wallace deemed it possible to separate both regions by a rather sharp line. This 'Wallace Line' which later became famous, runs between Kalimantan and Sulawesi in the north, and between Bali and Lombok in the south. West of this dividing line flora and fauna were said to show Asiatic characteristics, east of the line Australian species were said to prevail.
However, later research demonstrated that a delimitation greatly depends on the animal group studied, and that a sharp dividing line cannot be drawn. But it was established that east of the Wallace Line the fauna changes, and that, proceeding eastwards, one finds an increasing number of Australian species. The islands of Maluku Tenggara truly form an area of transition. As in the Lesser Sunda Islands, the animal world of Wetar, the most westerly island in this district, shows a predominance of Asiatic aspects, whereas the fauna of easterly Aru with its kangaroos (Macropodidae), cassowaries (Casuaris) – see illustration – and birds of paradise (Paradisaeidae), is practically the same as that of Irian Jaya.

◄ *Before the heavy rains of the West monsoon are unleashed, the gardens in the Babar archipelago are prepared for planting corn. In the years that the gardens have lain fallow, they became overgrown with bushes; these are now cut away and burnt.*

▲ *Every family in the Babar archipelago possesses heirlooms, usually gold objects and old textiles. When paying a fine for an* **adat** *offence, or on festive occasions, they are taken out of storage – with appropriate care.*

times. Thus the languages show characteristic similarities, and numerous traditions within the local east-Indonesian cultures have been shaped in a similar, clearly recognizable way.

In many cases the various fields that may be distinguished within a culture, such as the political system and the settlement pattern, are ordered by means of one comprehensive, dominant symbol. Sometimes this is the tree (of life), but very often it is the image of a boat that plays the integrating part. And where it does, as in house-building both in Maluku Tenggara and in the Lesser Sundas, the proa hardly ever appears as a separate, isolated metaphor; the arrangement of the village and the political system too, are then often ordered according to the model of a boat.

Among other islands in the South-East Moluccas, we find the proa symbolism in the Kai and Tanimbar archipelago, in Luang and Sermata, and within the Babar group. Here the boat models society at various levels, everywhere in a way peculiar to the area. Thus in the Babar archipelago we find a very specific pattern for the arrangement of the village, in particular in Dawera and Dawelor, two coral islands with characteristic, gradually ascending terrace layers. Seeing such a small settlement for the first time, one can hardly imagine a more tranquil scene. Beyond a row of coconut palms on the beach, the group of houses near the little church exudes an almost serene peace and quiet. In addition to the sound of the surf, only the monotonous pounding of the corn can be heard.

How different this situation actually was only recently: "With the exception of Tepa, the principal town, and a few native villages in Wetang, those in the various islands forming the Babar group are all built on steep heights and surrounded by thick walls, necessitated by the incessant state of war. But nowhere did I see walls as thick and high as in the islands of Dawera and Dawelor. The native village of Angkoeki for instance, has walls 3 metres thick and 6 metres high, entirely built of stacked sandstone blocks, and fitted with doors." The Dutch administration official Van Hoëvell was quite impressed by the 'eyries' he found in 1890. Soon after, the colonial authorities took action. All settlements on rocky plateaus were evacuated, and along the coast, in places easily checked, the current villages arose. Around 1920, after a massive conversion to Christianity, the last ramparts were demolished.

Helmsman, pilot and bailer-boy

Viewed from the limestone cliffs of Dawera, the 'new' village down below at the edge of the beach inadvertently reminds one of the model settlement of a transmigration project. The houses are neatly aligned, and even the rooftops point in one direction. Actually though, it conceals a pattern that is centuries old and based on the proa symbolism.

Once only one large clan lived inside the elevated fortress, in an impressive pile dwelling called the 'great house'. In this house (or in an annex) one was born, one married a relative, had children and died. The great house was a safe place in a

▲ *The village of Welora in Dawera. The traditional 'great house' is no longer found here; but there is a modernized version around which the Welorese live in smaller houses with separate kitchens outside.*

The 'great house'

In Dawera and Dawelor the traditional 'great house' is associated with a proa sailing from sunrise to sunset. The helmsman's part is found in the east, the pilot's in the west. Both halves of the house are separated by a central area, the ***ottuwlesol***, the 'sleeping-quarters of the unmarried men'; this also is the traditional spot for the men's common meal, and for entertaining the guests.

Indoors people orient themselves according to the 'direction in which the boat is sailing', with their backs to the east. Thus the right coincides with the north, and the left with the south. The names of the 'rooms' which in each half of the house are separated by a place for cooking, have been derived from this.

Lay-out and orientation of the great house:

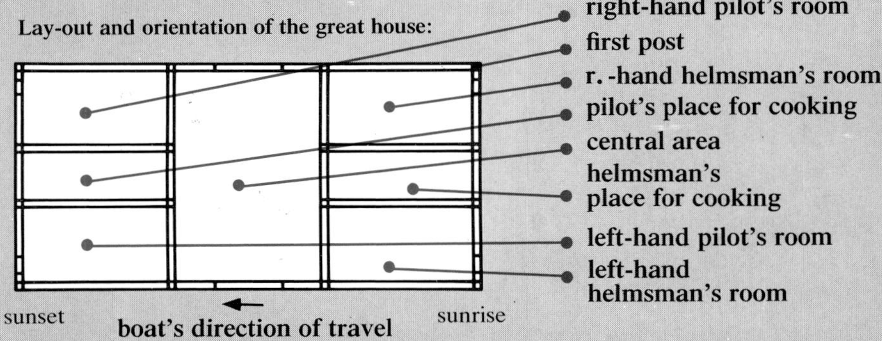

hostile world. Or in the inhabitants' terms: a proa on course, in rough water.

These symbolic words recurred in everything. Thus the house 'sailed' like a proa, following the sun's orbit, from east to west. The terms for the interior were in the same vein: the eastern half of the house was called the helmsman's part, and the western half was the pilot's. And the association of the house with a sailing proa was also apparent from the names of various elements of its construction. For instance, the first post, placed in the east, was called *mekamulol*, 'the one who holds the helm'.

The sun's orbit offered a religious basis on which to set the right course: this heavenly body was worshipped as a powerful, fatherly deity. The place where it rose, the east, was associated with life; where it set, the west, with death. Situating the first post (the 'birth') of a house, in the east, and the idea that the soul of a deceased person went to the west, to the island of Wetang, were based on this.

The marriage relations within the clan in the great house were closely linked with the division of the group into helmsmen and pilots. Probably a helmsman was obliged to look for a partner among the pilots, and vice versa. And again, the dichotomy was found in the political system. The helmsmen consider themselves the descendants of the original inhabitants of the place of residence; they were the progeny of the *warawluol*, the 'Lord of the Island'. The pilots, on the other hand, were said to descend from later arrivals. Hence the 'one' clan in the great house actually consisted of two separate groups. Two functions very common in eastern Indonesia were linked to this: the one who conducted rituals had to be a helmsman, and the wartime leader a pilot.

Thus many fields within society were ordered and interwoven by the proa symbolism. An extra dimension was added to this when (for lack of a more precise indication) after many years some isolated clans left their rocky cones to go and live together on larger mountain plateaus. The great houses placed together, jointly formed a new proa: the clan living to the east functioned as helmsman, the western clan as pilot. And in between, in the third great house, lived the bailer-boy. Such proa configurations were given names used in particular as battle cries that made the warriors invincible in war.

▲ *Ancestor statuettes carved from* **duyung** *bone.*

Surrounded by the sea

No inhabitant of Maluku Tenggara can get round the sea, hence its presence underlies a multitude of cultural expressions. Not only is the sea referred to indirectly, as in the proa symbolism, sometimes it stands out emphatically. In such cases the somewhat paradoxical relationship between Man and his surroundings is striking: though predominantly the sea is felt to be threatening, it has sometimes given Man life, provided him with ancestors. According to all kinds of myths the borderline between land and sea once was far less clearly drawn.

The origin of a number of food bans, aimed at sparing certain marine animals, sheds light on this side of the relationship. Thus members of various families in Maluku Tenggara are not allowed to eat **duyung**, *dugong (Dugong dugon); once an ancestor married a* **duyung**, *and by eating these animals they might partake of their own relatives.*

But in particular the sea is viewed as a world full of dangers. On its bed live octopuses with powerful tentacles that try and grasp every passing proa and drag it down. And in the shape of a ball of fire, all kinds of sea spirits may land on the foredeck at night, turn into an enormous rock there, and make the boat sink. On board, all sorts of magic means are kept ready to ward off this kind of hazard.

Nowadays, before their departure, the crew pray to God for a safe passage; under the influence of the Mission the ancestor statuettes one used to take along as personal protection, have disappeared from the cultures of Maluku Tenggara.

▼ *Ancestor statuette of coral limestone.*

The proa sails on

These kinds of 'proa' are now the lovely little villages on the coast. Nothing reminds one of the warlike times of old. With the kites flying their rounds high in the air, only the stories seem to have survived. Yet the great house of the pilot is still there in the west, the bailer-boy's in the middle, and the helmsman's at the eastern edge. Their dimensions have been reduced, the piles have disappeared from under them, but the rooftops still point east-west.

The idea of the proa lives on, not only in house-building and in village arrangement, but also in modern marine transport, or in soccer matches. Thus at sea, in the communal village boat, the helmsman must always be related to the clan that in the village occupies the symbolic position of helmsman. And the line-up of a village soccer team is reminiscent of the battle array in village wars (pilot up front, helmsmen to the rear); with the traditional proa names the teams are roused!

In addition, at least as fascinating are the symbolic dimensions of the human body as these seem to be embedded in the language of Dawera and Dawelor. This shows that not only the image of the community, but also that of Man himself originates from the model of a boat. Thus the local terms for nose and toe correspond to those for bow and rudder, and the shoulder blades are called *wedyol*, a word also meaning oar. In their wish to be buried according to the traditional orientation, some islanders still seem to refer to this image: the 'bow' of the deceased faces west, his or her 'rudders' face east. It is as if heaven lies in Wetang, the former 'Island of the Dead'.

Thus in many fields the familiar symbolism has survived, and despite the advent of Christianity the islanders have managed to maintain their own unique world view. For although they are subject to many changes, the house and the village, Man and community, still represent a very old and all-embracing cosmic order. The undisputed climax of village life, the New Year's celebrations, illustrate this.

The New Year's Feast

Under the Mission's influence, former seasonal ceremonies to extend the fertility of Man and fields with the aid of the ancestors and gods, have been reduced to an annual ritual that comes to a conclusion around Christmas. No one is allowed nor wants to miss this ceremony, hence everyone makes sure to be in the village before the beginning of December, at the end of the hot, quiet season. As Christmas approaches, the wind usually rises, bringing the first rains from the west. Suddenly everyone is busy at the cemetery. The graves are swept clean, inscriptions are touched up, and one night someone there hears the roll of drums, expected yet always frightening: time for the New Year's Feast!

Not only the living are now in their village, the dead have also returned. The drumbeats indicate that at night the *seka* is danced in the cemetery, and if one listens carefully in the evening, one can hear the sound of toe slippers shuffling through the village. Everyone is scared and stays indoors, out there the deceased are walking among the houses.

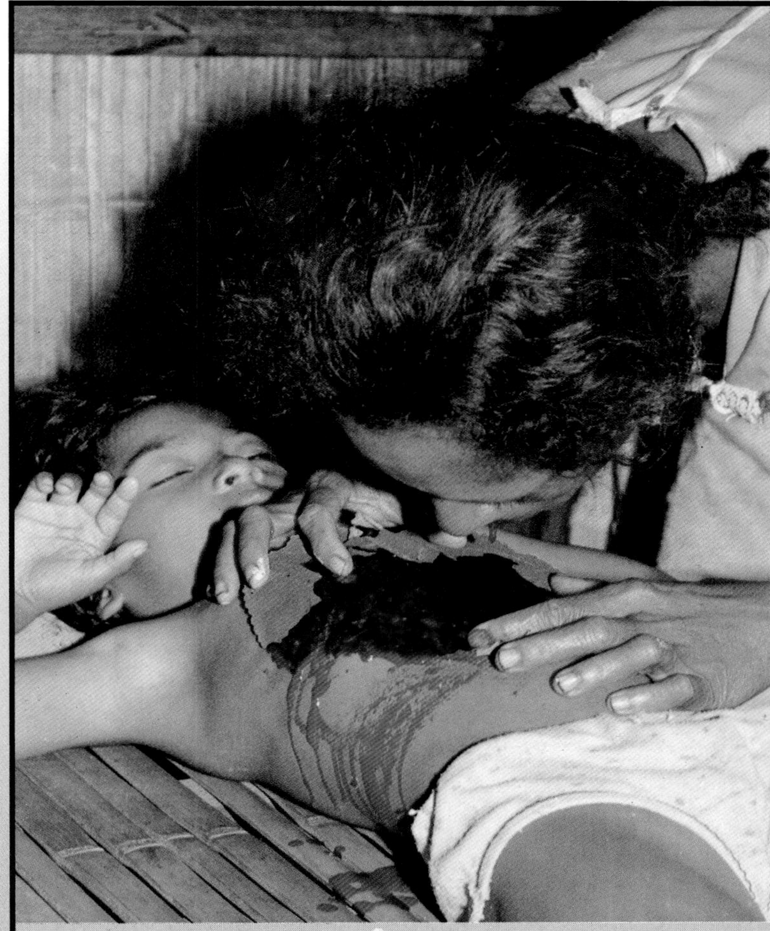

Illness and treatment

According to the Babarese a serious accident or a life-threatening disease nearly always results from an act of witchcraft, or is due to a lack of respect for the ancestors. Successful treatment is possible only if the precise cause is known.
Usually, in order to find the right treatment, a family gathering is organized; ***dukun*** like those working in the Ambonese ***pasisir***, are unknown in the Babar Islands. If it is concluded that the patient has been 'eaten' by a witch (that the spirit of the witch resides in the victim's body), it is tried to exorcize it by all sorts of means. In other cases it turns out that in a dream an angered ancestor has informed a member of the family about the background of the illness. In this way men who avoid the necessary repairs to the great house, often have their duties brought home to them.
However, one doesn't wait to help the unfortunate person until the real cause is known. In every island there are specialists who, each with a technique of his or her own, can bring bodily relief. For instance, in the village of Welora in Dawera, a few women are capable of removing 'dirty blood' from a diseased body by rubbing a rough tree leaf with their tongues. Others are known for their massage techniques, or can help the patient by treating the painful parts of the body with chewed-up ***sirih*** (Piper betle).

◄ *To reduce the stomach ache, the specialist rubs her tongue on a rough tree leaf that has been applied to the painful spot.*

(lower left) After a few minutes she already thinks she has removed all 'dirty' blood from the body of the little patient.

The treatment is over, the patient feels better. ▼

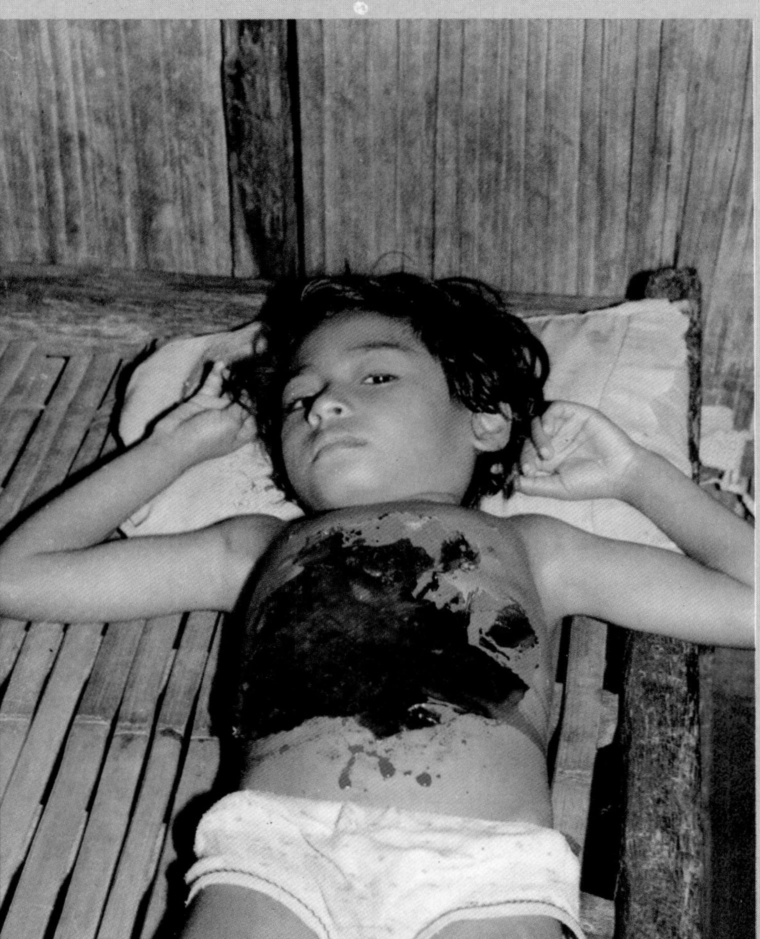

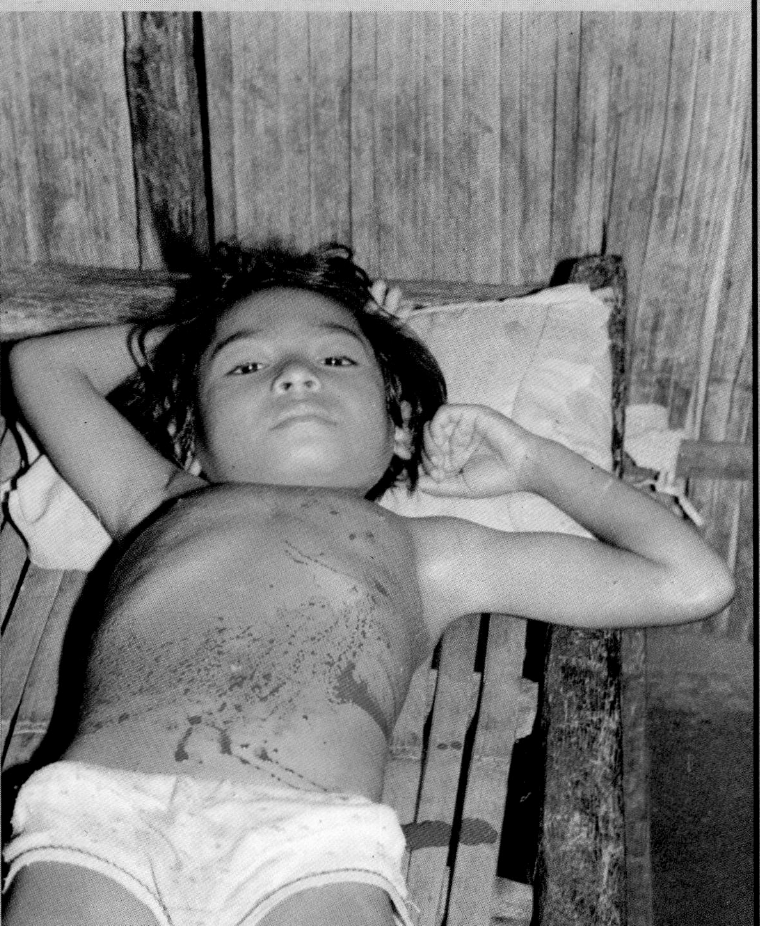

In order to replace ▸ the skins of dancing-drums, a dead goat is inflated by means of the hollow stalk of the papaya tree, so that its skin may be easily removed.

In the Babar islands no feast is complete without the ***seka****, the traditional dance. The men wear* ***basta****, very old cloths several metres long, largely of Indian origin. In these islands* ***basta*** *have both a ceremonial and an economic value.* ▾

No one dares to start a row, nor to leave the village, afraid as one is to meet an ancestor. The corn gardens lie deserted now. Then, when the moon is new, the helmsman's clan start the feast by slaughtering a pig and inviting all the village men to a common meal out in the open, beside their great house. Meanwhile, inside, various items are laid out: a small basket containing *sirih* and *pinang*, a bottle of *sópi* distilled in their garden, and a small bowl of sugar. These are a treat for the ancestors, and they enjoy their 'feast' in the empty house.

Before the meal begins, the head of the clan makes a speech, inviting those present to say whatever they might have on their minds, and to make a clean breast. Next he sings an old song, fills the *sopi* glass, and passes this *adat* drink around. The idea is for all men to drain their glass at one draught, after exclaiming: "oh...*tamparyol* (New Year)...hoi"! After the meal the men form a circle and dance the *seka* around the big drum, deep into the night.

A few days later the local bailer-boy's New Year's feast proceeds in the same way, followed by the pilot's. Finally the feast is concluded with an *adat* prayer of the 'Lord of the Island', said in the centre of the village in the spot where a great waringin tree (a Ficus species) used to stand, the village 'sail'. The festive gatherings have cleansed the 'village proa' of all evil influences, and prepared it for the coming year. The course has been set anew, the microcosm has been harmonized and expectantly one prays to the powers of the macrocosmic likeness: the deity, 'the one who holds the helm and the sail' is asked for a calm sea with small waves and little wind, meaning: no disease and death, but health.

Sopi

Far from the village, in a sheltered spot in a garden, the Babarese build their installations for distilling *sopi*. In an old oil drum sawn in half, palm wine is collected, the fermented juice tapped from the flowering stems of palm trees. Under the drum a fire is made, and the palm wine is brought to the boil. Then two thick bamboo pipes are inserted vertically in holes in the top of the drum, and at their tops these are connected to two sloping bamboo pipes several metres long. The alcohol in the palm wine evaporates, rises in the vertical bamboo pipes, and through condensation it settles in the sloping pipes. After some time the *sopi* drips from these, into a waiting bottle or pitcher. From half a drum of palm wine containing about 80 litres, more than 8 litres of this drink are distilled.

Along with *sirih* (Piper betle), *pinang* (Areca catechu) and tobacco, in the Babar archipelago *sopi* is indispensable in performing many *adat* ceremonies. In addition the drink should be served when group tasks are carried out. But *sopi* is not merely important for these purposes. By distilling it, many islanders also try and keep their food supply at an adequate level. The frequent crop failures in the smaller islands force the Babarese living there, to find something they can trade for food, and being the *adat* drink required everywhere, *sopi* is a product in demand.

▲ *In an oil drum cut in half, palm wine is brought to the boil. Then the bamboo pipes are installed,*
▼ *and the distillation process can begin. After some time the first* **sopi** *starts to drip into a great earthen jar.* ▼

▲ *Every morning and evening the Babarese climbs his palm trees to empty the bamboo palm-wine containers.*

▲ *Two forms of coastal fishing. From the beach the fisherman tries to catch small fish in a casting-net weighted at the edges; setting bamboo fykes covered with coral to prevent them from being washed away, serves to catch larger specimens.* ▼

Along the distant shores of the 'Realm of the Thousand Islands' the dug-outs still glide in peace: beyond the tourist routes life in the Moluccas hardly seems touched by modern time. Where no planes land nor ferries ply, the overwhelming splendour of Nature dominates the scene.

In the north and centre, the islands are mountainous and largely wooded, whereas more to the south they are often dry and eroded. But the underwater world is equally fascinating everywhere.

Breathtaking in their beauty are the coral gardens of Ambon, the throbbing heart of the Moluccas, and they are justly praised. Elegantly, multicoloured fish glide among the reefs, where corals 'bloom' in many hues of green and blue. But due to the tightening pressure of a growing population, natural sunken treasures such as these are increasingly brought to the surface and used as building material; the rapid changes in Kota Ambon are accompanied by an unforeseen exploitation of the reefs. Yet in many places off the coast the ocean's riches may still be admired, and the tourist can only be amazed at the multitude of enchanting colours.

Of course the Moluccas' real fame lies in their history. The praises of the 'Spice Islands' were sung in the West for centuries, and to this day the remnants of the European colonial past may be seen in many places. The ruins of Fort Victoria overlook the Bay of Ambon, in Saparua Fort Duurstede was recently restored, and in the Banda Archipelago the view of the Gunung Api volcano from Fort Belgica is the same as it was hundreds of years ago. To visit Banda Neira, untouched by the last world war, is to travel back in time. Here, at the end of the eighteenth century, the nutmeg monopoly resulted in an extravagant lifestyle still exuded today by the extraordinary architecture of the planters' residences. These men held the concessions to the nutmeg gardens. One will look in vain for tangible memories of the original population which in 1621 was practically annihilated by Jan Pieterszoon Coen, envoy of the Dutch East India Company. Descendants of the few Bandanese who escaped that massacre, now live in the village of Banda Elat in the Kai Islands.

The term Moluccas probably is a relic from pre-colonial days. The name derives from the Portuguese ***as Molucas*** which related to the North-Moluccan islands that were subordinate to the princes of Ternate, Tidore, Bacan and Jailolo. In turn, the Portuguese name is said to derive from ***djazirat al muluk***, 'Land of many Lords' as Arab traders in a remote past used to call the old principalities.

The last 'Lord of Ternate' died in 1974. No one succeeded him, and this Sultan's palace is now a museum. Cloves are still grown in the Moluccas. True, the world demand for spices has diminished considerably, because the refrigerator and cheaper means of conservation were introduced, yet in Indonesia the clove seems irreplaceable, not least because it is used in ***kretek*** cigarettes. The fragrance of the old Moluccas has become the aroma of a nation.

*In Maluku Tenggara ▲ the import of ready-made garments almost spelt the end of the art of weaving. Tourists came to the rescue: in addition to the traditional model boats made of cloves, the beautiful textiles of the southern islands are now available at the Ambonese **pasar**.*

7  Irian Jaya

Snow, and a wild tropical landscape: New Guinea. Here, perennially white peaks crown bleak, hardly accessible ridges. Mountain ranges that even in these modern times still conceal valleys, and possibly even hide amazing cultures from view. When will this island yield its last secrets?

At least as intriguing as the answer to this question is the way in which peoples recently discovered in Irian Jaya, reacted to the sudden presence of strange neighbours. Until now, tribal groups such as the Dani, who to our minds, live as in the Stone Age, have rejected nearly all pleasures the twentieth century could offer. In spite of increasing contacts with outsiders, they prefer an existence in accordance with their own traditions.

Ineke de Vries shows that many of these traditions can be linked to the condition of the soil in this province. Thus among the Dani, the scarcity of good soil in Irian Jaya has led to unique cultural achievements. But that same lack of fertile land also underlies the enormous problems confronting Indonesia in this region.

Harvesting in the east

To most travellers it is an exciting experience to arrive in Wamena, the only town in the elevated Grand Valley. From the air, the Earth at first seems covered all over in 'broccoli', an impression initially formed by the immense forests of the coastal plains, next by the wooded mountain slopes. Then, through a gorge, and after a sharp left turn, the plane suddenly reaches the Grand Valley, strikingly level and devoid of trees. In clear weather, for an instant the summits of Mounts Jaya and Trikora, covered in perennial snow, glisten in the distance. While the runway looms at the far end of the plain, a pattern of yellow-green mosaics emerges under the aircraft: the sweet-potato fields to which the inhabitants of this remote area owe their prosperity.

At least twice a day aircraft land on this vast plain in the Central Highland of Irian Jaya. They maintain contact with the outside world and bring in the goods a modern society needs. But once a week there is a group of curious tourists among the passengers, eager to meet the Dani, the self-willed mountain Papuas who so far have stubbornly rejected all attempts to modernize them. Numbering one hundred and eighty thousand, they also form the largest tribal group of Irian Jaya.

◄ *For Dani women, looking after children is difficult to combine with hard work in the fields. But for their continued prosperity, their work in the sweet-potato fields is indispensable, so the men agree to a limited number of children.*

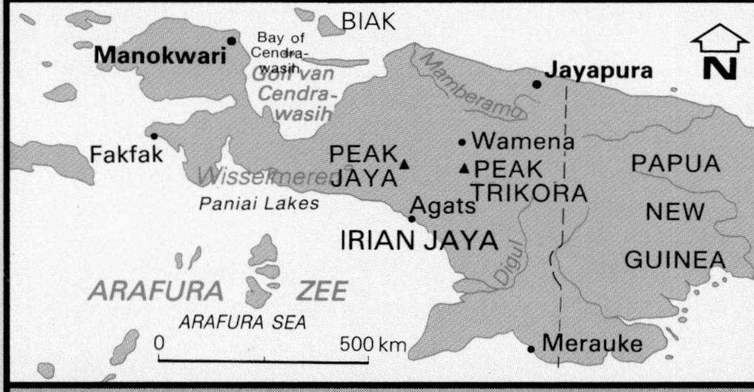

Glorious Irian

Indonesia's easternmost province, and also its youngest, consists of the western half of the island of New Guinea. On 1 May, 1963, the United Nations Temporary Executive Administration (UNTEA) transferred the sovereignty over this region to the state of Indonesia, after the Netherlands had relinquished control of its last colony in Asia, in 1962. In the eastern half of the island the Republic of Papua New Guinea was founded in 1975.

The province known as 'Dutch New Guinea' under colonial rule, was first renamed Irian Barat, West Irian. The literal meaning of the term ***irian*** is said to be 'hot climate' and to stem from Biak, a smaller neighbouring island. Once the people living there must have used the term to refer to the nearby 'mainland'. Nowadays the province is called Irian Jaya: the reference to western New Guinea has been replaced by ***jaya***, which means 'glorious'.

Potato beds in the Grand Valley.
▼ *The Dani distinguish no less than 43 kinds of sweet potatoes.*

▲ *Pigs are the Dani's most cherished possession. When the piglets are still small and weak, the women cuddle them and carry them around in a net on their backs, like babies.*

The Dani of the Grand Valley

The Dani are the last relatively large people to be discovered in New Guinea: as late as 1938 in fact, when an expedition led by Archbold, the wealthy American biologist, spotted the Grand Valley from a plane. Though early in this century field expeditions did locate a few smaller groups of mountain Papuas in narrower, neighbouring valleys. But such explorations never reached the Grand Valley. The footpaths leading to this part of the Central Highland were – and still are – barely negotiable, at least for Westerners. So the Dani in the Grand Valley remained unnoticed until the use of aircraft became a matter of course.

In appearance today's Dani hardly differ from the descriptions the members of the first expedition gave of them. Wearing almost nothing, they look very primitive. Apart from a few small body decorations, the men only wear the *koteka*, a penis sheath. The women are slightly 'better dressed', wearing a short hip skirt made of grass or tree-bark fibre, while outdoors a net of the same material covers their backs from head to upper legs. This piece of clothing also serves as a carrying-net. All sorts of things are transported in it: the day's harvest, the baby, or even a pet pig! The Papuas of the Grand Valley lack the spectacular buildings with which the top of a political or religious hierarchy distinguishes itself; the Dani are unfamiliar with this kind of structure. They build simple but sturdy wooden huts to live in, that trap enough of the heat of a small fire to protect the people inside from the night cold (some 15 degrees Centigrade).

The tools are simple, too. For their most important daily task, the cultivation of the sweet potato fields, the women use a simple dibble; the men's attributes are a bow and arrow and a stone axe.

Papua

All inhabitants of Irian Jaya, both the natives and the newcomers, are included in the collective term '*orang* Irian', Irianese. The term 'Papua' to indicate the indigenous population, is no longer used, as this name is now associated with a movement seeking independence for the region. But as the Introduction showed, this term – originally Malay and meaning 'frizzy-haired black person' – as yet seems indispensable to Anthropology.

There are some 800,000 Papuas in Irian Jaya, divided into over 240 language and culture groups. Usually, depending on where they live, they are distinguished into mountain and coastal Papua. The first category includes the Dani, the Ekagi of the Paniai Lakes and the Muyu of the Upper Digul. The best known coastal Papua groups are the Marind Anim and the Asmat in the south, and the Sentani and the Biak in the north.

▲ *The interior of a men's hut. Warmed by a wood fire, and with a gourd of water within reach, the men spend the night here. The women and children have a hut of their own.*

The pig as a status symbol

At the beginning of the fifties, more than ten years after the Archbold expedition, the pacification of the Central Highland around Wamena began. But even now, a few decades later, the Dani seem hardly interested in the material delights of modern life, and they are not at all impressed by the goods the newcomers in the valley use to try and gain a certain status.

The Dani stick to their own criterion for wealth: the number of pigs one owns. As they have a great many of these, their unequalled supreme possession, they do not envy their new neighbours. With justified pride they refer to the size of their pig stock; in such a densely populated valley it is no small achievement to feed so many animals.

Because of this enormous stock, neighbouring tribes in the Central Highland regard the Dani as a very

prosperous people. From far and near they come to the Grand Valley to persuade its inhabitants to exchange some of their pigs. Usually the Dani trade their piglets for stone axes, cuscus skins and shells. The men use the skins to decorate their bodies, and the shells are strung into precious bands.
As someone's stock of pigs determines his social status, maintaining it is a matter of constant worry to him. The women even hug and pamper young, vulnerable piglets, so that they may grow up in the best possible health.
The inhabitants of the Grand Valley have fully grasped Nature's opportunities to gain wealth and status. The soil structure enables them to practise sedentary agriculture, which is easily combined with pig-raising. But at least as important a pillar of prosperity, is their exceptional method of cultivation – with such a steady yield that both the population and their pig stock could expand to their present size.

The Bird of Paradise

Irian Jaya is famous for its birds. Over 700 species have been spotted. No doubt the best known is the Bird of Paradise (Paradisaeidae), even though few people will know that in New Guinea alone there are as many as 38 varieties of this bird. Birds of Paradise are seen both in the lowlands and in the mountains, but each variety is found at only one specific altitude.

The Dani harvest

The Grand Valley is marshy country, and the Dani have utilized the full potential of its fertile river clay. Yet the rich harvest of sweet potatoes would be impossible without the special horticultural method practised both by men and women. The potatoes are planted in mounds surrounded by deep canals. Due to the difference in level, any excess water is drained off, so that the crops won't rot in rainy periods. Whereas in dry periods the remaining water from the canals can be poured over the plants. Thus production is extremely stable, but this is no more than necessary, as sweet potatoes do not keep very long.
The women look after the gardens, but laying them out is a man's job. Now and again the gardens have to be moved, but there are no shifting cultivation cycles as used by the Dayak in Kalimantan. Thanks to the fertility of the soil, regeneration is swift.
This kind of intensive horticulture in Irian Jaya probably dates back to long before Christ. Archaeological excavations indicate that this method was used on the marshy plains of the Central Highland as early as 6,000 years ago, when agriculture was unknown to the Western world. At the time taro roots were grown instead of sweet potatoes. As far as could be established, this latter crop was not introduced into Irian Jaya until the seventeenth century.
Cultivating the gardens with the aid of irrigation and drainage canals, has long since enabled the Dani to share the Grand Valley with relatively many people; their number per square kilometre is now roughly 160 (400 per square mile), and even today this figure is higher than anywhere else in the Pacific. And, of course, the rich harvests enabled the people to raise the stocks of pigs that command so much respect among the mountain Papuas in neighbouring valleys.

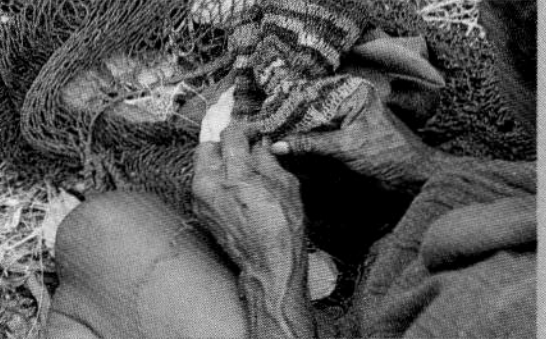

▲ *Agricultural attributes such as dibble and carrying-net are simple but effective. The dibble is used in the fields, in the self-knotted net the woman brings her* ◄ *harvest home.*

War and prosperity

In an interaction between culture and nature, the Dani have found various ways to extend their prosperity.
A restriction on population growth is the idea that a woman should not have more than two growing children at a time. Besides, two births must be spaced at least five years apart.
Such a limited number of children is what many women want. The work in the potato fields is heavy enough as it is. The extra burden of looking after a lot of small children, is something they can do without. To the husband as well, his wife's work in the field is more important. If she were to become pregnant again within the five-year period, he would perceive this as shameful. For that matter, Nature too, helps to keep family size down, though in a less desirable way: as in many other places in Indonesia, infant mortality is considerable here.
Ritual wars can also neutralize population growth in the Grand Valley. The Dani consider such wars necessary to satisfy their ancestors; in exchange these will use their supernatural power for the well-being of the people, and for the fertility of the fields and the pigs.
Though the impression is often given that it's only a spectacle, people do get killed in these skirmishes. However, a war has no essential significance for population density, unless the losing party is forced to leave the Grand Valley for a less fertile area.

The rich of the Earth

Wars do not only serve the prosperity of the Dani. The struggle offers men a chance to prove themselves, and bring status and wealth within their reach. A successful warrior makes a very attractive husband, and many wives are the mark of a war hero. As many women's hands make light work and harvest more potatoes, a *gain*, a warrior who has distinguished himself in action, can afford to keep many pigs. But noblesse oblige: being one of the 'rich of the Earth', on occasions such as the Great Pig Feast he is expected to confirm his position by contributing an extra large number of pigs and other goods to be consumed by the whole community. As a rule, the Great Pig Feast is held every five years. For a long time the exact date will be uncertain. Then, one day, the most important *gain*, the war leader of several Dani groups, will forbid the slaughter of pigs, and thus implicitly announce the Great Pig Feast. All the men and women of the groups he leads, participate in the feast; their numbers can run into a few thousand. They all celebrate together for about a fortnight. This period is used for, among other things, rituals that mark transitions: rites of initiation for boys and girls, wedding rituals and cremations.
According to the few Westerners who attended such a feast, they were most impressed when to the accompaniment of rhythmic chanting, the many pigs were shown to the community by their owners. For those involved these moments matter most, for they confirm these men's positions in society.

The Great Pig Festival

Due to modern influences the Dani hardly celebrate the Great Pig Feast in the traditional way any longer. Yet until recently this ritual was an absolute climax to them; it was the most important feast of all. And the festival was celebrated on a grand scale; an enormous number of people would participate, various ceremonies would alternate, the feasting would go on for many days, and last but not least: lots of pigs would be slaughtered and prepared in a braising-pit. The Dani's 'rites of passage' such as weddings, were performed only during this Great Pig Feast. At no other time was anybody in the Grand Valley allowed to get married. Such a feast was celebrated only once every few years, and those who had died since the last feast, could not be formally mourned until the next Great Pig Festival. For this purpose their remains would be exhumed and ritually cremated.
On the eve of any high point in the festival, such as a marriage or a cremation, some pigs would be slaughtered in the yard near a men's house. Two men would lift one pig to shoulder level, and from a few metres a third man would then shoot an arrow into the animal's carotid artery, so as to kill it almost instantly. As Dani men were (and still are) very skilled in the use of their weapons, this usually succeeded.
Nowadays the Dani converted to Christianity are reminded of the Great Pig Festival in particular during the celebration of Christmas. For the main ingredient of their Christmas dinner is great quantities of pork. The meat, braised in a pit in the traditional way, is appreciated by many.

The Land of Promise

Like no other people in Irian Jaya the Dani seem to have adapted to the ecological circumstances. The province only has small patches of fertile soil, a data that emerges in various expressions of their culture. The special method of horticulture, the voluntary family planning, the consequences of ritual wars: each of these instances visualizes the limits that the land sets to the population size.

But no longer are the Dani the only inhabitants of the Grand Valley. Over the past few years, in great numbers, all kinds of newcomers have settled on this plain. For lack of room, some Dani even found themselves forced to move to less fertile locations. But the majority go on living on the old land. Here, seemingly undisturbed, they continue their traditional way of life.

The traders and contractors making a new life for themselves in the Grand Valley, are called 'spontaneous' migrants. They came on the off chance, usually from Sulawesi and the Moluccas. But these newcomers to Wamena are only a fraction of all migrants who have taken the plunge and settled in Irian Jaya. Their number is estimated at over one hundred thousand, and they live mainly in the coastal towns.

Many of these spontaneous migrants are relatives of earlier migrants who by now have managed to make a living in the street trade or in domestic industry. But by no means everyone succeeds in realizing his dream of a better life. For instance in Jayapura, the rapidly expanding capital of the province, prestigious churches and shopfronts arise beside slums where corrugated iron is the main building material.

Apart from spontaneous migrants, nowadays large groups of poor families arrive in the province: the so-called transmigrants. From overpopulated islands such as Java and Bali, they have been resettled here within the framework of the massive government transmigration scheme. In sparsely populated Irian Jaya they are housed in settlements built especially for this purpose.

A people migrates

Between 1969 and 1984 over three million Javanese and Balinese were transferred to Sumatra, Sulawesi, Kalimantan and Irian Jaya. By April, 1989, the Indonesian government aims to have moved another 750,000 families, or 3.8 million people. Not without reason has this transmigration programme been called the world's largest, organized migration of a nation, as the numbers involved are great enough to form one. A country that pays so much attention to moving its inhabitants, must have a very urgent reason. And sc it has: the unbalanced distribution of the population. Two thirds of the 160 million Indonesians live in Java and Bali, while these two islands add up to a mere seven percent of Indonesia's entire territory. The great population density is a major cause of poverty and unemployment in cities such as Jakarta and Surabaya. The overpopulation is also exerting pressure on the natural environment in Java and Bali. Constantly, new land is prepared for cultivation, at ever higher altitudes, and this increases erosion. Even the climate

▲ *A Javanese transmigrant on his way to market in Merauke, the coastal town to be linked to Wamena by the 'Irian Highway'.*

On the way to modern life

In no other tropical region in the world is the jungle wilder, more treacherous and less penetrable than in New Guinea. Hence there still are unmapped areas whose inhabitants – if any – have never met a white man. Wherever possible, though, the interior is being opened up and small airfields are built for the benefit of missionaries and officials. The Grand Valley too, has become accessible, and representatives of both the government and the Church in Wamena now encourage the Dani to adjust to modern life.

So far, however, only few have exchanged their penis sheaths or grass skirts for Western clothes. A situation that may soon change, when the road to Jayapura now under construction, will open up the Central Highland more fully. This road is part of the 'Irian Highway', the ambitious project that is to link Merauke on the south coast and Jayapura in the north.

In Wamena the first few metres of the route have been constructed in the centre, right next to the market grounds. Here the exponents of the different lifestyles meet: the traditional and the 'modern' Dani as well as the newcomers. Every day this produces a spectacle full of contrast.

Plastic and penis sheaths. So far the Dani, ▼ *stubbornly clinging to their traditions, are not very impressed by modern articles.*

is subject to change. Java, famous for its many fertile *sawah*, runs the risk of turning into a desert. In transmigration and family planning ('two is enough'), the government hopes to have found a solution to the country's poverty and environment problems. Landless farmers and people who for any reason, have lost the basis of their livelihoods, are resettled in the outer districts, with their families and free of charge. At the moment Irian Jaya, with its population density of on average three people per square kilometre, is the main intake area. Hence all problems attached to the execution of these programmes, are piling up in this province.

The harvest of the transmigrants

Undoubtedly the biggest problem in Irian Jaya is the scarcity of fertile soil; primeval rain forest covers most of the land. Soil suitable for agriculture is found in few regions only: the Manokwari area, the north coast near Jayapura, a few valleys in the Central Highland, and the Skouten Islands in the Bay of Cendrawasih. Hence from time immemorial, this is where most local cultures were established. These parts are densely populated; as was observed above, the situation in the Grand Valley even is unique.

Due to this unequal distribution of fertile soil, large parts of Irian Jaya are sparsely populated, and the province appears to be the ideal region for the intake of transmigrants. But almost certainly, a resettled family will have to make a life for themselves on the poor, acid soil of what used to be the floor of the rain forest. And yet, transmigrants are expected to practise intensive rice cultivation on such soil. A practically impossible task, as was already indicated in the chapter on Kalimantan. And even though at first a transmigrated family may even seem to succeed, within a few years the soil productivity may drop after all. Disappointing harvests will then force such a family to cultivate another plot, but nowhere in the vicinity will they find suitable soil.

Next, in search of fertile areas, they clash with the interests of the indigenous inhabitants. Although the execution of the transmigration programmes may not be hampered by the claims the latter people assert, they will certainly not make room for their new neighbours without a struggle. Actually this is the same problem complex that caused the Kubu in Sumatra to submit a request for recognition of their land rights.

In spite of all these difficulties, transmigrant families in Irian Jaya sometimes do manage to make a life for themselves that would have been unthinkable for them in Java or Bali. Others have felt forced to move away sooner or later. If they are unable to return to their home region, the families will move to the nearest city. To survive here, they have to compete with the spontaneous migrants who came on their own initiative, and now dominate the street and distributive trade.

Dani from the Grand Valley rarely turn up in these coastal towns. Apparently they are not anxious to exchange their old lifestyle for that of the modern, urban dweller.

Ancient traditions, modern times

And yet, in the end, even the Dani won't be able to evade the confrontation with the outside world. For thousands of years they have lived in greater isolation than many other peoples of Indonesia. Until very recently, the Dani were oblivious of the process in which, due to interaction with other traditions, the *adat* was constantly changing – a process so typical of many of the Indonesian cultures described in the present book. In their development, these cultures demonstrated a flexibility that enabled them to preserve their own identities, in spite of being open to external influences: thus to this day, the ancient Hindu-Javanese motto 'unity in diversity' has remained relevant.

Such an interaction is far more difficult for peoples like the Dani who with their Stone-Age traditions are suddenly confronted with the modern world. It is to be hoped that the Dani – and comparable peoples such as the Mentawaians, the Kubu and the Punan – will get both the opportunity and the time to pass through the process in which the other peoples have preceded them. Then they too, will be able to flesh out their new, national identity with their own cultural heritage, strong and flourishing as it is.

▲ *Crowned pigeon (Goura cristata).*

Special animal species

As was mentioned in the Introduction, during the Ice Ages most of the area now covered by the China Sea was dry, and the islands of the Sunda Shelf were connected to the Asian continent. Similarly, a land bridge linked Australia to New Guinea, the largest island of the Sahul Shelf.

Hence it's not surprising that largely, Irian Jaya's fauna is of Australian origin, and that, from a zoogeographical point of view, the province falls within the so-called Australian region – in contrast to the Sunda Islands that are considered part of the Oriental region. As shown in the previous chapter, it highly depends on the animal group studied, where to draw the line between both regions; the Moluccas often are an area of transition.

Once New Guinea was cut off from Australia, many new animal species arose in this splendid isolation, and live fully adapted to their specific lowland or highland environment. For instance, apart from the species that are clearly of Australian origin – such as phalangers (opossums) and other marsupials – there are very special varieties of snakes, tortoises, crocodiles and large lizards.

New Guinea owes its name to the Spaniard Inigo Ortiz de Retes. Because in his view the Papuas resembled the negroes in West-African Guinea, he called this land Nueva Guinea, claiming it for the Spanish crown in 1545. Most Papuas will hardly have noticed anything of this or later European assertions of power. Only the population on the north coast underwent some influence; due to the inaccessible high mountain country, well into this century the great cultures remained isolated from the outside world. Interrupted by deep valleys, steep cliffs and narrow ridges, this natural barrier runs across the entire island, from east to west. The highest peaks are the summits of Mounts Jaya (over 5,000 m.), and Trikora (4,740 m.). The snow-line fluctuates around 4,500 m., which means that the peaks, close though they are to the equator, are covered in perennial snow. Of all the valleys in Irian Jaya the Grand Valley, stretching over a length of 45 kilometres, is the largest.
In this valley lies Wamena Town, the main tourist destination of the province. Here, on the old Dani footpaths around this town 'up on the flat roof of the Earth', a remote past meets the present.
Near the small administrative centre of Agats, in the vast lowland plains just south of the Central Highland, live the Asmat. These coastal Papuas, famous for their characteristic war-shields painted with white clay, live in bizarre tree-houses in a very marshy coastal region. The Asmat owe their fame in particular to the ***bish*** posts, several metres high, and erected in memory of the ancestors.
As this swampland can only be traversed by canoe, the Asmat region is not easily opened up to tourism on a large scale. Even so, the lowland marshes already seem to have yielded many of their riddles: it is only New Guinea's 'terra incognita' now that remains intriguingly shrouded in mystery.

▲ From the ocean, New Guinea is most accessible via the north coast; the population here has always been numerous, and here too, Irian Jaya's big cities arose. ▼

*▲ **Bish** post carved from mangrove wood. These posts, almost ten metres high, are erected by the Asmat during a memorial ritual. Afterwards they are left in the forest.*

Travelling in Indonesia

Indonesia has a very efficient system of public transport. If you like, you can travel twenty-four hours a day without ever having to wait long for a connection. At all times all important cities and islands can be reached either by train or bus, or by plane or ship. Only the truly remote destinations, such as the interior of Kalimantan and that of Irian Jaya, and the southernmost islands of the Moluccas require more travelling time.

For inter-island travel, Garuda Indonesia, the national airline, would seem the most obvious choice; the company serves some thirty national airports. Lines less frequently travelled, are served by smaller companies, such as Merpati Airlines, Pelita Airservice, Bouraq Indonesian Airlines, Sempati Airtransport, or Nusantara Airlines.

For longer distances overland in Java and Sumatra, one can choose train or bus. For short distances within cities and between villages, the traveller has a range of possibilities at his or her disposal.

Famous are the ***becak***, the beautifully painted tricycle taxis. Somewhat less romantic, but often cheaper, is to travel by ***bemo***, small motorized vehicles; like taxis they are found in nearly all big Indonesian cities. In smaller towns and between villages one can take the minibus, a small van or a pick-up with canvas cover, accommodating at least ten passengers with their market merchandise and other luggage. Like his big brother, a minibus has a fixed route, but no fixed times of departure. It sets off as soon as enough passengers have got in, or if someone has chartered the whole vehicle. The latter is often attractive, even for longer distances.

Photo Credits

The colour photos in Indonesia in Focus were taken by the following photographers.
The codes behind their names indicate the pages and the position on the page where the photos may be found.

Jet Bakels: 8, 41, 42, 43, 45

Jenne de Beer: 89, 93, 94 left, 95 top, 96

Lea Bolle: 8 lower left, 30 top, 32, 33 right, 34, 35, 36

Jorge Eduardo Cordoso Patuleia: 116 except lower left, 117, 118 left, 119

Vincent Dekker: large cover photo, cover: 'mysterious monuments', 30 bottom, 31, 38, 46, 51, 74 top, 76 top, 79 lower left, 79 right, 80, 86 left, 87 top, 102, 104

Toos van Dijk and Wim Wolters: 52 bottom, 69 top, 116 lower left, 120, 121 top, 125 right, 127 top, 129 centre, 131, 132, 136, 142 bottom, 143, 144 bottom, 145 bottom

Madelon Djajadiningrat-Nieuwenhuis: 47, 53 left centre, 53 lower left

Leonie Greefkens: 110, 111, 112, 113, 114, 115

Rens Heringa: 55, 56 lower right, 57, 58, 61 upper right

Peter Homan: cover: 'ceremonial richness', 2, 4 bottom, 5, 6, 33 upper left, 40, 48, 50, 59 left, 60 right, 61 left, 71, 72, 74 lower right, 75, 84 left centre, 77 left, 84 bottom left, 87 bottom, 91 top, 98, 99, 100 bottom, 101, 103 upper right, 103 lower left, 105, 106 upper left, 107, 109, 121 bottom, 152, 153 right

Nico de Jonge: cover: 'cultures in festive finery', 11 lower left, 69 bottom, 73 top, 74 left, 122, 128, 138, 139, 141, 142 top, 142 centre, 145 top

Joost Koedooder: colophon photo

Fred Kok: 103 lower right

J. MacKinnon: 94 upper right (from WWF archives, Zeist, The Netherlands)

Willy Nanlohy: 123, 124, 125 upper left, 125 lower left, 126, 127 bottom, 128 bottom, 129 top, 130 upper right, 130 lower right, 144 top

Hetty Nooy-Palm: 106 upper right

Gerard Persoon: cover: 'hunters in the jungle', 4 upper left, 8 upper left, 22, 23, 24 lower right, 24 lower left, 26, 27, 28, 29, 44, 96 bottom, back cover

Herman Rijksen: 9 upper right, 37, 90, 92 top, 149 upper centre (from WWF archives, Zeist, The Netherlands)

Reimar Schefold: 12, 14, 15, 16, 17, 18, 19, 20, 21, 108

Henk Schulte Nordholt: 73 bottom, 78, 79 upper left

Dik Teljeur: 134, 135

Hans Touwen: cover: 'struggle for status', 62, 63, 64, 65, 66, 67, 68

Annemarie Verkruisen: 9 bottom, 70, 76 bottom, 77, 81, 82, 83, 84 bottom, 85, 86 right, 158

Theo Vlaar: 56 lower left, 59 upper right, 60 lower left, 61 lower right

Ineke de Vries: 11 lower right, 137, 146, 147, 148, 149 except for box, 150, 151, 153 left centre, 153 lower left

Christine Waslander: 10, 106 lower left

Frans Welman: 88, 91 bottom, 92 bottom, 95 lower left, 95 lower right, 97

Cloths on page 9 upper left, 59 lower left, 60 right and 61 left from collection Rens Heringa

Photo on page 24 upper left from Hagen, B. *Die orang Kubu auf Sumatra*. Frankfurt, 1908.

Objects on page 25 from collection Gerard Persoon

Photos on pages 52 centre and 53 right from collection Madelon Djajadiningrat-Nieuwenhuis

Painting on page 84 upper left and objects on page 100 from collection Peter Homan

Prints on page 91 top from collection Jenne de Beer

Illustration on page 107 upper right Jowa Imre Kis-Jovak

Book on page 118 lower right from collection Multatuli Museum, Amsterdam, The Netherlands

Photo on page 130 left from VIDO archives of the Royal Tropical Institute, Amsterdam, The Netherlands

Objects on page 140 from collection Nico de Jonge

Cartography: Nelly van Betlehem and Michel van Elk

Glossary

A
Abangan 'red group' (also called *wong cilik*), Java's old class of small farmers; in Java the animistic heritage survives in particular in the daily religious practice of these 'little folk'
adat local customs and habits hallowed by tradition
Agama Hindu Bali Balinese religion, a mixture of pre-Hinduism, Buddhism and Hinduism
agama religion
alang-alang tough kind of grass
Aluk To Dolo 'the Rites of the People of Long Ago', the ancient faith of the Toraja in Sulawesi
aluk pia 'childhood ritual', first phase of a *dirapa'i*, the funeral festival of the Toraja in Sulawesi that includes a rest period
alun-alun open field north and south of the walled-in Central-Javanese *kraton*
angklung West-Javanese musical instrument
anteng white cloth used as a magic weapon by the witch Rangda in the Barong dance in Bali, to ward off attacks
aseuk dibble of the West-Javanese Baduy

B
Babad chronicle
bade Balinese cremation tower
bahasa Indonesia the Indonesian language
balian taksu Balinese trance-medium who acts as contact between the visible and the invisible worlds
banten flower- and food-offering in Bali
banteng wild cow
barang suci sacred objects belonging to a *balian taksu*
basta very old cloth several metres long, often of Indian origin, which in the Babar archipelago (South-East Moluccas) has both a ceremonial and an economic value
batik-lurik black-and-white chequered weave on to which in Tuban (North-East Java) dotted motifs are applied in batik technique
belian traditional healer and religious specialist (usually a woman) among the Dayak in Kalimantan
bish post carved post several metres high, erected by the Asmat in Irian Jaya in honour of their ancestors
bombo dikita 'the soul of the dead who is seen', the official name of an effigy of the deceased, *tau-tau*, of the Toraja in Sulawesi
boreh fragrant yellow beauty cream containing *kunir* (Curcuma)
bupati district head
buta Balinese demon who dwells in the underworld

C
Canting copper pen for drawing with wax in batik technique
carok violent satisfaction/revenge taken by Madurese man
cicak house lizard

D
Desa village
dirapa'i funeral festival among the Toraja in Sulawesi, in two stages separated by a rest period
djazirat al muluk 'land of many lords', old Arabic name for the North-Moluccan principalities
doa salamat ritual 'prayer for redemption' of the Giman in Halmahera, North Moluccas
duk black palm fibre, used in Bali as roofing for shrines of the gods
dukun specialist in magic, and religious healer
duyung dugong (Dugong dugon)

G
Gaba-gaba sago-palmleaf ribs
gain war leader of the Dani in Irian Jaya
gamelan Javanese music ensemble
gendi earthen pitcher
gogol owners of arable land, the social middle group in Tuban, North-East Java
gondang traditional music of the Toba Batak in North Sumatra

H
Hakim sara 'judge of Islamic law', collective term for the Islamic functions among the Giman in Halmahera
hampatong frightening sculpture of the Dayak in Kalimantan
hariara kind of Ficus, the 'tree of life' in the myths of origin of the Toba Batak in North Sumatra
hatib Islamic religious official
hukum tua village head in the Minahasa, North Sulawesi
hulahula bride-giving group among the Toba Batak in North Sumatra
huta Batak village (North Sumatra)

I
Ikat resist dye process in which designs are reserved by (repeatedly) tying off small areas of warp and/or weft yarns
imam Islamic religious official
ipoh vegetable poison related to strychnine, and used by the Punan in Kalimantan
irengan dark shoulder cloth for grandmothers in Tuban, North-East Java

J
Jaba 'outsider', Balinese not belonging to the *triwangsa*, the top layer of noble birth
jaha bars of rice heated in bamboo pipes and boiled in coconut milk (South Halmahera)
jambar part of the body of the largest animal sacrificed during a *tugu* feast of the Toba Batak in North Sumatra, and charged with a special meaning
jarik oblong hip cloth (Tuban, North-East Java)
jaro see *jaro pemerintah*
jaro pemerintah Baduy who mediates between the outside world and the *pu-un*, the highest authorities among the Baduy in West-Java
jejaitan palmleaf base for offerings in Bali
jenang trader linking the Kubu and the Sumatran world around them

K
Kain kentol hip cloth indicating social status (Tuban, North-East Java)
kaja 'direction of the mountains', term of orientation in Bali
kala demon who dwells in the underworld (Bali)
kalo see *kalo sara*
kalo sara usually called *kalo*, a plaited ring that among the Tolaki in South-East Sulawesi symbolizes the unity of the people
kamar suci a *balian taksu*'s consecrated room (Bali)
kancil mouse deer
kanda sacred drum in Benua, a Tolaki village in South-East Sulawesi
kanda house small structure in which the Tolaki in the village of Benua hang the *kanda*, the sacred drum (South-East Sulawesi)
kandaure fyke-shaped ornament made of beads (Toraja, Sulawesi)
kangin 'direction of the sunrise', term of orientation in Bali
kauh 'direction of the sunset', term of orientation in Bali
kawin lari marriage by elopement (Moluccas)
kawin minta marriage by proposal (Moluccas)
kawitan ancestral shrine in Bali
kebaya women's long-sleeved blouse
kelapa sekantet 'coconuts from one cluster', batik motif in Tuban, North-East Java
kelod 'direction of the sea', term of orientation in Bali
keter in do'ong 'the power and well-being of the village', name in a local Minahasan language, of the place where hunted heads used to be buried
kiyai religious leader in Madura
koteka penis sheath of the Dani in Irian Jaya
kraton walled-in palace complex of a Javanese ruler
kretek cigarette cigarette containing cloves
krotong scorched animal hide (Punan, Kalimantan)
kujur spear of the Kubu in Sumatra

Ladang field for dry (rice) cultivation
ladang cultivation shifting cultivation
lakkean house-like structure for a deceased in the 'village of the dead' of the Toraja, Sulawesi
lamanta old name for newly harvested sago; perhaps it is the origin of the name Kalimantan
laor sexually mature parts of the Palola seaworm, a delicacy in the Moluccas
lengsat root root whose juice causes infertility (Punan, Kalimantan)
leyak woman in the form of a witch, Bali
lis palmleaf used in Bali by a *balian taksu* to sprinkle holy water
lulo-ngganda dance of the Tolaki in South-East Sulawesi, related to the agricultural cycle
lurik Javanese chequered or striped weave

Ma'gellu' dance of the Toraja in Sulawesi, performed at a house-dedication feast
Malo Plim 'Five Landscapes', the name of the indigenous ethnic groups of South Halmahera, North Moluccas
mancapat hierarchically structured co-operative framework of 5 to 9 Javanese villages
mandala community small religious group living in isolation, whose members base themselves on an Old-Javanese belief with Hindu-Buddhist features
manteu (a) man, in the language of the Mentawai Islands
mantunu 'the slaughter of the buffaloes', the second stage of a *dirapa'i*, a Toraja funeral feast of the highest order (Sulawesi)
marga patrilineal descent group of the Toba Batak in North Sumatra
matakau a warning sign that has been cursed (Ambonese *pasisir*)
mateu 'matched to its essence', the outward appearance of a an object or a human being should express its/his/her essence (Mentawai Islands)
matundan 'waking (the deceased) from sleep' to conclude the 'childhood ritual', the first stage of the *dirapa'i* of the Toraja in Sulawesi
mekamulol 'the one who holds the helm', i.e. the first post of the 'great house' in Dawera in the Babar archipelago (South-East Moluccas)
***menurut agama dan menurut adat 'according to religion and to the** adat*', a saying that guides protestant life in the Ambonese *pasisir*, Moluccas
merajan small house temple of noble family in Bali
merajan gede temple of noble Balinese family in the mother yard
modin Islamic religious official
monahu-ndau Tolaki feast to conclude and re-open the agricultural cycle (South-East Sulawesi)
monconegoro the outer circle, the border regions of the realm of a Central-Javanese ruler; a realm structured like a system of concentric rings
mondok landless labourers, the lowest social group in Tuban, North-East Java
moyang sakti sacred ancestors in the Ambonese *pasisir*

Negoro agung the heart of the realm of a Central-Javanese ruler, a realm structured like a system of concentric rings
ngaseuk Baduy ritual preceding the sowing of rice, to propitiate Dewi Sri, the rice goddess (West Java)
ngurek part of the Balinese Barong dance, in which the dancers try to hurt themselves, but the Barong protects them
nipah palm palm species that the Punan in Kalimantan use in many ways
noah sago porridge rich in carbohydrates, the staple food of the Punan in Kalimantan

Orang asli term used in the Ambonese *pasisir* in referring to the members of indigenous families
orang Belanda Dutchman
orang pendatang term used in the Ambonese *pasisir* in referring to immigrants
orang human being
ottuwlesol central area in the traditional 'great house' in Dawera (Babar archipelago, South-East Moluccas)

Pa'barre allo 'the sun with rays', cosmological motif of the Toraja in Sulawesi
pa'rapuan family group of the Toraja in Sulawesi, often *rapu* for short
paabitara guardian of the *kalo*, a hereditary position in Tolaki society (South-East Sulawesi)
padmasana stone lotus throne of the god Shiva (Bali)
pangurei 'celebrating a wedding', a healing ceremony in the Mentawai Islands
pari rice stalk
parsantian sacrificial house of a branch of the *marga*, the patrilineal descent group of the Toba Batak in North Sumatra
pasar market
pasisir coastal region with a strong trading tradition, open to external influences, like Ambon-Lease and the north coast of Java
pedanda Brahman priest (Bali)
pela brotherhood relation between villages in the Ambonese *pasisir*
pinang a kind of nut (Areca catechu)
pinisi seaworthy wooden sailing vessel, built by the Buginese in South Sulawesi
pipitan 'close together', name for a shoulder cloth for mothers in Tuban, North-East Java based both on the motif and on their family situation
pisang jati high, cylindrical Balinese offering
pita 'yellowish' (Old-Javanese); part of the term *pipitan*
pitung bongi funeral festival of the Toraja in Sulawesi that takes seven nights
plangi resist dye technique to decorate textiles, but unlike *ikat*, applied to the woven material, by tying off small bunched-up parts of it, so that these will not receive colour.
priyayi aristocratic and ruling class in Java
pujangga court writer of Javanese rulers
punden grave of the (mythic) founder of a village in Tuban, North-East Java
pura dalem temple of the dead, one of three temples in any Balinese village
pura desa village temple, one of three temples in any Balinese village
pura puseh 'navel' temple, one of three temples in any Balinese village
pura temple
pura batur ancestral temple in Bali that houses the *kawitan*
pura dadia see *pura batur*
puri house of a noble Balinese family
pusaka sacred heirloom
pustaha sacred book of the Toba Batak in North Sumatra
putihan 'white'-and-blue batik cloth that offers protection against disease and evil influences (Tuban, North-East Java)
putus bujang-e saying in the Ambonese *pasisir* indicating the end of a bachelor's way of life
pu-un highest authority in the Baduy hierarchy

Raja king; in the Ambonese *pasisir*: village head
rapu see: *pa'rapuan*
real old Spanish coin in which the Tolaki express part of the amount to be paid as bride-price (South-East Sulawesi)
rupiah the Indonesian monetary unit

Sahala salutary spiritual power radiated by the ancestors of the Toba Batak (North Sumatra)
sang bongi funeral feast of the Toraja in Sulawesi lasting only one night
sanggah small house temple in Bali
sanggah gede Balinese temple in the mother yard
santri Javanese, usually traders and wealthy landowners, who strictly observe the Islamic laws
saringan bier of the Toraja in Sulawesi
saro-saro small biscuits which the Giman in South Halmahera swing in front of the faces of newly circumcised children
sarung hip cloth sewn into a tubular shape
sasi placing as yet unharvested crops in the Ambonese *pasisir* under Church protection against theft
sawah field for wet rice cultivation
sayut cloth worn by women diagonally across the shoulder like a sash, for carrying market merchandise or child in Tuban, North-East Java
seka traditional dance in the Babar archipelago, South-Eastern Moluccas
selamat well-being and blessing
selamatan common salutary meal on a special occasion (Java; Madura)
semen cement, concrete
sesamuhan biscuit of rice dough, included in many offerings in Bali
sirih kind of pepper (Piper betle), main ingredient for chewing sirih
slendang as *sayut*, but found throughout Indonesia

sopi locally distilled spirits (Moluccas)
stupa symbol of sacred Mount Meru, Buddhism
sunat 'recommendable' according to Islamic doctrine (Giman, South Halmahera)

Taksu deity who animates a *balian taksu*, a Balinese trance medium
tambak modern monumental 'family grave' of the Toba Batak, containing the remains of several ancestors (North Sumatra)
tamparyol 'New Year', exclamation during New Year's celebration in Dawera (Babar archipelago, South-East Moluccas)
tanah kosong 'empty land' (term used by farmers to justify their annexation of) stretches of forest not officially claimed by its inhabitants, the Kubu (Sumatra)
tanah kopi 'coffee land', term for parcels of land in Minahasa, where coffee was once grown (North Sulawesi)
tau-tau wooden effigy of deceased Toraja placed by his grave in cliff face (Sulawesi)
tedun 'descent' of a Balinese deity into the body of a believer going into a trance during a temple feast
tempel flat-bottomed boat to transport commodities along the rivers of Kalimantan
to 'human(s)' as part of the term *toraja*, which according to the Toraja means 'people of kings'
tonaas traditional priest in Minahasa, North Sulawesi
tongkonan *adat* house of the Toraja in Sulawesi, the status symbol of a *rapu*, the family group
toraja Buginese term for 'mountain dweller' or 'inhabitant of the interior' (Sulawesi)
tortor ritual dance of the Toba Batak (North-Sumatra)
trah Javanese family group based on kinship on both father's and mother's side
tritik resist dye technique for the decoration of textiles, in which the motifs are laced up with thread; the thread line does not receive colour
triwangsa Balinese upper class of noble birth, comprising Brahmana, Satria and Wesya
tugu modern, often tall monumental ancestral grave of the Toba Batak in North Sumatra, usually containing the mortal remains of one, very early ancestor
tukang banten woman who produces offerings (*banten*) in Bali

Ulos ritual cloth of the Toba Batak in North Sumatra
uma communal pile-dwelling in the Mentawai Islands
umat simagere 'toy for the soul', a bird carved out of wood to cheer the souls of men and animals (Mentawai Islands)
umoara war dance of the Tolaki in South-East Sulawesi

Wa'ilan 'blessed one', Minahasan title of honour gained by completing as a host a series of nine festivals of merit; *wa'ilan* were buried in a *waruga* (North Sulawesi)
warawluol 'Lord of the Island', the founder of the first settlement in Dawera (Babar archipelago, South-East Moluccas)
waruga old Minahasan mausoleum; see *wa'ilan*
watu tumotowa 'sacred stones of the village', spot where Minahasans used to bury hunted heads when founding a village
wayang Javanese drama played with (shadow) puppets or by people; the stories acted out may be inspired by Javanese versions either of Indian epics such as the Ramayana, or of Islamic stories
wedyol shoulder blade or oar, term used in Dawera and Dawelor (Babar archipelago, South-East Moluccas)
wong cilik 'little folk'; see *abangan*
wong kentol village aristocracy in Tuban, descendants of the first people to reclaim the land (North-East Java)
wopal traditional return gift handed over after receiving a bride-price in the village of Pulilo, South Halmahera

The Balinese worship their gods in many ways: with music, with dancing, but in particular with offerings. These vary from small to very large, and from simple to exceedingly complex. Flowers often form a fragrant and colourful part of them. ▸

Index

In addition to geographical names, personal names and the names of ethnic groups, the following Index includes all catchwords, i.e. the keywords printed diagonally at the top of a page.